Techno Feminism

TECHNO FEMINISM

S Thakur

MD PUBLICATIONS PVT LTD
NEW DELHI
www.mdppl.com

Published by :

MD Publications Pvt Ltd
"MD House", 11, Darya Ganj,
New Delhi - 110 002
Phone : +91-11- 45355555
E-mail : contact@mdppl.com
Website: www.mdppl.com

ISBN : 978-81-7533-344-4

Published and Printed by Mr. Pranav Gupta on behalf of **MD Publications Pvt Ltd** at Repro India Limited.

PREFACE

Feminist ideas develop partly within their own area of debate, acquiring their own momentum. They also, however, interact with other intellectual currents. The changing paradigms in scientific thought are sites for just such a crossover. Indeed sometimes it can be difficult to distinguish social critiques of science from strands of feminism which assume that 'feminism' by definition is to be equated with a rejection of science, technology and indeed reason.

The recognition that values are embedded within the social processes of scientific study and technological innovation has challenged the assumption that these are neutral forces. This has an obvious relevance for understanding the peculiar difficulty women have confronted in gaining access to the theoretical and practical scientific and technological worlds. This awareness of gender has contributed to new insights into the history of science and technology in western thought and society. Instead of wondering what is wrong with women, with capitalism, or with 'patriarchy', feminist enquiry has shifted during the last decade to what is wrong with the tradition of modern western science.

The feminist critique of the tradition of western science has come from several perspectives, anti-utopian as well as utopian. Scepticism about essential female values, utopias and grand plans has combined in 'postmodernism' to undermine the very possibility of objectivity. This too has had an unforeseen effect in paralysing any effort at strategic resistance. It is important to recognize that while women adopts labour casualisation, the higher is the number of women employed and the greater is their vulnerability to exploitative conditions. The impact of economic globalisation on women needs to be assessed in light of women's multiple roles as productive and reproductive labour in their families, as well as their contributions towards overall community cohesion and welfare, and maintaining the social fabric. Because of deep-rooted differences in gender roles and socio-cultural expectations, the impacts of economic globalisation are felt quite differently by women and men.

One of the biggest challenges of tracing and fully understanding the ways in which globalisation affects women is the absence of sex-disaggregated indicators and data in key sectors such as agricultural production and employment, services, and the informal sector. While independent researchers and institutions such as UNIFEM are gathering information and showing how women are affected by current economic trends, many of the indicators and methods used to monitor these trends are in and of themselves not gender sensitive.

I am very grateful to Mr. Pranav Gupta, Director of MD Publications Pvt Ltd, New Delhi, for his kind cooperation and support for this book.

S Thakur

CONTENTS

1

Technology and Sexual Difference

A riddle might ask what technology has to do with activities such as speech, consciousness of the inevitability of death, and the ability to lie: all have been mobilized at one time or another in the attempt to specify what constitutes the crucial difference of "Man." The epistemological or ontological project here is to mark aboundary or even a barrier against other species - "Man" is the one who speaks, the one who is aware that he must die, the one who is able to use language not only as it is dissociated from referentiality but as it contradicts it intentionally, and finally, the one whose use of tools is extensive, elaborate, and sophisticated enough to constitute a technology.

Because the relation to technology has been invoked consistently as one of the fundamental problematics in the delineation of human subjectivity, its implications for the conceptualization of sexual difference should be of considerable interest to feminist theory. The ongoing saturation of culture by technologies of imaging, information, and computation makes a consideration of this history an even more compelling project for feminisms at the turn of the century.

Historically, technology has been inextricable from certain explicit or implicit assumptions about the body and its limits and limitations. The conceptualization of that body - whether it is viewed as flawed (marked by castration) or as the site of a contingency that guarantees freedom and hence as the last refuge of humanness - is what is at stake. To the extent that pervasive new technologies of information continue to harbor a latent dream of disembodiment, it is perilous for feminist theory to neglect them. Nevertheless, the term "technology," despite its widespread deployment in analyses of modernity and postmodernity, is extraordinarily vague.

Etymologically, it can be traced to the Greek techne, the craft or art of making something, and is frequently opposed to physis, or nature. But as Jean-François Lyotard has pointed out, techne is also "the abstract from tikto which means to engender, to generate [tekontes, the genitors; teknon, the offspring," a lineage which would seem to mark the phrase "technologies of reproduction" with redundancy. Jacques Ellul (xxv) has argued that although technology is often reduced to the notion of the machine, it is more properly associated with "technique" as the method or methods imbued with the greatest degree of efficiency and rationality in any field (allying technology inevitably with the very process of rationalization). The machine is merely the purest incarnation of that efficiency and rationalization.

However, it has become increasingly difficult to dissociate technology from the concept of the tool or instrument. And the tool is most frequently conceptualized in relation to the human body as either its extension or replacement. Grounded in the analogy of the body, discourses on technology consistently return, quite uneasily for the most part, to questions of sexual difference. Despite the mechanistic and scientistic assumptions of many of these discourses, sexuality and sexual difference emerge as seemingly unavoidable tropes to an astonishing degree, allowing or disallowing the configuration of certain arguments.

Theoretical speculation about electronic and digital technologies, in particular computerization, is haunted by the possibility of a technology -i.e., artificial intelligence - that would eliminate altogether the status of the body as discursive ground and limit. As Donna Haraway has compellingly demonstrated, it is the intimate alliance between "man" and technology - the notion that "man" is above all a tool-using animal - that has been crucial in the development of primatology as a discipline in the twentieth century. Haraway points out that "primatology is about primal stories, the origin and nature of 'man,' and about reformation stories, the reform and reconstruction of human nature".

The discourse of primatology is particularly illuminating in its construction of a relation between technology and the body. A critical stake in primatology is the elaboration of a complex series of connections and differentiations between the animal and the human within the category of primate behaviour. One of the first and most persistent conceptualizations of differentiation, continuing to influence primatology well into the post-war studies of the 1950s, was the notion of upright posture. Bipedalism in itself was not necessarily perceived as determinant in hominization, but it refashioned the body in such a way that the hands were freed for the tool-use that would be constitutive of culture. In this view, technology emerges as a consequence of a specific adaptation of the body. As Haraway points out,

Technology has, therefore, an extraordinary scientific-mythic significance, built into the comparative anatomy of the bones and muscles of the pelvis. Stories about technology and skill are here the key guarantors of human unity, where the typological genius [sic] of race or nation is made to give way to the universal story of plasticity, culture as tool-using skill, language as instrumental naming, and self-making humanity. Almost immediately, sexual difference seems to become a theoretical stake insofar as the use of tools is synchronized with the dichotomy of hunting versus gathering, it perceived as one of the most primitive forms of the sexual division of labour. And despite arguments about the baby sling as the first practical tool, it is the masculinized trope of the toolweapon associated with hunting and defense that comes to dominate discussions of what it is to be human.

In a first movement, the tool in primatology is conceptualized as an extension of the human body, adding to its capabilities and sharpening its efficiency. But the tool can also be a form of substitution or a supplement in the Derridean sense of supplying a lack. Thinking about technology often seems to be predicated on the positing of a body that is haunted by lack or failure. This is the case in relation to speculation in physical anthropology about the appearance of smaller canine teeth in fossils perceived as transitional between ape and man. The first tools, then, would be compensations for a body shorn of its effective weapons. Haraway sees a certain feminization at work here: "at the dawn of hominization, culturally made weapons supplied the body's new biological lacks.

Yet, in the movement from animal to human being, the female body suffers a loss as well, although it is of a significantly different nature. While the male body is deprived of a kind of built-in technology, the female body "loses" estrus in favour of a constant "receptivity" that allows for the operation of "choice" in sexual behaviour. Hence, in the species-defining transition from animal to human, the male body is delineated by technology or, more properly speaking, its absence, while the female body loses sexuality as an isolatable sign-more precisely, it loses the differentiating ground of a non sexual temporality. In other words, there is no time when that body is not sexual. Haraway reads this primatological discourse somewhat differently:

> Sexuality and technology, each marked in the appropriately gendered bodies, from which physical marks of animality had been erased, were both part of logic of culture, which rested on the transfer of social causation from the determined body to the disembodied realm of free choice. Physical anthropology was witness to this transfer. Ironically, for a science born in the eighteenth-to-mid-twentieth century practices of marking the body of man to produce the bodies stained by sex and race, post-World War II evolutionary physical anthropology took up the task of erasing these marks to create a more versatile, biologically authorized universal man for the open society. As a result of a species-defining loss, sex and weapon moved from the anatomically marked bodies of female and male animals to universal, unmarked human bodies.

Here Haraway suggests that the male body's relationship to technology and to the female body's relationship to sex undergo a strictly parallel transformation in anthropological discourses after the war. Because the tool is separable from the body for the male and sexuality is not localized temporally for the female (in estrus), the body for each becomes unmarked, universalized in support of a liberal ideology of choice. Yet it certainly seems that discourses of technology encourage fantasies of disembodiment much more emphatically than those of sex. The "loss" of estrus does not necessarily mean the loss of sexuality or its disembodiment.

Rather, it indicates the reduction of its localization and specification, its general diffusion across the female body. On the other hand, the dissociation of technology from the body in the narrative of male ascension to humanity allows technology to assume the sheen of the purely pragmatic or operational, which seeks results in the nonideological bliss attributed to science. Yet, despite these divergences, there are crucial and often incoherent links between discourses on technology and discourses on sexuality. The body returns as the inescapable common denominator against which each is measured.

Primatology's origins can be traced to the eighteenth century with the birth of the category of the primate. It blossomed in the twentieth century, but the conditions of possibility for the emergence of this burgeoning discipline were established in the nineteenth century with a unique convergence of endeavors, including Darwinian evolutionary theory, thermodynamics, psychophysics, and time-and-motion studies.

Anson Rabinbach argues that with the centering of the concept of energy and the metaphor of the human motor, the period witnessed a concerted effort in various fields to desexualize or degender the human body, to abstract it in a move designed to graph, measure, and thus instrumentalize its energies (this would be a different form of desexualization than that suggested by Haraway). The human body became the working body and all other attributes, including sexuality, were bracketed in the hopes of perfecting this machine. The master discourse here was thermodynamics.

Although elaborated within the realm of physics in the 1840s, the two laws of thermodynamics have had an extraordinary impact - both subtle and explicit on a range of different fields including literature, biology, psychoanalysis, and information theory. The first law, commonly known as the conservation of energy, stipulates that energy may change in form but the total quantity of that energy always remains constantit cannot disappear altogether.

The second law recognizes that usable energy ultimately and irreversibly exhausts itself in the process of transformation and dissipates, leading inevitably to the degeneration and death of a closed system - this is the law of entropy. The two laws are at least seemingly inconsistent, and it could be said that their apparent contradiction, in fact, conditions the terms of understanding of the late nineteenth century. Rabinbach argues that the tension between the two laws or their "paradoxical relation" defines the contours of modernity. On the one hand, the law of conservation fuels the optimistic view of progress, of an ever increasing efficiency and rational control over nature.

On the other, the law of entropy supports theories of inevitable decline and degeneration, of an ultimate descent into disorder and chaos that seems to be accelerated by developments within modernity. However, the two laws are only apparently contradictory since the first concerns the quantity of energy while the second deals with its quality (i.e., whether it is "usable" or not). The first law describes a system that has no necessary relation to temporality - whether progressive or regressive. It is the second law that makes the temporal dimension inescapable.

Hence, it would be more accurate to revise Rabinbach's argument to claim that both the idea of progress and the idea of degeneration or decline are intimately linked to each other and to the second law of thermodynamics. As soon as the theory of energy is injected with temporal directionality, the ideas of both historical progress and historical decline become possible.

Such formulations about energy as pure force, about quantities, measures, and the maintenance of a balance would seem to exclude decisively the terms of sexual difference (as Rabinbach suggests) and, indeed, to suggest the possibility of a neutral or neutered discourse. However, it is instead the case that the concepts and rules of thermodynamics are continually aligned with the categories of sexual difference. This might be anticipated from the fact that Helmholtz identified the body with a thermodynamic machine: "The animal body therefore does not differ from the steam engine as regards the manner in which it obtains heat and force" (quotd in Rabinbach 61).

This thermodynamic body was from the beginning explicitly unspecified and implicitly white and male. At its foundation, thermodynamics' forging of a relation between heat and energy was infused with calculations about racial difference. Robert Mayer, whose work preceded Helmholtz's by a few years, based his findings concerning the energy principle on his "discovery" (which was never verified) that human blood in the Dutch Indies contains fewer red corpuscles than it does in northern climates.

This proposal was consistent with a pervasive discussion in the early 1800s that linked heat with low energy levels and idleness with savagery and uncivilized societies, and later ethnological descriptions of the "primitive's" inclination to laziness and inertia (in the context of speculation about fatigue as "resistance to modernity"). And more implicitly, because the body of thermodynamics was above all a working body, it was preeminently and incontestably male.

But beyond the specification of the body within a thermodynamic problematic, the component aspects of thermodynamics itself, its laws and equations, are orchestrated with narratives of sexual difference. The allegory of the steam engine, relayed by Dolf Sternberger as a fundamental moment in his analysis of the "panorama" of the nineteenth century, is a case in point.

The steam engine, which acts as a massive historical reference point in the delineation of the impact of the industrial revolution, is also frequently designated the originary machine of thermodynamics. In other words, the working of the steam engine is said to have inspired the laws of the transformation and conservation of energy. Sternberger relates the story presented by a famous German statistician in 1875 at a banquet celebrating the centennial of James Watt's invention of the steam engine. The narrative appears in the form of a toast to a married couple on the occasion of its hundredth anniversary:

> The husband is a true child of Nature, of ancient stock. His forebears claim to have witnessed the first and proudest of all foundings, the Creation of the world. All the offspring of this dynasty have one thing in common: they are very hot-headed. Now, to be sure, our man was forced to be somewhat wellbehaved upon entering matrimony, and he still is, on the whole.
>
> However, at times, when neglected, and especially when short of drink, he gives vent to his native temperament, smashing everything around him to smithereens and sparing nothing that stands in his way...The wife is altogether different. Her family is much younger than her husband's, although her ancestors could easily go back as far as the Freytags. Still, ages and ages ago, they were very simple and roughhewn people...One hundred years have elapsed since then. The marriage performed in 1775 is, despite the vast differences between the spouses, one of the happiest on the face of the earth and is still in its heyday.

The allegory is transparent, almost immediately legible - the hushand in this marriage is the steam which provides the energy while the wife is the engine which controls and directs that energy. Sternberger provides a provocative analysis of the allegory; nevertheless, in the process he desexualizes its terms in order to stress the success of the copulation between the natural and the artificial: "both elements, the natural and the artificial, adhere as tightly to one another as the Magdeburg hemispheres and are so inextricably enmeshed that the seams [cannot] be detected".

Yet, the way in which the attributes of the thermodynamic machine are distributed here is quite curious. On the one hand, the allegory's division is explicable by the fact that the male element represents power, and the female element constraint (aligning the woman fully with domesticity, taming, and the conservative values). On the other hand, the association of the male with Nature and the female with Culture or the artificial is more startling. Also, it is the male here who, in the light of the everpresent possibility of industrial or technological accident, represents instability and unpredictability - the perpetual potential of catastrophe and disorder.

These are attributes usually associated with the woman and her Pandora-like function. In the steam engine allegory, there is a metonymic chain connecting nature, disruption, and the male, while the female signals the rationalization, direction, and control of nature. This would situate the woman as the basic principle of industrial and technological progress, keeping at bay the man's unruly and aberrant proclivities. Technology here confuses the classical tropes of sexual difference (particularly the fundamental Nature/Culture opposition) and confounds the traditional clear-cut lines of differentiation. Just as technology always harbors within it the potential for physical or material crisis, it also poses the discursive threat of epistemological or representational crisis.

It might be tempting to propose that Sternberger was right to emphasize the success of the copulation in the allegory rather than its distribution of the terms of sexual difference. However, the allegory's confusion and reversal of the classical tropes is consistently reinscribed in discourses about thermodynamics. This is particularly visible in the incorporation of thermodynamics in the disciplines of sociology and biology where the two laws of energy conservation and entropy are explicitly linked with sexual identity. In The Study of Sociology, Herbert Spencer claimed that there was a "somewhat earlier arrest of individual evolution in women than in men; necessitated by the reservation of vital power to meet the cost of reproduction".

In other words, the economics of the first law of thermodynamics (the conservation of energy) dictated that the energy women expended in reproduction was unavailable for any other social or individual purpose. But Patrick Geddes and his student, J. Arthur Thomson, in an influential 1889 text, The

Evolution of Sex, went much further in reinscribing within the domain of biology a thermodynamic logic of sexual difference. According to Geddes, maleness and femaleness were differentiated at the level of cellular metabolism (where one could witness the minutest distributions of energy).

Male cellular metabolism was "katabolic," that is, it favored disruptive processes that result in the dissipation of energy. Female cellular metabolism was "anabolic" - favoring constructive synthetic processes. Ultimately this meant for Geddes that males were more active, energetic, eager, passionate and variable;" whereas females were passive, conservative, sluggish and stable" (stability here, as in the steam engine analogy, has negative connotations). Geddes embedded his thermodynamic logic in an evolutionary theory that allowed him to resist emerging feminist arguments: "To obliterate them sexual differences it would be necessary to have all the evolution over again on a new basis. What was decided among the prehistoric Protozoa cannot be annulled by Act of Parliament".

Hence, a biological explication of sexual difference that at first glance seems to denigrate maleness ultimately corroborates male superiority:

Males live at a loss, are more katabolic, - disruptive changes tending to preponderate in the sum of changes in their living matter or protoplasm. The females, on the other hand, live at a profit, are more anabolic, - constructive processes predominating in their life, whence indeed the capacity of bearing offspring.

Femaleness and maleness are hence explicitly aligned with conservation of energy and its inevitable dissipation, the first and second laws of thermodynamics respectively. Again, within a techno-scientific discourse, it is loss, failure, and breakdown which are characteristic of the male who, it would appear, bears the mark of castration. Why is it the second, pessimistic law of entropy that becomes the masculine principle, hurtling the universe toward destruction and dissolution? To complicate matters further, entropy becomes, when thermodynamics is transformed into information theory, "a measure of the information content of a message evaluated as to its uncertainty".

The masculine here connotes ambiguity, the inability of a form to hold steady its boundaries, the gradual bleeding away of meaning. The only recompense, if it could be thought of as such, would be that in the antagonistic thermodynamic relation between the sexes, the male principle ultimately wins in an apocalyptic finale of the universe - it is the male principle that controls the teleological direction of the system. From the first primate to stand upright and grasp a tool to the catastrophic end of time, the masculine would predominate - if not in practice, in the realm of a heavily charged symbolic order.

The logic behind the tropological displacement in thermodynamics is in a slightly different direction. Beyond the specific instances of sexual metaphor or analogy, what happens to the scientific conceptualization and representation of the human body toward the end of the nineteenth century and the beginning of the twentieth? Thermodynamics stipulates that the body is a machine like any other - regulating and transforming energy to produce work.

Figures like Etienne-Jules Marey, who were very much concerned with the careful and detailed depiction of the body in movement, were heavily influenced by Helmholtz. Inventor of a number of at first mechanical graphic inscriptors and later photographic inscriptors (which he called chronophotography, the photography of time); Marey was interested in charting the most minute movements of the human body through time. During the 1860s and 1870s, Marey conducted a number of experiments including attempts to record the movement of birds in flight and a variety of gaits of the horse.

After exposure to the work of Eadweard Muybridge, an AngloAmerican photographer who was also interested in the decomposition of motion, Marey switched from graphic notation to photographic notation. In the work of both Marey and Muybridge, the body becomes the object of a scientific discourse whose aim is to make visible the previously invisible facets of movement. Marey and Muybridge accumulated a vast arsenal of documentation of bodies in motion. For each of them, the point of contact with Helmholtz and thermodynamics is a fascination with the deployment of energy in the body. Muybridge made successive photographs of children climbing stairs, of women carrying baskets or water jugs, of men lifting, throwing, and wrestling.

Muybridge's bodies are consistently set against a black and white background that allegedly provides a means of graphing their movements. Despite his obsessive attention to the forms and positions assumed by the body in a variety of habitual (and staged) situations, Muybridge's colossal effort has only the veneer of a scientific endeavor. It is often quite difficult to determine how the background graph allows meaningful measurement. And, as Marta Braun has pointed out, Muybridge often fudged his results, covering over the absence of certain sections of a series and publishing them despite the gaps.

At some level, Muybridge was more interested in a photographer's aesthetics of the body in motion than in scientific procedure hence, the importance of the traces of narrative, costume, and mise-en-scène in his work. Confronted with the plethora of images that constitute his life's work, it is easy to see why many film histories locate him as the major scientific precursor of the cinema. The exhibits look precisely like strips of film, each still image differing slightly from the one preceding it. Linda Williams has argued that in his clearly differentiated treatment of men and women in the series of photographs, it is the woman who is associated with an excess of mise-en-scène or "a much greater degree of diegetic illusion".

With props like classical urns and veils, the woman's body is narrativized and eroticized more strongly. Nevertheless, in comparison with what happens to the body in Marcy's work, Muybridge's images are characterized by an insistence upon the body's presence - its details and idiosyncrasies. The representational aspirations are those of a classically inflected realism. It is almost as though the body acted as a kind of refuge for Muybridge - an optical haven from modernity.

In contrast, Marcy gave scrupulous attention to scientific procedure and has been seen by a number of recent historians (Braun, François Dagognet, and Rabinbach) as a crucial figure in the representational ruptures of modernity. Marcy's experiments were designed to pierce through the illusions of human vision (and its incarnation in classical realism) and to document the otherwise imperceptible movements in time and space of a human body conceived as a complex machine. He was, in fact, adamantly opposed to the cinema for simply confirming and perpetuating the illusions of the senses.

Marcy made use of photography not for its representational realism but for its accuracy as a record. He was more interested in the indexical relationship between the object and photographic image than in its property of iconic resemblance. In this scientistic context, the body disappears. Marcy's work generates a denial of the body at two levels. First, he disables the eye of the subject and replaces it with a mechanical eye with the power to freeze temporal progression.

He spoke of mechanical inscription as "a new sense endowed with amazing precision". Secondly, his work, unlike Muybridge's, quickly moves beyond the representation of the bodily form recognizable as such and becomes increasingly abstract. Blurred and overlapping bodies are common in his images, and he developed the technique of attaching lights or luminous strips to parts of the body and photographing it against a dark background so that only series of dots and lines are visible, with only a hint of a ghostly bodily presence.

For instance, Marey placed a brilliant point at the base of the spine of a man walking away from the camera to record what he called "a luminous trail, an image without end, at once manifold and individual". The photograph of Georges Demeny (a collaborator of Marey's) in a black hood and black suit with luminous striping and points for what Marey called geometric or partial chronophotography has become indissociably linked with Marey's endeavor. The body itself merges in blackness with the background. The resulting photographs resemble abstract modernist paintings.

Much of Marey's work was in the service of an attempt to understand the most efficient and productive utilization of the body's energy. Its effects thus merged with those of Frederick W. Taylor in the U.S. and the notion of scientific management. One of Taylor's disciples, Frank B. Gilbreth, was heavily influenced by Marey's chronophotography and pursued his abstraction of the human body. Gilbreth attached a small electric light to the limb of a worker and used a time exposure to photograph the movement as a continuous line in space - he called the result a "cyclograph" (or a chronocyclograph if a motion picture camera was used).

For instance, one photograph, entitled "Cyclograph of an Expert Surgeon Tying a Knot" represents the operation as several Moebius strip-like lines of light against the background of the stable figures of doctor and nurse. In "Girl Folding a Handkerchief", however, the girl has completely disappeared and only the movement's progress itself is registered as curves of light. Gilbreth's comment on the picture of the surgeon reveals the extent to which he perceived his work as having a certain aesthetic value: "The path of the motion is shown, but not the speed or the direction. The record does show the beautiful smooth repetitive pattern of the expert".

This trend toward abstraction in the representation of movement though time is intensified by Gilbreth's translation of the photographed movements (i.e., streaks of light) into wire models. One such wire model, entitled "Perfect Movement", is simply an elaborate white curve against a black background. The particularities of the worker's identity or the type of labour involved have completely disappeared in the abstraction of perfection. In his monumental book, Mechanization Takes Command, Siegfried Giedion juxtaposes Gilbreth's cyclographs with paintings by Paul Klee and Joan Miro. Time and motion studies, the obsessive concern of a science of work in the late nineteenth and early twentieth centuries that appears to be about the body, in effect cause it to disappear.

This may have to do with certain uneasiness with the evolving perception of the body as a limit. Unlike a machine, the human body is subject to fatigue and fatigue-induced error.

Rabinbach, in the course of his analysis of the metaphor of the human motor, has extensively documented the evidence that fatigue was viewed as a form of resistance to modernity (as well as its enabler in certain respects).

Fatigue was something to be controlled, contained, and directed. But Rabinbach also argues that the central place of the working body in the problematic of thermodynamics gradually gives way in the second half of the twentieth century to the more "cerebral" and postmodern work associated with the circulation of images, communication, and cybernetic systems: "The appearance of the cerebral worker whose material and product is 'information' is emblematic of the vast distance traversed between the worker who surveys complex technologies of communication and the 'man-beef of Taylor'".

In Rabinbach's analysis, it is the working body which disappears - leaving room for the emergence of a gendered body and a racially inscribed body. Yet, if the move in information theory is away from the body that occupies the realm of the physical, tangible, and the material, any body would find it uninhabitable. From this point of view, the place or non-place of the body in information theory may have more in common with that of thermodynamics than Rabinbach suggests.

If the body is confronted as a limit to the progress, efficiency, and rationality seemingly promised by technology, there would appear to be two solutions to such a dilemma - eliminate it as a category, or transform existing notions about the body. At the turn of the century and beyond, anxieties about this body are played out partially through the newly emerging technology of the cinema. It is intriguing that the "scientific" pursuits anticipating the cinema should be focused on the human body, both inscribing it insistently and erasing its presence, causing it to emerge as a graphable and measurable entity.

There is a sense in which this double logic is reinscribed in the cinema. In some of the earliest films, the very sight of the female body - particularly in some state of tantalizing undress - constitutes the raison d'être of the spectacle. In a series of one-shot dance films made by Edison in 1895 and 1896, films which strikingly resemble one of Muybridge's photographic series (entitled "Woman Pirouetting"), the object of the film is simply a woman with long flowing skirts dancing in front of a black background as the colour tinting of her costume is varied.

In What Happened on Twenty-Third Street, Trapeze Disrobing Act, and Pull Down the Curtains, Suzie, the incipient voyeurism is not entirely unlike that of the fully developed classical cinema, anticipating a stable point of view for a male spectator.4 Much of the fascination of George Meliès's films, of course, hinges on the continual disappearance and reappearance of bodies - both female and male.

Yet, it was the newly emerging avant-garde of the 1910s and 1920s that was fascinated by the technology of the cinema as well as the idea of technology and that activated most fully the second moment of the double logic, absenting the body completely (as in Marcel Duchamps' Anemic Cinema (1926) which, although taking its title from a bodily pathology, is constituted solely by revolving spirals and word play) or banishing that body to the margins of the discourse and focus briefly on one particularly well-known example of the avant-garde's obsession with technology, Fernand Leger Ballet mecanique, and to trace the vicissitudes of the body in this film.

As its title suggests, Ballet mecanique is a somewhat ironic merger of a classical art concerned with rhythm and form and the industrialized context of modernity, where things become animated and machines impose their own temporality. Produced toward the end of what art historians label Leger's "mechanical period" (1919-24), the film evinces a fascination with gleaming metal, the movement of machines, industrial objects.

Consistent with the French obsession with Charlie Chaplin, the film is introduced by a collage figure representing "Charlot." Following an idyllic shot of a woman on a swing (shots of this woman bracket the film), the film deals primarily with objects that move themselves or appear to move and change shape as an effect of accelerated editing -a straw hat, shoes, kitchen implements, geometric forms, bottles, and a vast array of machines and mechanical devices, with a concentration on their reflective surfaces. Excluding all traces of a narrative logic, Ballet mecanique is more concerned with the temporality of objects than with their recognizability.

A few references to the human body are interspersed among the objects - shots of the eyes and smiling mouth of an androgynous model named Kiki, two shots of Leger's collaborator, Dudley Murphy, emerging from a chaos of mechanical moving parts, a loop of a washerwoman climbing the same stairs over and over again, endlessly repeating the same gestures, a pair of legs cut off from any body performing a cinematically induced dance. Yet, it is the shock-like effect of the editing that seems central to the film's project. The thermodynamic logic of its structure is reflected in the deployment of forces and energies and their manipulation across time.

Leger himself conceived of the film as a kind of assault on the spectator: "We 'persist' up to the point where the eye and the mind of the spectator'can't take it any more.' We exhaust its visual power at the very moment when it becomes unbearable". In this respect, it is the body of the spectator that is placed in the balance, put at risk. Leger's strategy here is fully consistent with the avant-garde's understanding of the cinema in this period as pure kinesis, energy and movement unadulterated by content. Force is chosen over meaning.

Despite these manifestly abstract tendencies, it is interesting to note that Leger himself described the film as "objective, realistic, and in no way abstract". Standish Lawder, who has constructed a detailed shot by shot analysis of Ballet mecanique, argues that Leger's experience of World War I was the decisive factor in his move away from an analytical cubism concerned only with processes of vision at the expense of content. Lawder traces Leger's obsession with the machinery of modernity to the shocks of a highly technologized battlefield. Leger claimed, "Once I bit into this reality [war], the object never left me," and "the breech of cannon, the sun beating down, and the rawness of the object itself. That's where I was formed".

The object may never have left Leger, but it is not entirely clear what happens to the subject. Like Anemic Cinema, Ballet mecanique contains a section that might be characterized as word play. Yet, while Anemic Cinema manipulates and matches sounds and meanings, Ballet mecanique reduces the words to their sheer materiality as letters, as psychic traces. This section begins by taking its material from a sentence that might well be derived from another privileged site of modernity - the newspaper headline: "On a vole un collier de perles de 5 millions [Pearl necklace worth 5 million stolen]."

The following shots proceed to break the sentence into fragments, severing the letters and isolating them (particularly the O's) so that they seem to dance across the screen, to appear and disappear unpredictably. The subject-spectator is positioned in this context as the site of pure registration rather than understanding or the production of meaning. In this respect, the avant-garde's use of language is reminiscent of the goals and strategies of a discipline that emerged in the late nineteenth and early twentieth centuries, referred to variously as psychotechnics or psychophysics.

One of the earliest and most structuring of the experiments in this field involved placing a subject in front of a machine that generated random letters or syllables in order to measure the subject's memory of these material traces without any recourse to meaning. The subject here becomes a mere surface for inscription. Friedrich Kittler's analysis of psychophysics in Discourse Networks 1800/ 1900 demonstrates that it is based on the assumption that "all sense making has its frontiers in domains of nonsense and in automatized operations that no longer belong to a subjective authority".

In the processes of both psychophysics and the avant-garde, there is a certain evacuation of subjectivity that necessitates a conceptualization of the body as a site of inscription rather than as the vessel or conveyor of meaning. As Kittler points out, "Psychophysics advances, beyond all attribution of meaning and its transparent arbitrariness, to the meaningless body, which is a machine among machines". In this case, the machine that the subject mimics, as pure recorder or surface of inscription, would not be dissimilar to the cinema itself, an asubjective memory.

There is a sense in which Ballet mecanique does represent the body as a "machine among machines." Its parts are subjected to the same filmic operations as the mechanical parts and kitchen implements. Kiki's eyes are open in one shot, suddenly closed in the next, with all transitional moments elided. Her facial movements are as mechanical and expressionless as possible. The disembodied legs in the film perform a mechanical dance that differs in no way from that of the film's other objects. The mechanicalness of human movement becomes most apparent, however, in the loop of the washerwoman climbing the stairs.

As she climbs the stairs, she performs the same movements each time, looking up at the camera and talking, moving her arm outward for effect. But she never advances further than a certain stage and is then condemned to a seemingly infinite repetition of the action. The section lays out the terms of filmic representation itself - where a movement that is apparently singular, unique, and spontaneous is inscribed as infinitely repeatable, as the collusion (or perhaps collision) of the contingent and the meaningful.

Nevertheless, the most relevant body here is the one that both opens and closes the film and is the representation that is the furthest possible from that of the machine. This is the idyllic scene of the woman on the swing that, eschewing any links to the fragmentations and discontinuities of modernity, aligns itself with an exaggerated Romanticism. Despite the fact that a few shots later this woman reappears, still swinging, from a disconcerting and defamiliarizing high angle, she continues to represent, through negation, what the film is not about -the type of body that its discourse disallows, a body outside the boundaries of a technological paradigm.

The film ends on this negative note as well, its final shot presenting the same woman, carefully and elegantly smelling a blossom in a garden. Despite Lawder's claim that the purpose of the shot of the woman swinging is to establish a rhythm and that "the content of the image is of incidental importance," it is not surprising that the body is that of a woman and that the mise-en-scène is infused with a somewhat stale femininity.

For Ballet mecanique, born out of the confrontation with the rawness of the object experienced in war, masculinizes itself through the violent collisions of metal, machinery, and time.

The woman is the body; the body is that which must be rejected. The woman swinging in Ballet mecanique functions both as a reminder of what is to be replaced and as a return to that which seems inescapable, which continues to haunt any discourse on technology - the body as limit, as obstacle. The metaphor of the body as machine has been with us so long that it has become banal, uninformative. But it is not this metaphor itself that I see as the crux of technology's intersection with the body.

Rather, a technological discourse has always only been possible on condition that it endeavor to think the radical absence of the body (and perhaps in the process to tell us something about the very operation of metaphor). Cultural theorists like Kittler and Mark Seltzer have pointed out that the typewriter was invented by and for the blind, the phonograph by a nearly deaf Edison ("Media, like psycho-physical experiments, begin with a physiological deficiency").

The anxieties attendant upon the idea of a disappearance of the body become most acutely visible, perhaps, in 1950s discourses about automation and its consequences, activating in the science-fiction imagination horror stories about technological take-overs at the expense of the human. Underlying the thermodynamic theories of energy that support and direct technological expansion is an apocalyptic notion of the end of the universe - of degeneration, dissipation and the annihilation of anything at the level of the physical or material that might be construed as a body.

The body, in fact, has been theorized as an island of resistance to the second law of thermodynamics, as an incarnation of "negentropy". Yet, it might be more accurate to argue that this formulation of the problem neglects the first law of thermodynamics in favour of the second, the law of entropy, and that the first marks a certain reassertion of the body and its claims. From this point of view, modern technological discourses would be characterized by a tension between the desire to think away the body and the apparent impossibility of conceptualizing the absence of the body.

This would explain the persistence of a double logic of inscription and erasure of the body in the time and motion studies of Marey and Gilbreth, which liken the body to a machine, and in the early cinema, particularly that subset of the avant-garde that understands the specifically cinematic as pure energy or kinesis. Technological representations of the body obsessively return to this play between presence and absence, to that originary moment isolated by primatology as the dissociation of technology from its bodily origins - the moment when the razor sharp canines became tool-weapons held in the hands of an upright being. Technological discourses seem to succumb continually to the temptation to repair that initial separation.

The sexual logic of thermodynamics is not confined to the nineteenth century and its immediate aftermath. It is very much with us in contemporary elaborations of information theory in which the pair energy/entropy is simply displaced by information/noise in a signifying economy where, as Rabinbach argues, communication replaces labour as the basic cultural paradigm.

Michel Serres argues that information theory simply takes the theoretical armature of thermodynamics and applies it to a different object, replacing the macroscopic scale of motors and general systems or producers of movement (resulting in speculation about "the cosmos in general" or "organic life in particular") with the microscopic scale of the ordinary activities of reading, writing, and the transmission of messages. Entropy operates here as well: "It immediately became obvious, or was taken as such, that a store of information transcribed on any given memory, a painting or a page, should drift by itself from difference to disorder".

In Serres's own rewriting of the thermodynamic logic of information theory, "noise" (which is the embodiment of entropy) is anthropomorphized and designated the "third man." And this "third man," although despised and denigrated by the two who are attempting to communicate, is an absolutely crucial support of the very idea of dialogue or communication: "To hold a dialogue is to suppose a third man and to seek to exclude him; a successful communication is the exclusion of the third man".

The question persists: why is entropy - disorder, degeneration, ambiguity, uncertainty, noise, unpredictability - consistently aligned with the masculine in the tropological scenarios of thermodynamics and information theory? Why, in the steam engine allegory isolated for analysis by Sternberger, is the husband Nature and the wife the engine? Entropy has the advantage of determining a direction, of commanding teleology.

A technological order changes the terms of the conceptualization of Nature. Nature is no longer the benign and submissive partner in a philosophical conversation but the mute and inescapable final cause with tremendous and potentially uncontainable energy. Binding and control (in technology, in information theory's tenuous hold over noise) become feminine when control and power are no longer synonymous, when catastrophe is the constant measure of a system that cannot succeed, allowing the reassignment of failure to the woman. When entropy becomes noise, the scenario is repeated at the microlevel of the body (rather than the cosmos).

Serres muses about the tremendous noise that must be generated by the series of thermodynamic systems that compose the body, where a roaring din would be the effect of a continual drifting of information into background noise. One of the questions that guides his inquiry is - why don't we hear it? A discussion of a complex series of rectifiers between different levels, which transform noise into information, reveals that it is the body as a meta-thermodynamic system that uneasily and fragilely contains and subdues this noise.

Insofar as the body is aligned with the feminine (which is also aligned, in a thermodynamic logic, with the conservation of energy) a technological discourse's desire to eliminate the body might seem quite transparent. And this desire would foster the appeal of entropy as the complete annihilation of the material/physical realm - the Ur-fantasy of a patriarchal symbolic order with an idealist agenda. The only problem is that this is a rather self-defeating scenario.

The terms and quandaries of this problematic are laid out explicitly in an extraordinary essay by Lyotard that rewrites the sexualized allegory of the steam engine. The title - and structuring question - of the essay is Can Thought Go on without a Body? The fundamental problem confronting and determining the direction of techno-science, according to Lyotard, is the inevitability, in 4.5 billion years, of the most catastrophic event conceivable - the explosion of the sun. Solar death is pure event," "disaster"; unlike human death, it will be unthinkable after it happens because no thought will exist. The direst consequence of solar death, in Lyotard's view, is not that it will annihilate all human life as we know it but that it will make philosophy impossible.

All technical and scientific research now organizes itself around this problem: how to make thought materially possible after the catastrophe of materiality or, in other words, "how to make thought without a body possible". This leads Lyotard to a series of ruminations about computer hardware and software and the possibility or impossibility of artificial intelligence. The first part of the essay ends with a reassuring "no" to the question. The body is not simply the physical support of thought; it provides its grounding analogy - vision. Or, more precisely, thought and vision are analogous because both proceed analogically with respect to their environments - symbolic and sensible.

The second part of the essay further refines the reasons why thought is not separable from the body, extending the discussion of analogy and the status of vision as a model for what happens in thinking. Vision is, above all, incomplete: "A direct, focused vision is always surrounded by a curved area where visibility is held in reserve yet isn't absent". It is as though visibility constituted a veiled but always deferred promise of the possibility of the empirical grounding of knowledge. A complete recognition, identification, or description of an object is therefore never possible and thought proceeds hesitantly, in trials and by degrees. Analogy is the term that defines this progression, grounded as it is in "this blur, this uncertainty, this faith in the inexhaustibility of the perceivable".

Lyotard goes on to present an astonishing yet very familiar discussion of thinking, writing, painting as a form of receptivity to the "givable" and therefore as a waiting, a discomfort, suffering. And it is inconceivable to Lyotard that a machine could suffer - pain announcing the immediate certainty of a body. But the final and most decisive move in his argument, the transcendent move from his point of view, is the insistence upon the fact of sexual difference as that which "launches thought". The presumption of heterosexuality is quite manifesting here as Lyotard defines sexual difference as "a paradigm of an incompleteness of not just bodies, but minds too".

Recognition or description of the other is impossible for the same reason that vision is incomplete, uncertain; and that inability to unify or completely determine the object is the source of a suffering and unhappiness that is determinant in thinking. Lyotard argues that "your thinking machines will have to be nourished not just on radiation but on the irremediable differend of gender" and that "not only calculation, but even analogy cannot do away with the remainder left by this difference. This difference makes thought go on endlessly and won't allow itself to be thought".

Sexual difference is the apex of the uncertainty, the blur, the inexhaustibility of perception that makes analogy possible. And thought proceeds above all by analogy, not by logic - a thinking that entails suffering because it must wait for the approach of the "givable." Entropy here is what makes possible the acknowledgment (if not the thinking) of the originating force, the critical importance of a sexual difference that cannot be thought (but that "launches thought"). But sexual difference also appears in the essay in a different form. Part one is entitled "He"; part two is entitled "She."

There is no explanation of this bifurcation, and it is not easily understandable. Is this a conversation between an anonymous man and an anonymous woman who represent only their respective sexual identities? Is part one "about" masculinity and part two "about" femininity? Does each part manifest the incompletion of the other? Or is Lyotard making it clear that sexual difference is the structure allowing him to think this apocalyptic scenario? Part one, labeled "He," poses the problem of techno-science as that of impending and inevitable solar death and lays out the terms of the question, "Can thought go on without a body?" It ends with the first obstacle to such a project: the central importance of analogy in human thought and perception.

This part is addressed to a "you" who seems to represent the philosopher with his unanswerable questions, the philosopher whose enterprise is made laughable by the fact of solar death. Part two, labeled "She," is addressed to the techno-scientist and is a kind of lyric to the body as an enabler of thought. This is where Lyotard presents his theory of thought as incompletion, as pain and suffering, as waiting, and as grounded in the most determinant form of incompletion - sexual difference.

Quite predictably, the section entitled "She" marks in full force the return of the claims of the body and also of its ineffable haze of suffering and pain that limits that which is programmable. On the other hand, the section entitled "He" is an elaboration of an inevitable teleology, an entropic process leading to the absolute catastrophe - "pure event." Linking the masculine with entropy seemingly recapitulates the terms of the steam engine allegory discussed by Sternberger, where the male is an unpredictable, unruly and disruptive Nature and the woman a controlling Engine, a thermodynamic system.

Entropy is a measure of leakage, excess - what cannot be controlled by the system. But in fact, Lyotard's scenario reveals the instabilities and contradictions of the steam engine allegory, its inability to hold together. If the woman represents the irrevocability of the body, its pure presence, it is difficult to align her with a technology that also always strives for disembodiment for a radical absence of the body. The tropology goes awry and seems to suffer the entropic fate of information slowly disintegrating into noise. What remains and provides the point of discursive stability is the "fact" of sexual difference as grounding the possibility of thought. It is not the substance or content of the sexual identity (which continually shifts and changes form) that matters but, rather, the relations (of incompletion, of demand, of desire) between sexually defined entities. Lyotard's essay reveals how it is the "fact" of sexual difference that will not go away as a tropological support for thought itself.

Technology in a first stage always confronts us as a form of rationalization and control over nature whose temporality is that of progress. To that extent, as the time and motion studies of Marey and Gilbreth and the avant-garde work of Fernand Leger demonstrate, it harbors a somewhat perverse dream of disembodiment, of eliminating a body marked by failure, lack, and limitation. Assigning the body to the woman quarantines this failure and contingency. But a curious nostalgia for the body intervenes in this scenario, indicating the degree of difficulty and stress involved in thinking disembodiment, in giving up one's own body.

Technological efficiency and rationalization are counterbalanced by the theorizing of failure, lack, and incompletion as enabling. It therefore becomes a question, in Lyotard's science-fiction scenario, not of building the perfect computer to house intelligence, but of transporting the body away from a doomed earth (to transport, to transfer, bear, carry - we are in the etymology of metaphor and back to the processes of analogy). The cost of the dream of disembodiment emerges as the apocalyptic vision of solar death. The sacrifice entailed in thinking away one's own body prompts an attempt to make that body something else - or at least to place it somewhere else. For the body also protects even the philosopher of science against the tremendous noise within, the roaring of entropic processes.

2

Identity Construction

The study of identity forms a critical cornerstone within modern sociological thought. Introduced by the works of Cooley and Mead, identity studies have evolved and grown central to current sociological discourse. Microsociological perspectives (social psychology, symbolic interactionism), perspectives focused primarily on the individual, dominated work published through the 1970s. Sociologists focused primarily on the formation of the "me," exploring the ways in which interpersonal interactions mold an individual's sense of self. But identity research of the past two decades proves antithetical to traditional concerns, a shift largely fueled by three important trends.

Social and nationalist movements of the past three decades have shifted scholarly attention to issues of group agency and political action. As a result, identity studies have been relocated to the site of the collective, with gender/ sexuality, race/ethnicity, and class forming the "holy trinity" of the discursive field. Writings attend, in particular, to that which constitutes a collective and the political implications that result from collective definitions.

Intellectual concerns with agency and self-direction have re-energized the study of identification processes. At the level of the collective, scholars are examining the mechanics by which distinctions are created, maintained, and changed. New communication technologies have freed interaction from the requirements of physical copresence; these technologies have expanded the array of generalized others contributing to the construction of the self. Several research loci emerge from this development: the substance of "I," "me," and the generalized other in a milieu void of place, the establishment of "communities of the mind," and the negotiation of copresent and cyberspace identities.

THE NATURE OF COLLECTIVE IDENTITY

Collective identity is a concept grounded in classic sociological constructs: Durkheim's "collective conscience," Marx's "class consciousness," Weber's Verstehen, and Tonnies' Gemeinschaft. So rooted, the notion addresses the "we-ness" of a group, stressing the similarities or shared attributes around which group members coalesce. Early literature approached these attributes as "natural" or "essential" characteristics - qualities emerging from physiological traits, psychological predispositions, regional features, or the properties of structural locations. A collective's members were believed to internalize these qualities, suggesting a unified, singular social experience, a single canvas against which social actors constructed a sense of self.

Recent treatments of collective identity question the essentialism of collective attributes and images. Anti-essentialist inquiries promote the social construction of identity as a more viable basis of the collective self. Other works stress the problems inherent in collective categorization, presenting a postmodern challenge to arguments of unified group experiences.

SOCIAL CONSTRUCTIONISM

In concert with theories of WI Thomas, Peter Berger, Erring Goffman, Howard Becker, and others, the social constructionist approach to identity rejects any category that sets forward essential or core features as the unique property of a collective's members. From this perspective, every collective becomes a social artifact - an entity molded, refabricated, and mobilized in accord with reigning cultural scripts and centers of power.

Social constructionism informs much of the work on gender identity. Such studies challenge essentialist dichotomies of gender and dismiss notions of gender's primordial roots. Constructionists conceptualize gender as an interactional accomplishment, an identity continually renegotiated via linguistic exchange and social performance. From this stance, researchers also explore subjective definitions of femininity and masculinity, attending to the symbols and norms that initiate and sustain either/or classifications.

Constructionist works often scrutinize agents of socialization, delineating their role in gender identity acquisition: the family. While such studies reflect numerous intellectual traditions, all are concerned with the ways in which socialization agents organize and project the affective, cognitive, and behavioral data individuals use to form a gendered self.

An important outgrowth of gender constructionism rests with works that problematize the gender-sex link. Researchers dissect the differences in male and female biology - the body and reproductive system in particular. By questioning the meaning of biological distinctions, scholars expose the social rituals, symbols, and practices that transform such differences into social facts. In so doing, this literature demonstrates the inscription of gender on the body, simultaneously dismantling notions of gender as emergent from the body.

In highlighting the subjective nature of gender, constructionists do not deemphasize the effects of gender categories. Rather, they argue that socially defined maleness and femaleness severely constrict human behaviour. Subjective definitions imprison individuals in spheres of prescribed action and expectation. Dorothy Smith writes of this effect within scholarship, dubbing it "the alienation of utterance...models of speaking, writing, and thinking that took (women's) powers of expression away from us even as we used them". Gender scripting attitudes, behaviors, emotions, and language, and treating these scripts as natural signals, ensures that social members both succumb to and recreate the "armor" of gender identity stereotypes.

Constructionist approaches to sexual identity complement the gender literature. Important entries include the work of Verta Taylor and Nancy Whittier on lesbian identity and lesbian social movements. Taylor & Whittier map a three-step process, itemizing (a) the construction of boundaries that both insulate and differentiate nonmainstream groups from the dominant sexual collective, (b) the emergence of shared consciousness and goals among nonmainstream sexual groups, and (c) processes of politicization that valorize a group's minority status. Janice Irving (1994) takes a similar approach to adolescent sexual identity.

Irvine identifies nine "axes of constructed domains" that contribute to identity building and identity-based experience: gender relations, sexual identities, reproductive strategies and behaviour, sexual language and public discourse, the role of the family, nonreproductive sexuality, the purpose of sex and the role of pleasure, knowledge and meaning of the body, and sexual violence. Irving also explores the cultural differences that can colour sexual identification as it occurs in varying social locations. These works exemplify a much broader literature exploring the origins, meaning, and renegotiation of sexual communities.

Race and ethnic studies represent another stronghold of constructionism. F. James Davis, for example, provides a fascinating historical excursion that charts definitions of blackness in America. Davis documents the history of the "one drop rule," a vehicle for racial classification. He unpacks the rule's development and highlights its triumph over competing alternatives. Davis follows the one drop rule in action, itemizing its role in the struggle to maintain the slave system. He also contrasts the US classification experience with racial categorization in other nations.

Davis concludes with thoughtful speculation regarding the one drop rule's impact on the future of US race relations - particularly in light of developing demographic shifts. In another arena, Balibar & Wallerstein view racial identity within a broad analytical landscape, considering race in conjunction with nation and class. Blending constructionist premises with the socioeconomic lenses for which the authors are renowned, Balibar & Wallerstein thoughtfully analyze both imposed racialization and self-racialization, variantly considering racial identity and collective repression, the struggle for collective autonomy, and the search for collective shelter.

Several works on racial and ethnic identity incorporate the subject's voice into their inquiries. Examples include Richard Alba's work on European-descended Americans. In keeping with constructionist premises, Alba argues that ethnic identity is no longer anchored in strongly ethnic social structures. Rather, he presents ethnicity as a symbolic entity "concerned with the symbols of ethnic cultures rather than with the cultures themselves".

Alba argues that symbolic ethnicities are easily reshaped in response to varying situational contexts and growing social needs. His data suggest one such reconstruction - a renegotiation that unites European descendents under the broad umbrella of a European-American identity. Alba argues that this identity shift bears significant social benefits for those it encompasses; the shift provides white-Euro descendents with a larger, more comfortable base as they face a rapid influx of non-Euro, nonwhite immigrants.

Identity shifts and their implications are also central to Mary Waters's (1990) research. Like Alba, Waters brings forward a constructed, symbolic ethnicity. However, her work problematizes the relentlessness with which individuals cling to ethnicity. Waters scrutinizes ethnic identification in light of its social payoff rewards, she argues, that prove negligible for white, Euro-descendents and potentially negative for Americans of nonwhite, non-Euro lineage. Ultimately, Waters comes to understand ethnic identity as the product of personal choice - social category individuals actively decide to adopt or stress. Her research documents the ways in which those of mixed ancestry switch and amend their primary ethnic affiliations.

In this way, Waters locates the attraction of ethnicity within a double-edged American value. Commitment to ethnic identity stems from a culturally based need for community -

community lacking individual cost. In another arena, Joann Nagel examines ethnic identity shifts as a sociopolitical phenomenon. Using US Census figures, Nagel documents changing patterns of Native American identification. She explains identity shifts with reference to three sociopolitical factors: changing federal Indian policy, increased American ethnic politics, and growing American Indian political activism. Nagel argues that these factors raised Native American ethnic consciousness, and she traces the ways in which policy and politics encouraged an ethnic renewal.

Social constructionism drives a multifaceted literature on national identity. A rich collection of sociohistorical works on commemoration, narrative, and symbolization chart the ways in which actors, particularly elites, create, manipulate, or dismantle the identities of nations, citizenships, allies, and enemies. In related work, several studies grapple with constructionist issues as they consider the constitution of the American self. One also finds innovative elaborations of constructionism, such as Benedict Anderson's work on imagined community. Anderson approaches national identity as a sociocognitive construct - one both spatially and temporally inclusive, both enabled and shaped by broader social forces. He documents key moments of identity construction, times during which cultural (language) and social factors (capitalism, print technology) convene in a particular historical moment, effectively remaking collective images of the national self.

Yet, more than any arena before the identity scholar's eye, national identity work presents a multivoiced excursion. Works probing nationalism with reference to the state and world markets continue to thrive. "New institutionalism" brings middle-range questions to bear, examining political structures and organizational principles and their influence on policy, political agenda, and ultimately collective self-definition. Newer trends include Yasemin Soysal's "postnational model," which addresses changing definitions of national membership.

Soysal examines the different strategies by which Western European nations incorporate guestworkers into the national citizenry. She argues that citizen collectives increasingly are defined not by their primordial ties to a territory, but according to entitlements emerging from both a transnational discourse and a set of structures celebrating human rights. Anthony D Smith poses perhaps the greatest challenge to constructionism. Smith adopts a middle-ground approach to national identity, linking social constructionism to more essentialist views.

He defines national identity as a product of both "natural" continuity and conscious manipulation. Natural continuity emerges from pre-existing ethnic identity and community; conscious manipulation is achieved via commemoration, ideology, and symbolism. Smith compliments this duality with a social psychological dimension, citing a "need for community" as integral to identity work. In Smith's view, this tri-part combination distinguishes national identity, making it the most fundamental and inclusive of collective identities.

DECONSTRUCTING CATEGORIES

While supporting the antiessentialism that drives constructionist inquiries on identity, postmodernists cite serious flaws in the school's approach. Some find constructionism's agenda insufficient, suggesting that it simply catalogues the identity construction process. Further, many contend that the constructionist approach implies identity categories built through interactive effort. Such a stance underemphasizes the role of power in the classification process, mistakenly suggesting "a multidirectional flow of influence and agency".

These weaknesses leave postmodern identity theorists skeptical of social constructionism's trajectory, fearing that the paradigm ultimately approximates the very essentialism it fights against. Diane Fuss elaborates in evaluating the constructionist approach to gender: "specifying more precisely these subcategories of 'woman' does not necessarily preclude essentialism.'French bourgeois woman' or 'Anglo-American lesbian,' while crucially emphasizing in their very specificity that 'woman' is by no means a monolithic category, nonetheless reinscribe an essentialist logic at the very level of historicism".

In an effort to broaden the social constructionist agenda, postmodernists examine the "real, present day political and other reasons why essentialist identities continue to be invoked and often deeply felt". Further, in the study of identity, they view the variation within identity categories - i.e. women, African-Americans, working class - as important as the variation between identity categories. Finally, postmodernists advocate a shift in analytic focus, deemphasizing observation and deduction and elevating concerns with public discourse.

In the spirit of Jean Baudrillard, Jacques Derrida, Michel Foucault, and Jean-Francois Lyotard, the postmodern-identity scholar deconstructs established identity categories and their accompanying rhetoric in an effort to explore the full range of "being." Works in this tradition call into question models that equate discourse with truth; they expose the ways in which discourse objectified as truth both forms and sustains collective definitions, social arrangements, and hierarchies of power.

For students of identity, postmodern works on gender and sexuality prove richest. Judith Butler (1990), Patricia Hill Collins (1991), Jane Flax (1990), Marjorie Garber (1992), Donna Haraway (1991), Bell Hooks (1984), and Trinh T Minh-Ha (1989) reconsider gender identity, giving voice to women of colour, those of various social classes, and lesbian and bisexual women. They expose the dangers in approaching gender collectives as homogeneous entities and urge careful consideration of the complex, often contradictory, nature of collective existence.

In contrast to the social constructionist, postmodern gender theorists challenge the dualistic, oppositional nature by which gender is traditionally framed. Patricia Hill Collins (1991), for example, notes that elements such as race and social class produce multiple variations of "women" and "men," distinctions that many societies use to build complex hierarchical stratification systems. The existence of these multiple categories alerts us to the flaws of binary gender conceptualizations, focusing us instead on the ways in which multiple identity affiliations qualitatively change the nature of human experience.

Core postmodern works on sexual identity follow a similar thrust, problematizing sexual categories and contesting sexual hierarchies. In contrast to prior treatments of sexual identity (i.e. studies exploring the construction of a particular sexual identity or community - e.g. homosexual, lesbian, etc), current "queer theories" advocate an inclusive approach. They suggest, first, simultaneous considerations of heterosexual and homosexual identity construction, and second, serious focus on identities excluded by the hereto/homo duality - e.g. bisexual or transgender identities.

These basic tenets carry a provocative methodology. Queer theorists advocate a new "reading" of materials using an "inside/outside" opposition. In such an analysis, the reader must assume the connotation of homosexuality in the denotation of heterosexuality; the reader must reinterpret a product in terms of a homosexual presence. Further, the explication of a cultural product's hetero/homo opposition must direct readers to all excluded forms of sexuality as well.

Any work under analysis must be read with an eye for that which it itemizes and thus simultaneously implies. When queer theorists read television sitcom Laverne and Shirley or Alfred Hitchcock's film Rope from a homosexual "subject-position," they contest current hierarchical structures of sexuality. Constructing alternative readings of a work's sexual implications deconstructs the taken-for-grantedness of the dominant sexual model. Reminiscent of Garfinkel's approach to identifying "invisible" normative structures, queer theory's subject-positioned readings jolt the very process of classification.

Despite their differences, the issues raised by social constructionists and postmodernists alike direct scholarly attention to a collective's struggle to self-name, self-characterize, and claim social prerogative. Such concerns underscore the politics of identity.

IDENTITY POLITICS AND COLLECTIVE MOBILIZATION

Collective identity and the political movements it spurs constitute an important concern for identity scholars. Issues of politics are raised in previously cited works on gender/ sexuality and race. Identity politics also provides the focus for many works on the formation and experiencing of social class. However, concerns with identity politics move scholars beyond this "holy trinity" of the discursive field. Animal protectionists, environmentalists, the health conscious, the homeless, members of the 1960s student counterculture - in current literature, these groups too exemplify collectives moved by issues of collective definition, signification, and power.

When moved by identity, collectives take on distinct properties. Spurred not by ideology or resource mobilization, identity-based movements act rather than react; they fight to expand freedom, not to achieve it; they mobilize for choice rather than emancipation. Alberto Melucci, central in this area, notes:

The freedom to have which characterized...industrial society has been replaced by the freedom to be. The right to property has been, and remains, the basis of both industrial capitalism and its competitor model, 'real socialism'. In post-material society, there emerges a further type of right, the right to existence, or rather, to a more meaningful existence.

In this way, identity politics creates "new social movements," collective initiatives that are self-reflexive and sharply focused on the expressive actions of collective members. Identity politics and new social movements suggest a special form of agency - a self-conscious "collective agency." Identities emerge and movements ensue because collectives consciously coordinate action; group members consciously develop offenses and defenses, consciously insulate, differentiate, and mark, cooperate and compete, persuade and coerce.

In such a context, agency encompasses more than the control and transformation of one's social environment. Rather, borrowing from Charles Taylor's discussion of agency and the self, suggest that collective agency includes a conscious sense of group as agent. Further, collective agency is enacted in a moral space. A collective pursues the freedom to be because that which frames the collective's identity defines their existence as right and good.

In connection with issues of identity politics and collective agency, David Snow, Robert Benford, William Gainson, Doug McAdam, and others address the framing and schematization of identity as it occurs within social movements. Studies in this area delineate the frame alignment processes that bring both group focus and shared identity to particular collectives at specific historical moments. Further, these works itemize the ways in which resulting collective identities then direct movement participants by defining the parameters and appropriate arenas of collective action.

Such analyses remain fully mindful of the ways in which movement participants' perceptions of history, social structures, and cultural arrangements constrain or enhance the interpretive processes. This work's appeal rests in its multifaceted theoretical base. By merging sociocognitive construction processes with concerns for structural and organization factors, this literature creates an exciting conceptual bridge, linking micro and macro analyses, linking cultural and social concerns. Such works provide a model that forces the simultaneous consideration of thought, articulation, and action.

Recent literature raises concerns regarding the long-term social consequences of identity politics. Michael J Piore, for example, writes of identity-based movements as isolated, cohesive "communities of meaning." Because such groups are narrowly focused and formed relative to distinctions, Piore argues that they find themselves incapable of cross-boundary exchange.

Further, he believes such groups often remain unaware of the economic conditions that may constrain their collective goals. Based on these observations, Piore locates identity movements in America's ideological roots of individualism. He suggests that current socioeconomic conditions beckon a change in this stance. Using cognitive theories derived from sociology and anthropology, Piore presents a five-step plan aimed at replacing identity politics with a shared commitment to a unified national structure.

IDENTIFICATION PROCESSES

Attention to collectives and the establishment of their identities have re-energized scholarly interests in the identification process itself. A growing literature explores the mechanics by which collectives create distinctions, establish hierarchies, and renegotiate rules of inclusion. Such works are closely linked to important knowledge theories, including Bourdieu's theories of distinction, Derrida's focus on difference, Foucault's genealogy of epistomes, the semiotic models of Saussure and Pierce, and Zerubavel's work on sociomental classification.

This section elaborates on a variety of identification processes currently under study. Michele Lamont documents the role of symbolic boundaries in the construction of valued identities. Using rich data drawn from interviews with upper-middleclass men in France and the United States, Lamont specifies the conditions under which moral, socioeconomic, and cultural boundaries successfully create objective conditions of socioeconomic inequality.

In contrast to Bourdieu, Lamont maintains a tri-part focus, demonstrating that the importance of boundary types varies across space and time. Her work also emphasizes boundary strength; her findings indicate that only those boundaries firmly grounded in widely shared meaning prove sufficiently strong to generate hierarchy and confer relative value to collective identities. In related work, Jill Quadagno & Catherine Forbes use cultural and social lenses to explore identification and distinction among US Job Corps participants.

The authors examine the workings of both symbolic boundaries and structural barriers as these factors contribute to gender reproduction and gender inequality. Concerns with symbolic boundaries characterize recent inquiries in life course research as well. Works by Gaines, Jeffreys, Modell, Postman, Waksler, Winn, and Zelizer help to refocus sociologists on the cultural contexts within which age categories are constructed, age identities are built, and age transitions occur.

Margaret Somers and Harrison White approach issues of identification by specifying the cultural repertoires or systems of meaning that characterize various symbolic communities. These authors are especially concerned with the ways in which social context and social location enable the invoking of such repertoires. In this regard, Paul DiMaggio's landmark research on the arts also proves important. DiMaggio demonstrates the ways in which art acquisition and classification solidify status categories and distinguish the elite from the ordinary.

In a different arena, Jane Bachnik & Charles Quinn (1994) focus on indexicality and its role in the construction of Japanese identity. Building on the Japanese concepts "uchi" (inside) and "soto" (outside), various authors explores the ways in which these boundary distinctions direct collective orientation and pattern behaviour. In probing identity, all authors consider both linguistic communication and social practice through their linkage to context. Elsewhere, Eviatar Zerubavel (1997a) offers a special edition that brings his concepts of lumping and splitting to life. Authors chart these complementary sociomental processes as they explore identification and distinction in monetary exchange, fetal classification, the construction of sexual identities, and other interesting areas.

Among social psychologists, John C Turner presents depersonalization as a process enabling collective identities. His work maps the ways in which depersonalization permits social stereotyping, group cohesiveness, ethnocentrism, cooperation and altruism, emotional contagion and empathy, collective action, and other processes. Finally, James Aho (1994) invokes Berger & Luckman's five steps of reification to elaborate both the construction and deconstruction of political enemies.

Aho situates his analysis in a variety of recent incidents, including the Ruby Ridge affair, the dissolution of the Soviet Union, and a case study of a KKK defection. Using media reports, government documents, and interviews, Aho carefully explores the development of collective moral righteousness. He notes the processes by which such sentiments legitimate the destruction of the "other." Grappling with the question "Can one struggle effectively against evil without become tainted by it?", Aho builds an interesting case for an enemy that is both "them" and "us."

The study of objects also proves key to recent research on identification. Several works note the ways in which individuals and groups use art objects, commodities and commodity signs, or clothing to articulate and project identities. Complimenting this agenda, Dauber's work on Pueblo pottery, Mukerji's studies of formal French gardens, and Zukin's exploration of city structures use objects to better understand the political, cultural, social, and economic contexts in which the objects are produced. Finally, Nippert-Eng and Silver offer especially interesting excursions on the role of personal possessions in bridging identity transitions.

Several works, anchored in the study of discourse and symbolization, provide a multitiered analysis of collective identification and the ideologies that support it. In contrast to deterministic theories, such studies approach identification as a process that unfolds in relation to economic, historical, and political contexts. As such, multitiered investigations view identification at critical junctures in a collective's history, including periods of identity production, its institutionalization, and periods of identity interpretation.

Further, these works cast identity discourse and symbols as mediators of structure and action. Robert Wuthnow's work on communities of discourse exemplifies the approach. Wuthnow explores the general cultural, political, and economic conditions that enabled three specific ideologies: the Protestant Reformation, the Enlightenment, and Marxist socialism. After charting the historical sources of these agendas, Wuthnow traces the modes by which each ideology was institutionalized, taking readers through the schools, religious and scientific groups, and the governments and media that modeled and disseminated each perspective.

Finally, Wuthnow examines audience reception and reaction, analyzing the collective application and experience of the three ideologies through the decades. Wuthnow's rich inquiry demonstrates the complex chain by which movement ideologies and resulting identities are both born and sustained. Following Wuthnow's example, Valentine Moghadam adopts the multitiered approach, analyzing fundamentalist discourse and its relationship to gender and national identities.

Other multitiered works include Michele Dillon's studies of discourse on divorce and abortion. Her works explore the ways in which political climate and the institutional status of discourse producers relates to both the nature and the effect of discursive strategies. In a similar vein, David Campbell examines the American "discourse of danger," exploring the ways in which such a discourse shapes visions of the American "us," the enemy "them," and ultimately, the form of American foreign policy.

Cerulo, too, applies a multitiered perspective in her study of national identity symbolization. Probing the various contexts of anthem and flag adoption, she identifies a set of social structural variables that appear to delimit general rules of symbolic expression. Cerulo also explores the institutionalization of identity symbols, suggesting a new theoretical model for predicting symbol change. Finally, her inquiries on symbol reception and interpretation elucidate faulty identity symbolization, thus specifying the conditions under which symbols can fail to capture the fervency of those they portray.

TECHNOLOGY AND IDENTITY

In the present environment, one cannot consider identity without reference to new communication technologies (NCTs). NCTs have changed the backdrop against which identity is constructed; they have reframed the generalized others and the "generalized elsewheres" from which the self takes its cues. Joshua Meyrowitz was among the first to fully explore the NCT/identity link. His works examine the ways in which electronic media reorganize the sites of social interaction. According to Meyrowitz, NCTs weaken or sever the connections between physical and social "place." In this way, NCTs locate the self in new hybrid arenas of action;

they mesh public and private, beckon new types of performances, and form new collective configurations:

> Television has fostered the rise of hundreds of "minorities" - people who in perceiving a wider world, begin to see them as unfairly isolated in some pocket of it. Television has empowered the disabled and the disenfranchised by giving them access to social information in spite of their physical isolation. Television has given women an outside view of their incarceration in the home. Television has weakened visible authorities by destroying the distance and mystery that once enhanced their aura and prestige. And television has been able to do this without requiring the disabled to leave their wheelchairs without asking the housewife to stop cooking dinner, and without demanding that the average citizen leave his or her easy chair.

According to Meyrowitz, the places enabled by NCTs reconfigure the boundaries that distinguish collectives. Thus at the present social moment, the differences dividing children from adults may be less stark than those that distinguish the computer literate from the nonliterate. The line that separates home from work may now pale in comparison to online/offline borders.

David Altheide (1995) poses complementary positions in his work on NCTs and the self. He argues that NCTs enable new communication formats - new modes of selecting, organizing, and presenting information. In turn, these new formats reshape social activity; they modify or dismantle current practices, and spur or shape new ones. In this way, NCTs create new environments for self-development and identification; they present new opportunities for collective affiliation and mobilization. Altheide's writings on keyboard technology illustrate these ideas.

In considering human experience with telephones, ATMs, computers, video games, calculators, and television controls, the author casts the keyboard as a new door to interaction. He argues that keyboard technology initiates a large majority of modern exchange. But while keyboards may transport us to places not easily accessed in the past, Altheide argues that the technology limits and directs the form and substance of the social interaction it enables. For example, keyboard technology reduces the distance between children and adults, often promoting a type of reverse socialization. Similarly, keyboard technology homogenizes work and play sites; keyboards merge adult work and play worlds, link adult workspaces and children's play spaces, and reconfigure children's play via the world of adult tools.

Beyond specific communication tools, Altheide also explores the intersection of communication, power, and social control. He considers the ways in which technology and its resulting communication formats provide some with the power to define a social situation while leaving others vulnerable to the reality of crafted images. In these and similar discussions, Altheide outlines the ways in which communication formats can "block" the social stage, scripting emergent action even in realms thought to possess an internal logic.

In the spirit of Meyrowitz and Altheide, many explore the impact of NCTs on community formation and resulting collective identity. Beniger initiated this agenda, suggesting specific ways in which media-generated communities provide a "pseudo-gemeinschaft" experience. Subsequent works describe technologically generated communities as more tangible and real. Several authors document the processes by which NCT's build "we-ness," demonstrating the concrete effects of techno-links and charting emergent cultures of reference that can unify once disparate social actors. But others are less enthusiastic regarding the impact of NCTs on community and identity.

Schlesinger, for example, notes both the potential and the surprising failure of electronic media in constructing a unified European identity among the nations that comprise the Euro-community. Similarly, Fisher's sociohistorical research on the telephone suggests that community structure can be remarkably resilient to technological change. Overall, Fisher remains skeptical of NCT's ability to reconfigure social bonds. These contradictory positions have led some to initiate multidimensional models, models designed to address and distinguish varying forms of NCT-generated bonds.

Related works magnify identification processes within specific NCT domains. Sherry Turkle, for example, explores online communities and their impact on personal identity construction. She follows members of a virtual community as they interact in "multi-user domains" (MUDS). Testimony of MUD members, along with Turkle's keen insights, provides a unique picture detailing the building and experiencing of online persona. Further, Turkle documents the ways in which individuals negotiate online identities relative to other facets of the self.

By probing the balance between "virtual" selves and "real" selves, Turkle's work forces us to question any perspective that places virtual experience second to the concrete. In another arena, Byron Reeves & Clifford Nass (1996) approach communication media as objects relevant to identity-building interactions. In essence, the authors find that media objects become a viable "other" in the building of self, and they outline the ways in which humanto-machine relationships mirror purely human relationships.

Reeves & Nass discover, for instance, that people treat computers with female voices differently than those with male voices; people are polite to computers even though they don't need to be; the size and movement of TV screen images affects physical responses and perceptions of personal bodyspace in ways identical to real-life motion. These patterns hold implications for identity studies and beyond. Indeed, relevant to communication efficacy, the authors suggest that the human brain has not sufficiently evolved relative to technology's rapid advancement. Reeves & Nass suggest ways in which this knowledge can improve future technological products.

The literature here reviewed constitutes an antithesis to traditional identity studies, an antithesis built upon several research fronts. The works cited here refocus scholarly attentions from the individual to the collective. These works often prioritize discourse over the systematic scrutiny of behaviour. Many studies approach identity as a source of mobilization rather than a product of it. Finally, the analysis of virtual identities now competes with research on identities established in the copresent world. In considering the old and the new of identity, one finds a field ripe for synthesis. This section suggests potential avenues for synthesis, noting works that exemplify such efforts. The works chosen here are not "ideal types," but rather suggestive models - models that illustrate what can be gained when the future is mined from careful reflection on past and present.

Some have achieved a productive synthesis of identity work through the reconciliation of theory. In recent work on gender identity, for example, Judith Lorber synthesizes constructionist and postmodern concerns of the day with issues raised by sex role theorists and Marxist feminists of past decades. Her efforts result in an interesting theory that frames gender as a social institution - a free-standing entity that establishes patterns of expectations, orders social processes, and drives social organizations.

In another arena, Norbert Wiley merges Peircian and Meadian paradigms to form a neopragmatist view of the self - the self as a three-dimensional dialogue between "I," "you," and "me." Wiley then works with pragmatist notions of reflexivity and Durkheimian solidarity concepts to create a model of "a semiotic self," a sui generis self resistant to social determination. In a historical era spurred by identity politics, Wiley argues that conceptions of a sui generis self may prove vital to the defense of democratic principles.

Others attend to macro-micro linkages in promoting the cause of synthesis. Indeed, several recent theoretical advances relevant to identity studies rest on successful macro-micro linkages: Bourdieu's work on habitus, Giddens's structuration theory, or Habermas's theories of communicative action. Further, a number of the works heretofore discussed have successfully established the links. Research on social movements or several of the multitiered identity projects represent prime illustrations. Other macro-micro initiatives are underway.

For example, determined to eradicate the micro-macro divide, Deidre Boden innovatively combines elements of each arena, thus building a unique analytic approach to organizational identity, form, and function. Boden maps conversational exchanges across varied organizational settings, using these data to configure the structure of talk in organizations. She then examines talk structures as vehicles that constitute organizations, analyzing organizations as they emerge within daily interaction. Boden argues that "the ways in which organizational actors realize both the constraints and opportunities in their working environments is critical to what actually constitutes an 'environment'".

For Boden, the micro-processes of talk become the macro-structure of the organization. In another arena, Cerulo pursues macro-micro linkages in analyzing narratives of violence. She explores the institutionalization of storytelling formats in this area and documents the impact such formats can have on audience evaluations of violent acts. In essence, her study elucidates the conditions under which macro-social norms of communication can direct complex micro-patterns of cognition and identification. Among social psychologists, Peggy Thoits & Lauren Virshup propose a macro-micro merger that hinges on social theories of the mind.

Specifically, they suggest ways in which self-schema theory might unify inquiries on individual and collective identity. In the cause of synthesis, scholars of collective identity also might revisit traditional micro-level studies in the area. Much common ground exists between traditional and new approaches to the topic.

During the 1980s, social psychologists' addressed similar themes, focusing on multiple roles, their resulting identities, and the impact of both on human experience. To be sure, collective and micro-level inquiries pursue different elements of "human experience." Yet, knowledge of the cognitive processes, social practices, and symbolic tools with which identity is constructed, enacted, and projected is integral to each school of thought. Knowing this, focused efforts to translate certain findings from the social psychological realm to the macro level could hold rich rewards for collective identity studies.

At the broadest level, an important site of synthesis rests in the careful blending of intellectual perspectives. Within the past two decades, the humanist or cultural studies approach to identity has dominated the field. To be sure, sociologists of identity cannot afford to ignore these works, for they provide a rich and thorough treatment of the symbols, rituals, and world views that constitute identity. At the same time, the sociologist must consider this literature with some care.

At present, the cultural studies position appears somewhat trapped in a singular conclusion that locates the constructed nature of culture in the sole service of power. Further, such works frequently frame social action as a process that is fully culturally constituted. In tapping identity materials garnered from the cultural studies approach, sociologists must diligently maintain the critical analytic distinction between the social and the cultural. Via careful consideration of actors, collectives, and broader social institutions, via thoughtful attention to lived experience and the cultural products and rituals associated with such experience, the sociology of identity can fully elucidate the intricate links between the social and cultural domains.

TECHNOBIOGRAPHY

In his Introduction to Cybercultures, David Bell argues that cyberspace is created through the stories we tell about it: material stories (about hardware and software histories); symbolic stories (in popular culture, for example, films); and experiential stories (about cyberspace encounters, which are mediations of material and symbolic stories). Bell draws on the work of N. Katherine Hayles to define his three types of stories as stories about what cyberspace and cyberculture are, stories about what they mean, and stories about what they do.

Stories are important, he writes, because cyberspace is "something to be understood as it is lived"; cyberspace is culture, "made from people, machines and stories in everyday life". In particular, individual experience stories, or technobiographies, are significant because of the subtle and nuanced differences in each individual's techno-experiences

(Costigan). This is an argument that Carolyn Steedman has made for autobiographical stories more generally: the purpos e of autobiographical projects, she writes, should nor be to draw generalized conclusions which can be used to theorize the lives of many, but rather, to understand the many and varied ways in which individuals negotiate social experiences.

The aim should not be to universalize and subsequently simplify, but to specify and then render complex. Technobiographies, this chapter proposes, are kinds of experience stories through which it is possible to do just this. This chapter, therefore, is an argument for technobiography as a useful method for studying digital experiences in general, and the relationship between online and offline lives in particular. After beginning with an outline of what technobiography is, and two important contributions that a technobiographical approach can make to the field that some scholars call cybercultural studies.

First, technobiography makes it possible to examine online lives in offline contexts, and so facilitates moving beyond a focus merely on virtual representations of lives and selves, to a fuller understanding of the social relations of the production and consumption of Information and Communication Technologies (ICTs). Second, technobiography allows access to the context in which online lives are produced, to lived experience and to living experience-that is, what it feels like to live certain experiences of digital multimedia from the inside, or to occupy privileged and non-privileged identity positions within the micro-power dynamics of technology-rich environments.

The first project is Project Her@, named after the Greek goddess Hera, worshipped by women at every stage of their lives. Project Her@ was an experiment in the use of computer-mediated distance learning to enhance access to university level education for women from disadvantaged backgrounds. The project involved the delivery of the Her@ course, a part distance-learning foundation course which prepared students to undertake undergraduate degrees.

The course itself was founded on the principles of experiential education: Her@ students were asked to produce reflexive autobiographical narratives about their experiences, which served both as assessed work and as research data. Fourteen mature women took part in the Her@ course, part of which was delivered via networked computers loaned to the students for the duratio n of the program, and installed in their homes. Willingness to participate in associated research projects was a condition of acceptance in the course.

The Memex center houses a range of courses in multimedia, new media and digital media as well as research, production and consultancy activities in these areas. Aiming to connect the university and its community with global developments in information, communication, and media technologies, the center combines teaching, learning, and research with professional and creative practice and production activity. Establishing the Memex center was a collective development project involving myself and colleagues as teachers, researchers, and professional multimedia practitioners.

The term was first used in a collection entitled Cyborg Lives? Though a number of the first-person narratives in Cyborg Lives are playful explorations of technological experiences, all have a serious message about the intersections between gender, power, technology, and subjectivity which shape the experiences at the center of the narratives. Our aim was to produce a collection of life-stories about the place of technology in everyday life, a book of experiences which, while not a "theoretical" book, "spoke to" theory, opening up "a space where the relationship between theory and experience might be explored".

The broad theoretical context in which original technobiographies project was located is the discipline of science and technology studies (STS), and particularly gender and technology studies. STS starts from the premise that technologies are "social through and through" -that they are socially constructed, just as the social is technologically constructed and mediated. Since there is a mutually constirutive interplay between societies and technologies, it is therefore necessary to explore not only how digital and online technologies affect lives, but also how lives affect, and indeed construct, these technologies. Another STS premise is that technology is not just "something that hurts when you drop it on your foot", but is also constituted by the knowledge that creates it and uses it, and by its symbolic meanings.

Consequently, when examining socio-technical relations through technobiography, it is important to consider skills, knowledges, and the meanings assigned to material artifacts, as well as the artifacts themselves. A number of technobiographical trends can be traced in STS, such as biographical attempts to recover previously invisible contributions of women scientists and technologists in feminist technology studies (for example, Sadie Plant on Ada Lovelace), or the use of autobiographical anecdotes to illuminate techno-social relations (for example, Susan Leigh Star on McDonalds, standardization, and her allergy to onions).

Despite these examples, however, just as autobiography rarely has technology at its center, so too autobiography remains relatively absent from STS. Technobiography, on the other hand, recognizes that there is much to be gained from a closer interplay between these fields. Haraway proposes the cyborg, or cybernetic organism comprised of both human and machine, as a tool for taking responsibility for gender-technology encounters in a way that challenges, and indeed transforms, existing power relations.

Her argument that feminists are not in a position to reject technologies, and that technologies in fact are intertwined with our identities, led us to explore the usefulness of the concept of the cyborg for understanding our technobiographical experiences. Indeed, there are a number of similarities between technobiography and what Haraway calls cyborg writing. Both are reflexive processes, reflecting on experiences themselves and on the act of constructing those experiences through writing. Both "facilitate the interrogation of positionings, the recognition of partial standpoints and the assumption of accountability". In other words, both are constructed stories reflecting partial versions of events.

Clearly, technobiography is located in the context of autobiography, a methodology and a field of analysis well established in gender studies, cultural studies, and elsewhere in the humanities and social sciences. The possibilities that autobiography offers for understanding lives and selves will be familiar to readers of this journal. If autobiography is the process of writing the story of the self; if, in effect, selfhood is constructed through the production of autobiography; if the autos, or self, does not exist as a complete entity outside the written autobiography and the act of writing it, then this will indeed be a fitting method with which to study cyber-subjectivities, digital identities, and online lives.

Describing individuals as "active agents who are not simply stamped with the imprint of their given social relations", but who "construct themselves into existing social relations", Haug explains how the collective uses memory work to examine the extent to which theories that attempt to explain social relations adequately "capture" experience. Similarly, Steedman uses autobiography to explore the adequacy of theoretical frameworks, such as Marxism, feminism, and psychoanalysis, for understan ding an individual's lived experience. This interest in the subject-in-society, and in the extent to which the "central interpretative devices of the culture" account for individual subjects' experiences, is also central to technobiography.

Another common reason scholars work with autobiography is to retrieve silenced and marginalized voices, or at least to create a space where counter-hegemonic voices can emerge (Swindells). As Liz Stanley suggests, socially useful forms of autobiography need to highlight the lives of ordinary people in order to enhance understanding of forms of social organization. At the same time, however, it is important to keep in mind Steve Jones's argument that new digital technologies are in some ways the territory of elite groups, or at least groups who have access to the technologies and the skills to use them, and that to enhance understandings of the place of ICTs in society, these technological elites need to be "studied."

Indeed, Stanley's implied argument that "ordinary" or "marginal" experiences need to be studied instead of elites is especially problematic given the important role played by cyber-elites in shaping cyberspaces. Such elites have everyday practices as well, and we should apply the same rigor and derail to researching their practices as to the experiences of 'ordinary' people." In fact, a technobiographical approach can help us to unpack and problemarize this binary opposition between "ordinary" and "elite." In his recent book Cyberpower, Tim Jordan distinguishes between online and offline, new and old elites, arguing that people with access and skills relating to digital technologies are a certain kind of elite, even if they do not occupy elite status in non-digital terms.

Given the now relatively common proposition across the humanities that we live different aspects of our identity at the same time, one of my aims in using technobiography has been to examine what it feels like to occupy both privileged and non-privileged identity positions simultaneously. As a research method technobiography has a number of origin stories- in modern notions of the self (Smith); in feminism and its proposal that the personal is political (Stanley); in reflexive research which interrogates a researcher's choice of research subjects (Walkerdine); in the premise that knowledge is situated, and that, as James Costigan writes, "everything that I have seen, heard, and experienced has brought me to this point, and I understand nothing but in relationship to me at this point." The types of autobiography presumed to emerge from these origins are varied.

For some, like Julia Swindells, autobiography includes a broad range of personal accounts, including ethnography and oral history; for others, autobiography more specifically involves "mining (one's own] memory, subjectivity and life history for research purposes". My use of technobiography to date has been twofold. My research on Project Her@ involves drawing on technobiographical material produced by Her@ students -both written and oral narratives, and home pages, combining textual and visual content-about their experiences with technology.

ONLINE LIVES IN OFFLINE CONTEXTS

A number of scholars of digital culture advocate a kind of methodological approach which has much in common with technobiography-this is another reason for my use of this method. Many argue that long-term biographical studies are needed which tell personal stories about personalized new media such as the Internet.

Acknowledging the autobiographical character of her own study, which compares her own research practices with those of her other research subjects, Christine Hine suggests that methodological innovation incorporating biographical studies will be needed in the future in order to increase our understanding of Internet practices. Several of Hine's ten principles for virtual ethnography suggest that a technobiographical approach would be fruitful: for example, that virtual ethnography can only ever be partial and can never reflect the totality of the Internet; or that the ethnographer also participates in using the media of cyberspace, so reflexivity about online experiences should be foregrounded.

In describing his book as a "personal telling of cyberstories", David Hakken reveals his own autobiographical approach to ethnography. And echoing the words of James Costigan quoted above; Steve Jones also argues that Internet research must be personalized:

If the Internet is a form of "personalized" mass media, perhaps researchers, too, should in some sense "personalize" their efforts, in two ways. First, to be sensitive to and aware of, their own experiences on-line and second, to focus not only on community but on individuals within social groups as well.

To me, all of this adds up to technobiography, but technobiography of a certain kind. In advocating mobile, adaptive, and multi-sited methods, Hine points to a central argument of this chapter: the need to study online lives in offline contexts. Hine uses this description to characterize the methods that she moved towards in her own Virtual Ethnography, and which she implemented more fully in later research about Web pages, their authors, and audiences.

Hine gives several reasons why researchers must apply such multi-sited methods to go beyond the online text, whether a newsgroup posting or a Web page, to the producer of the text. Such an approach, she argues, enhances understanding not only of the online text, but also of its context of production. In addition, Hine points out that "to understand the form of WWW pages it is crucial to understand their significance for their authors". In her own work, Hine has applied such adaptive methods in two distinct ways. In her work on Internet covera ge of the Louise Woodward case, which provides the focus of Virtual Ethnography, she goes beyond the online text to carry out online interviews with the producers of those texts, whereas in her later research on the production of institutional Web pages, she engages in face-to-face interviews with the Web page producers.

Lori Kendall has also advocated studying online lives in online and offline contexts. She stresses the importance of both online considerations (such as the understandings, norms, and variations of specific online groups) and offline environments (for example, the conditions of participation in online forums). While acknowledging that access to offline environments may not always be possible, Kendall emphasizes the latter, offline contexts. She favors a methodology of participant observation, which, she suggests, facilitates study of the social contexts in which online lives are lived and produced.

Her research into the online forum BlueSky was based on three years of her own participation in the forum, thirty face-to-face interviews, and attendance at face-to-face gatherings of the BlueSky community. Online life cannot be divorced from life offline, argues Kendall, because the latter may be constraining the former. We need to know whether people have the access, training, interest, or desire to live certain kinds of online lives. In addition, participants in online communities draw on their offline experiences to negotiate their virtual interactions. For as Kendall points out, "[n]obody lives only in cyberspace".

After carrying out a range of preparatory activities, including thinking about the uses, advantages, disadvantages, and potential dangers of home pages, and participating in the production of a collective, group home page, the students produced personal home pages. The Her@ students did not receive any guidance about the specific content that should be included in their home pages. Instead, by considering issues such as quantity of text and size of images, they were encouraged to determine themselves what was an appropriate amount of content for a home page. Students were also assessed on how well they provided "evidence of building on observations relating to other homepages." Thus, although the students were free to choose their own content, their familiarity with the personal home page genre shaped their decisions about their own home pages.

For example, in a classic early study of online lives, Life on the Screen: Identity in the Age of the Internet, Sherry Turkle drew on the experiences of her research subjects in MUDs to explore the relationship between postmodern, fragmented identity and virtual spaces. Turkle proposed that in anonymous MUDs, people could hide or disguise those aspects of identity which, for example, might lead to discrimination, such as race or gender, and so could engage in identity experimentation.

We can be anyone in cyberspace; we can hide our marginal identities, and become part of the mainstream. Turkle concludes that the opportunities for anonymous playing with identity offered by MUDs and other virtual spaces lead to empowering experiences of li fe online, often characterized by fluidity and fragmentation, by the dissolution or transcendence of boundaries. Mark Poster reinforces Turkle's claims when he writes that within the "techno-cultural landscape" of cyberspace, "instead of supporting a stable, centered identity, subjects are constituted as diffuse, fragmentary, multiple". Rob Shields also supports the claim that boundaries are dissolved or transcended in virtual identity:

The Internet creates a crisis of boundaries between the real and the virtual, between time zones and between spaces, near and distant. Above all, boundaries between bodies and technologies, between our sense of our self and our sense of our changing roles: the personae we may play or the "hats we wear" in different situations are altered.

And Cheris Kramarae summarizes the empowering possibilities opened up by online anonymity as follows:

> At least for periods of time, the new technologies let us be our own representations of whatever animal, vegetable, sex, race, nationality, or tribe we wish to try to be. Differences, disabilities, defects, and dominance seem, at first reading, to be basically irrelevant on the Internet.

These generalized claims about virtual identity that I was seeking to examine in my own analysis, therefore, could be summarized as follows: virtual identity is anonymous, fluid, fragmented, and transcendent of traditional boundaries such as self/other, or human/machine.

In my initial analysis of the Her@ students' home pages, I questioned the claim that online, people can hide aspects of their identity, such as race or gender, which might otherwise lead to discrimination, and that this possibility is empowering. My critique was based on a number of factors. First, it was important to differentiate between distinct types of virtual spaces. Turkle's findings in relation to text-based spaces like MUDs did not necessarily apply to the more visual and multimedia form of the World Wide Web home page, and the different types of online identities and experiences it makes possible.

Second, on the whole, the ten Her@ students who created personal home pages showed no signs of wanting to hide such aspects of their identities as their gender and ethnicity, and thereby "benefit" from the possibility of anonymity that cyberspace offered them. I reached this conclusion as a result of the explicit and implicit references to gender and ethnicity that these students i ncluded in their home pages.

These references came in a number of forms: images (for example, a picture of an African mother and child); links (to a black cultural bookshop, for example, or BlackNetUK, an online network for the black British community); or text (for example, students' discussion of their experiences of motherhood, or the decision of one student to share her home page with her daughter). Virtual identity does not have to be anonymous to be empowering, in fact, in the case of the Her@ students, the contrary seemed more applicable.

That many of them clearly identify as black women in their home pages could be said to empower them and other black women more than hiding their identities would, as their home pages give a voice to black, working-class women in a technical medium dominated by white male voices. Here the importance of who the Her@ students are offline is clearly shaping who they are online, suggesting that the online lives are lived and produced in the context of lives of fline.

However, despite these findings, the confessional style of some of the Her@ students' home pages seemed to suggest that they felt anonymous online. In addition to including such personal details as first names, surnames, email addresses, and photographs within the home pages, a number of students also demonstrated a propensity to be "extraordinarily frank and revealing," to use Daniel Chandler's description of the home page authors he studied.

One student wrote at length about the lack of support she received from her husband, who insisted that she continue her domestic duties whilst studying full-time, even though he was out of work. A central aim was to ask the former Her@ students about the issue of virtual anonymity. I noted that in their written reflections prod uced to accompany their home pages, a number of the students had demonstrated an awareness of the need for caution when including personal detail on home pages. Had they wanted to preserve their anonymity?

Or to remove it, by stating openly who they were? Their responses problematized my earlier reading of the home pages, which had depended heavily on a textual analysis of the students' online selves. At that time, I had felt that their explicit and implicit references to their gender and race, as well as the inclusion of personal data like their names and surnames, meant that their virtual identities were not anonymous. As I discovered during these interviews, however, the concept of anonymity is more complex than this, as some of the students insisted that there was more anonymity in their home pages than I had originally thought.

For example, one student I'll call Tessa took issue with my conclusion that the image of a Trinidadian flag and her reference to Caribbean foods such as plantain and avocado on her home page indicated her blackness. Since, as she pointed out, there are white Trinidadians and white people who like Caribbean food, she insisted her ethnicity actually was more hidden than my reading had assumed. Noon, the student who wrote critically about her husband, said that she still felt a degree of anonymity in her home page, despite including her name and surname.

These responses suggest that for some home page producers, there is a distinction between being anonymous and feeling anonymous-a distinction deriving from what David Chandler describes as the dual role of the World Wide Web as both public (publishing thoughts, feelings, and identities to a potentially large audience) and private (located in the home, a medium used to construct thoughts, feelings, and identities).

Though some Her@ students gave their names and surnames, they still apparently felt a degree of anonymity in their home pages, indicating the need for more complex understandings of virtual anonymity that move beyond a simple acceptance of the claim that while people experiment with anonymous identities in virtual contexts like MUDs, by including photographs and other autobiographical detail in home pages, they reveal their "true" identities and thus erase the possibility of anonymity (Tetzlaff).

Such understandings will need to take account of the Web's status as simultaneously public and private, and of the importance of going beyond online lives and selves to consider the offline context of their production and consumption. This means not just acknowledging who the producers of online selves are offline, but also considering how they feel about their online selves-to use Hine's phrase, to think about the ways in which online selves are socially meaningful to their offline counterparts ("Web Page"). Technobiography can play a role in facilitating such understanding.

DIGITAL TECHNOLOGIES

Cyberculture as a field of study is relatively new. In a short space of time, it has matured from an area made up of a handful of publications to an established, ever proliferating discipline. One consequence of its newness is that apart from the few examples already discussed, there has been comparatively little empirical, ethnographic, or biographical study of experiences in cyberspace. In the absence of a varied and diverse range of studies of online lives, Turkie's conclusions about her own research subjects, which were no doubt valid for them, seemed to serve as characterizations of all online lives and experiences.

As the quotes from Poster and Shields indicate, at least for a while, claims which simultaneously confirmed and grew out of Turkle's study seemed to proliferate. At worst, such claims can now be characterized as sweeping and unsubstantiated, as the evidence on which they are based is not always apparent. A growing recognition of these gaps within cybercultural studies has led a number of writers recently to stress the need for more grounded investigations of online lives against which to test out claims like Turkle's. Such new studies would move beyond a focus on online identity play to consider a broader range of social and cultural factors, and so arrive at a more comprehensive understanding of cyber-experiences.

For example, whilst noting the importance of debates about virtual identity, Eileen Green argues that there is a need for more empirical projects which examine the place of new technologies in everyday practices, of the kind undertaken by Kendall and Hinc. Though small in number, such recent studies have mapped out a more diverse set of propositions about life online than those originally set out by Turkle.

For example, despite prevailing claims about multiple and fluid identities in such environments, Kendall concludes from her study that participants in the o nline forum BlueSky "continually work to reincorporare their experiences of themselves and of others' selves into integrated, consistent wholes". In other words, virtual lives are not always fragmented but often stable; in some forums, relatively unified cyberselves are presented. Drawing on the findings of her research into online soap fans, Baym similarly calls into question the assumption that online selves are primarily fictional and detached from the offline world:

Judging from the scholarly attention paid to anonymous CMC [Computer-Mediated Communication] interaction and its uses in identity play, one would think most on-line interaction is anonymous and few people ever interact as themselves. The reality seems to be that many, probably most, social users of CMC create online selves consistent with their off-line identities.

Many more grounded, empirical studies like these are needed for us to comprehend the full complexity of socio-technical phenomena like online lives and virtual selves. Furthermore, as I have suggested above, such studies need to move beyond the online and the virtual to examine techno-experiences in both online and offline settings.

Since experiences of the Internet, hypertext, and digital multimedia are necessarily offline as well as online phenomena, research into offline experiences of these digital technologies should form the context for developing a greater understanding of online experiences. Researchers should hold life online and life offline in dialectic tension; one should not be privileged at the expense of the other. My argument in this chapter is that technobiography is a good tool for doing this, and that cybercultural studies needs technobiography, in part because of the need for more studies of the relationship between online and offline lives in this field.

This claim makes us insecure about whether what we know still has value, and if it does, how long this value will endure. In such an environment, insecurity about our multimedia knowledge and our futures is difficult to resist- even for me, where my apparent knowledge (of the latest digital multimedia software) could be seen as new, and therefore, according to the hype, more valuable than the old. Richard's construction of my multimedia identity as one of limitless, admirable skill and potential could thus be seen as an example of the insecurity that pervades these technologies, rather than a reflection of my actual technical skill.

His responses to my work and knowledge may arise from his own feelings of disempowerment in the face of multimedia, as he attempts to digitize his own analogue identity, to overcome feelings of insecurity, and to feel a sense of belonging, and inclusion in, not exclusion from, the digital future that multimedia technologies seem to promise. In this context, constantly proclaiming the death of the old leads to feelings of career instability for some people, who may then project their imagined desires onto real others. Richard, for example, projected total employability onto me, regardless of the fact that I d not experience this for myself.

On the contrary, I was still describing myself as a technofraud eighteen months after starting my multimedia career, as the more I knew, the more I felt I did not know. Only two years after starting work in this area did I begin to acknowledge my multimedia knowledge, and even now, with a portfolio of digital media production and theorizing, I do not really feel like the cyberchick others, like my analogue video friend, seem to perceive. Discourses about the fast pace of change in digital multimedia, and the even faster redundancy of technical knowledge, assign symbolic value to multimedia. Such discourses lead to feelings of insecurity, which in turn shape experience, so that, in my case, my feelings of technofraudulence never leave me completely.

Characteristic of the offline cont ext in which online lives are produced is the circulation of symbolic discourses about digital technologies, and the engagement with these discourses at the level of emotion in which individuals engage- as a number of scholars of autobiography have insisted, occupying certain categories of identity and participating in certain social experiences are questions of feeling and emotion, nor just of abstract concepts.

TECHNOBIOGRAPHICAL ISSUES

Like all research methods, technobiography has its problems of course. One criticism of autobiography is that it indulges the individual subject at its center in a kind of "confessional self-indulgence". Academic rigor is thus required to ensure that our purpose in using technobiography goes beyond simply telling stories about our quirky lives, interesting though they may be to us, to a quest for a greater understanding of how socio-technical structures are experienced.

Another problem arises from the issue of voice. Since the "other" voices in technobiography are usually edited and interpreted by the researcher, there is always the danger that the researcher will privilege his or her own voice and version of events. To avoid this privileging, it is crucial that researchers make their own positioning explicit-and one of the strengths of technobiography is its capacity to highlight the partiality and locatedness of the researcher's point of view.

Permission to use the words and actions of research subjects as research data is also an issue for technobiographers. We acknowledge that autobiographies incorporate the biographies of others, but to what extent do we, or should we, seek consent to use this "material"? In my case, in addition to fictionalizing most of the people who populate my technobiographical studies, but it is not clear if all technobiographers do this. Anonymity is therefore a methodological as well as a conceptual issue-I may attempt to preserve the anonymity of my research subjects, but if I quote verbatim from an online text, the knowing reader can often track down the source by typing the quotation directly into a search engine.

How then can the claims of the confessionally self-indulgent, partial, and situated technobiographer be trusted? Though this question could also be asked of all researchers and all methods, from my examples in this chapter, it is evident that this concern has led me to triangulate my technobiographical material with interviews with other technobiographical subjects, in the Memex center and on Project Her@.

Technobiography is the only possible method for studying online lives, but rather that technobiography has a contribution to make to such studies. As a tool, technobiography can enhance our understanding of digital experiences in general, and the relationship between online and offline lives in particular. A technobiographical approach which holds online lives in dialectical tension with life offline can be extremely illuminating-my use of my own experiences in a digital multimedia production center has been a way of moving beyond a focus on online, virtual representations of selves to an examination of the contextual social relations surrounding the consumption and production of ICTs in which these online lives and selves are produced.

This allows an exploration of what it feels like to live experiences of new networked technologies from the inside, suggests the importance of symbolic stories about these technologies in shaping our ex periences of and feelings about them. The fear and insecurity about technical skill and knowledge in the face of fast-changing digital technologies extending across a range of subject positions that have been identified in a number of research projects, including my own, indicate the importance of such feelings in mediating digital experiences, whether these experiences take place online or offline.

My research has also ventured beyond a focus solely on online lives and selves by moving away from merely the online texts of the personal home pages produced on Project Her@ to consider not only who their producers are offline, but also the meanings of those home pages for their producers, and even their readings of my readings of their technobiographical practices.

The resulting data suggest that supposedly simple concepts like "anonymity" are actually complex, and acknowledging this complexity allows us to appreciate the intricacy of online lives and selves, and to move beyond the simplistic understandings of virtual environments which suggest that while anonymity prevails in some, like MUDs, in home pages it is wholly absent. Technobiography can contribute in a variety of ways to our understandings of cybercultural landscapes; understandings which, to date, are far from full.

3

Reading the Body in Contemporary Culture

From Mary Shelley Frankenstein, published in 1818, to Maria, the robot in Metropolis, to Frankenhooker, the possibilities of human hybrids have fired our cultural imagination as the Western world has developed through the industrial revolution into the age of high technology. But the decade of the 1980s stands out as the historical moment when a high-tech human hybrid moved off the pages of science fiction novels into everyday life: it was in many ways the decade of the cyborg. In 1986, Max Headroom stuttered his way onto American television and the cover of Newsweek.

That same year Elektra Assassin, Frank Miller's celebrated antihero, challenged the revitalized comic book industry's vision of a proper heroine. By Christmas 1990, it was clear that Transformers TM were the toy of the decade, edging out sales of plastic figures of other popular cyborgs such as RoboCop, Terminator, and Captain Picard's Borg. During the 1993 Christmas season, The Mighty Morphins PowerRangers TM flew off the shelves of U.S.-based Toys R Us discount stores; some parent went so far as to bribe toy store workers to find Mighty Morphins TM for their videogame-weary children.

Cyborg, a shorthand term for "cybernetic organism," usually describes a human-machine coupling, most often a man-machine hybrid. Cyborgs are alternately labeled "androids," "replicants," or "bionic humans." Whatever label they attract, the cyborg serves not only as the focal figure of the mass-mediated popular culture of American techno-science, but also as the figuration of posthuman identity in postmodernity.

From children's plastic action figures to cyberpunk mirrorshades, cyborgian artifacts will endure as relics of an age obsessed with the limits of human mortality and the possibilities of technological replication. This requires a discussion of certain developments within cultural theory, by Michel Foucault, Mary Douglas, and Donna Haraway, as well as other feminists, all of whom contribute to a framework for interpreting the body as a cultural text. This detour is necessary for a second reason. It shows how the female body historically was constructed as a hybrid case, thus making it compatible with notions of cyborg identity promulgated by more recent cultural theorists.

READING THE BODY

When the body is said to be "inscribed," "painted," or "written," it makes sense to write of the "discourse of the body," meaning the patterned ways that the body is represented according to broader cultural determinations and also the way that the body becomes a bearer of signs and cultural meaning. Following the work of Michel Foucault, several scholars -including Bryan Turner, Catherine Gallagher and Thomas Laqueur, and Emily Martin, among others - address the relationship between the body, culture, and society to enumerate the ways in which the body is put into discourse. Using a variety of strategies, these scholars study modes of representation of the body: its iconography, its aesthetic and symbolic functions, or its discursive repression.

Although they propose different body projects - Turner, for example, is concerned about reconstructing the problem of order as a problem of the government of the body, while Martin presents an ethnographic investigation of women's experiences with reproduction and menstruation - each scholar enacts a reading process that supports the theoretical understanding of the body as a signbearing (textual) form. To claim that the body is a discursive construction, and therefore can be read, already effects a deconstruction of its natural posture. Such is the first act of thick perception.

Michel Foucault is not so much interested in the truth of the body as he is in elaborating the apparatus that produces truth effects at the level of the body. His concern is to describe the discursive systems that produce serious truth claims about bodies. Thus, in his genealogical projects he annotates the intelligibility of the body in terms of the discursive, social, and political practices that construct it as an object/subject with meaning.

For example, in The History of Sexuality, he describes the four central apparatuses of control that mark the transition between a traditional order and one constituted by "scientific biopower": (1) the hysterization of the female body; (2) the construction of homosexuality; (3) the creation of distinctions among infant, child, and adolescent sexualities; and (4) the establishment of a discourse of perversion. These "apparatuses" organize the deployment of power; control is established through the cultural transformation of the meaning of body practices and bodily markers of identity. In short, these apparatuses identify a "conjunction," or what I understand as an "articulation of discursive practices" that produces body knowledges.

Foucault goes on to delineate the means by which power is exercised. Central to his work is the assertion that the means of the production of discourse include a more ambiguous process of the construction of knowledge claims. For example, the hysterization of the female body, as one way in which scientific biopower is organized and reified, was accomplished through the exercise of new discursive practices (of science, of psychoanalysis), institutionalized social relations (the family under capitalism), and knowledge claims (the medicalization of the female body).

This is to say that the meaning of the female body as a "hysterical entity" - a corpporeal being susceptible to hysteria - was a meaning constructed through discursive practices, i.e., not only in the discourses of science and medicine, but also through the establishment of social institutions. These institutions, in turn, reproduce specific knowledge claims through the practices established by the profession and as part of the education and socialization of practitioners. Foucault suggests the term "apparatus" and later "technology" to name the process of connection between discursive practices, institutional relations, and material effects that, working together, produce a meaning or a "truth effect" for the human body.

In this sense, an apparatus or "technology" articulates power relations, systems of communication, and productive activities or practices; "articulate" here is used both in the sense of "expressing" that which is already given or operative and in the sense of conjoining or connecting. So, following Foucault's logic, the notion of "technology" describes the workings of a collection of practices that produce specific cultural effects. Technology names the process whereby discursive practices work interdependently with other cultural forces to produce effects at the level of the body.

These effects, in turn, become part of an apparatus of control. Foucault goes on to argue that the notion of technology allows for the analysis of power in terms of a number of concrete relations: (1) systems of differentiation, (2) types of objectives, (3) means of bringing power relations into being, (4) forms of institutionalization, and (5) degrees of rationalization - all of which are rooted in social networks, language use, and the human body. I find this notion of a technology and his enumeration of concrete relations particularly useful as a framework for investigating the way in which certain taken-for-granted "truths" are, in fact, culturally constructed and eventually institutionalized.

As many feminists have argued, Foucault evades direct consideration of gender as an "effect" produced at the level of the body. His broad-sweeping account of the disciplinary practices that produce subjugated bodies neglects to consider gender as an underlying organizing framework for deciphering the disciplined body. Thus, although he can identify the "hysterization of the female body" as one of the apparatuses of control of the body, his grid of analysis fails to consider gender itself as an organized, institutionalized, system of differences that constitutes the individual body and renders it meaningful. In a way that contradicts his analytical intentions to consider the system of differentiations that make the body meaningful, gender often functions for him as a natural given.

If Foucault's project is to deconstruct (in his own fashion) the most commonsensical, taken-for-granted "truths" about the workings of power, it is clear that he runs into problems with his elision of gender. This fact has provoked several feminists to reevaluate the history he offers. For example, in Diamond and Quinby Feminism and Foucault Francis Bartkowski argues quite directly that "what Foucault has done is to reproduce and produce as history the patriarchal history of sexuality." It is clear that throughout his project he treats the gender identity of the female body as a naturally occurring bodily characteristic instead of a "truth effect" produced by cultural discourses that constructs some bodies as active and disciplines others to be passive.

Within his analysis, gender materializes as a key "dividing practice" that objectifies the human body and makes it intelligible to him, yet he fails to consider it a technology of power/knowledge in its own right. For all his concern to elaborate systems of power and resistance, Foucault ends up writing not so much from a site of resistance but from a site of power - male-centered discourse. Given this, perhaps it is unavoidable that the more radical promise of his project would not be realized by him. Several feminist scholars are doing what he could not -articulating a history of sexuality from a site of resistance by addressing the construction of the feminine, femininity, and Woman to describe how gender is, in Foucault's terms, a primary apparatus of scientific biopower that constructs the body as an intelligible object.

For example, in Susan Suleiman collection of essays The Female Body in Western Culture several scholars implicitly rebuke Foucault's oversight by showing how gender is one of the primary effects of the discursive construction of the human body. Suleiman herself poses the question of the female body this way: "what place has the female body occupied in the Western imagination, and in the symbolic productions of Western culture over the past two thousand years?" Foucault would have us believe that "she" was hardly present, marginal and uninteresting at best.

The authors in Suleiman's collection collectively argue the contrary; they examine the many different sites of the ideological inscription of sexual difference by looking at representations of the female body in different cultural texts. The essays are organized thematically rather than historically, on the topics of eros, death, mothers, illness, images, and difference. The primary purpose of Suleiman's collection is to argue that the female body is not an essentially unchanging, given-in-nature, biological entity, but rather is symbolically constructed within different cultural discourses situated within different historical conjunctions.

Following Foucault, Suleiman underscores the importance of reading the body as a symbolic discursive construction:

> The cultural significance of the female body is not only (not even first and foremost) that of a flesh-and-blood entity, but that of a symbolic construct. Everything we know about the body - certainly as regards the past, and even, it could be argued, as regards the present - exists for us in some form of discourse: and discourse, whether verbal or visual, fictive or historical or speculative, is never unmediated, never free of interpretation, never innocent.

The analyses offered in Suleiman's book are textually grounded and politically motivated; taken together, they articulate an understanding of how the relation between the body and culture is mediated through discourse such that the body is transformed into an epistemological issue - knowledge about the body becomes a matter of representation of the body. The critical point Suleiman stresses is that there is no "natural" approach to the female body that is rooted in an essentialist female nature.

All understandings of the body are mediated through representations which, in turn, are constructed through interpretive frameworks. This approach, like Foucault's, keeps the body contained within discourse and subject(ed) to determinate systems of power and knowledge. But in many respects, this collection skirts the dangerous line of suggesting that knowledge of the body is only discursive. Or, put another way, when Suleiman writes that the "cultural significance" of the body is a matter of its symbolic construction, not its "natural femininity," she comes close to asserting that this is the singular definition of the female body.

This approach inadvertently ends up invoking a dualistic logic, that the female body is either a "flesh and blood entity" or a symbolic construct. I stress the term "inadvertently" to remind readers of the historical situation of the production of this approach to the study of the female body. It was an approach that sought to correct the overreliance on an essentialist definition of the female body as a biological or "natural" entity.

Since that time, feminist discussions of the constitution of the female body have been often sidelined by debates about the effectivity of essentialist versus anti-essentialist perspectives. I would like to sidestep this debate by focusing attention on the ways in which nature and culture are mutually determining systems of understanding. While it is true, as Suleiman says, that "everything we know about the body...exists for us in some form of discourse," this discourse is not entirely divorced from the material manifestation of the "flesh and blood" entity.

AS A SYMBOLIC CULTURAL RESOURCE

Building on the work of Marcel Mauss, cultural anthropologist Mary Douglas describes the relationship between symbolic systems, social structures, and the body by analyzing the way cultural systems rely on the body's expressive resources to formulate social relations. In her book Natural Symbols, Douglas asserts that social perceptions of the human body are never free from determining cultural influences; the body is always comprehended as an interaction between the materiality of what is given in a particular body and the symbolic constructions of the "body" embedded within a given culture.

But the most important point she makes is that although the meaning of the physical body is itself structured by the symbolic representation of the body, it is at the same time an experiential resource for the construction of such representations:

> The social body constrains the way the physical body is perceived. The physical experience of the body, always modified by the social categories through which it is known, sustains a particular view of society. There is a continual exchange of meanings between the two kinds of bodily experience so that each reinforces the categories of the other.

In this statement, Douglas follows Mauss by asserting that the human body is always defined according to cultural beliefs about social relations. But even as Douglas asserts that "most symbolic behaviour must work through the body" (vii), she argues that the meaning of the body, and thus the meaning of different systems of body symbols, is, in fact, constructed through "a continual exchange of meanings between two kinds of bodily experience" - of the physical body and of the social (or symbolic) body.

While I don't want to belabor the point, it is important to note that Douglas keeps the notion of the physical body at the heart of her account of the cultural construction of the symbolic body. Her broader point, of course, is to argue that although the physical body is in many ways a naturally occurring referent for symbolic systems, its meaning is not "naturally" determined. In this sense, there are no natural symbols, although there are plentiful symbolic representations of nature and of the "natural body."

Douglas offers an important contribution to an understanding of the cultural construction of the gendered body. "There can be no natural way of considering the body," she writes, "that does not involve at the same time a social dimension." This assertion denaturalizes both the body and gender and provides a basis for accomplishing what Brown and Adams identify as a critical feminist project - the deconstruction of the "natural" female body. Following this, gender identity can be redefined as a body attribute that is assigned, organized, and acquired through the process of social perception; in short, it can no longer be considered a "natural fact" of the human body.

Rather, we must consider how the human body is "gendered" through a series of social acts that often begin long before physical birth and are determined only partially by personal (selfdecipherment) perception of physiological body parts (the genitals, for example). But the important issue here is not only that gender is "denaturalized" but that so too are definitions of gender that rely on appeals to the natural body. Behind the construction of representations of "natural bodies" and "natural" gender identities, Douglas claims are beliefs and anxieties about the social body.

In keeping with Douglas's line of analysis, Thomas Laqueur argues that the female body was at the center of a radical 18th-century rein-terpretation of the patriarchal social hierarchy. Sexual difference was reconsidered such that the female body was no longer considered merely an inferior, underdeveloped, and infantile version of the male body (ovaries as underdeveloped testicles, for example); rather a complementary relation between the male and female body was established, such that writers of all sorts were determined to base what they insisted were fundamental differences between male and female sexuality, and thus between man and woman, on discoverable biological distinctions.... Thus the old model, in which men and women were arrayed according to their degree of metaphysical perfection, their vital heat, along an axis whose telos was male, gave way by the late 18th century to a new model of difference, of biological divergence. An anatomy and physiology of incommensurability replaced metaphysics of hierarchy in the representation of women in relation to men.

Since Laqueur explicitly draws on Douglas in his analysis of the construction of the female body, it is not surprising that he situates this transformation of the cultural understanding of the "nature" of the female body within the changing constitution of the 18th-century social order, "when the basis for a new order of sex and gender became a critical issue of political theory and practice". Laqueur points out that the new order (which replaced the divine right of kings, a similar point of analysis in Foucault's historical genealogy) was concerned to establish naturalized hierarchies among human bodies.

He explains how such a cultural imperative and the use of metaphors (of heat, of oestrus) functioned to define the female body in terms of its reproductive biology. The hierarchical relation between the male body and the female body was not overturned; rather the political, economic and cultural transformations of the 18th century created the context in which the articulation of radical differences between the sexes became culturally imperative. In a world in which science was increasingly viewed as providing insight into the fundamental truths of creation, in which nature as manifested in the unassailable reality of bones and organs was taken to be the only foundation of the moral order, a biology of incommensurability became the means by which such differences could be authoritatively represented.

Here Laqueur offers an account of the exercise of scientific biopower on the female body. The turn toward a biologically based definition of the complementarity of the female body raised new questions about the relationship between that body and social control. For if female bodies are fundamentally different from male bodies, not just an inferior version, and the issue of control becomes more critical: how does one control a body that isn't entirely knowable?

In her examination of medical textbooks of the nineteenth century, Mary Poovey illuminates the historical construction of the female body as the object of medical attention and control. Moreover, she explicates how medical discourse constructed the female body as excessive and threatening to the epistemological boundaries of the prevailing social order. Specifically she focuses on the medical debates concerning forms of anesthesia to show how they function as a discursive site of the struggle for authority over the female body between obstetricians, midwives, and other medical practitioners. Not incidentally it is a site in which the female body is thoroughly silent/silenced:

> The debate presented itself as an argument about the nature of women and medicine's proper relation to them.... First, does the woman in labour properly belong to the realm of nature, which is governed by God, or to culture, where nature submits to man? Second, how can a man know - so as to master - the female body, which is always other to his own?

If the female body properly belonged to nature, the argument went, then midwives were better positioned to serve the laboring maternal body, being female bodies themselves and skilled in reading the natural labour signs of that body. If the female body could be secured as belonging to the cultural order, then, by extension, it was beholden to the cultural authority of medicine and medical discourse and would be properly served by the administration of chloroform during labour (one of the two forms of anesthesia being debated).

At this point, Poovey implies that the articulation among new technologies (forms of anesthesia), social debates about medical authority and the status of medicine as a scientifically rational practice, and a definition of the female body as governed by its reproductive capacity, establishes a definition of the female body as "always lacking and needing control":

> This set of assumptions - that woman's reproductive function defines her character, position, and value, that this function is only one sign of an innate periodicity, and that this biological periodicity influences and is influenced by an array of nervous disorders - mandates the medical profession's superintendence of women....[quoting Dr. Issac Ray:] With women, it is but a step from extreme nervous susceptibility to downright hysteria, and from that to overt insanity.... Seen in this way, hysteria is simultaneously the norm of the female body taken to its logical extreme and a medical category that effectively defines this norm as inherently abnormal.

Furthermore, Poovey explains:

> On the one hand, representing woman as an inherently unstable female body authorizes ceaseless medical monitoring and control. But on the other hand, this representation of woman as always requiring control produces her as always already exceeding the control that medicine can exercise.

Consequently, the female body is defined as simultaneously belonging within the "proper" domain of medical discourse and yet always threatening its epistemological boundaries. Here we read the conflation between the political contest to establish the physiological facts of female nature, and the physiological consequences of symbolic representations of the female body.

The female body that is an effect of the construction of identity/ authority of obstetricians in nineteenth-century medical discourse is a hybrid creature formed through the articulations among social practices, the development of new knowledge, and changing patterns of power and authority. In this sense, the female body functions as a border case; it is at once defined as part of a natural order and as an intensely fascinating and yet threatening object of cultural control. Its excessiveness strains the cultural authority of medical knowledge. As such it is a site of potential transgression against the boundaries of social order, at once constituted within the dominant discourses of science and medicine but threatening to the epistemological certainty of that discourse.

PANIC POSTMODERNISM AND THE DISAPPEARING BODY

The story about the female body doesn't change much in more recent history, especially in cultural narratives of postmodern identity. In *Body Invaders*, a collection of essays on panic sex in America, Editor Arthur Kroker also seeks to intervene in the reproduction of a dominant discourse of the body that would define it as an organic, natural entity. Following Marshall McLuhan, Kroker argues that the "natural" body has disappeared, replaced by a technologically produced simulacrum. Kroker reads the current list of "panic" body issues (AIDS, anorexia, addictions of all sorts) as signs of significant social anxieties concerning control and safety.

The "panic body" marks "a declining culture where the body is revived, and given one last burst of hyper-subjectivity, as the inscribed text for all the stress and crisis-symptoms of the death of the social". With this statement he reasserts Douglas's understanding that "cultures think themselves through the body." He sees the proliferation of rhetorics that work feverishly to invest the body with meaning as a symptom of a culture in decline - a culture where meaning has been banished. For Kroker the body is simply obsolete, replaced by numerous technological extensions of its senses.

The prevalence of body rhetorics masks the disappearance of the natural body (now replaced by technological devices) which in turn, masks the disappearance of the social - the final death of social solidarity that comes from daily living with the apocalypse. Discourse, now objectified as communication technologies, and literally replaces the material body with simulated body senses. Whereas Foucault's project was to explicate how the discourses of modernity redefined the body as machine, in postmodernity what we discover is that technology now transforms the body into nothing more than discourse.

With the disappearance of the material body in McLuhan's analysis of media culture and Kroker's reading of postmodernity, gender too presumably becomes ephemeral, or at best an artifact of an outdated rhetoric that seeks to invest the body with meaning. And yet, we can read in both McLuhan's and Kroker's analyses a submerged discourse of gender that continues to organize and make intelligible the discourses of the body in late capitalism. Even as he claims that the velocity of cultural change blurs the boundaries upon which identity is constructed, Kroker identifies the special status of the female body in postmodernity:

Because now as ever, the play of power within and against the text of women's bodies is an early warning sign of a grisly power field that speaks the language of body invaders. As privileged objects of a domination that takes as its focus the inscription of the text of the body, women have always known the meaning of a relational power that works in the language of body invaders. This is not, though, the wager of an old patriarchal power that announces itself in the transcendent and externalized language of hierarchy, univocity, and logocentricity, but a power field that can be multiple, pleasurable, and indeed, fully embodied....women's bodies have always been postmodern because they have always been targets of a power which, inscribing the text of the flesh, seeks to make of feminine identity something interpellated by ideology, constituted by language, and the site of a "dissociated ego."

Kroker elaborates this language of body invaders as the conspicuous consumption of late capitalism, which turns all bodies into sign vehicles for fetishistic commodities. As a companion to McLuhan "Mechanical Bride," "The Capezio Woman" figures as a final icon in Kroker's analysis. Whereas the Mechanical Bride symbolizes the female body of American media culture that is docile, traditional, and subjected to "the wager of old patriarchal power," the Capezio Woman symbolizes the female body that is stylish, pleasure-anointed, and happy to find a snappy pair of new shoes.

Both images testify to the persistence (nonobsolescence) of gender in a postcorporeal world. Even when the body is reduced to a discursive effect, notes Kroker, the female body functions as the privileged sign of the "body debased, humiliated, and inscribed to excess by all the signs of consumer culture". Upon closer reading, the female body hasn't been transformed at all; it is still constructed as the message-bearing and silent form of the (eighteenth and nineteenth centuries') unruly body, produced through the formation of the cultural imaginary; only now the cultural imaginary is expressed through the rhetoric of "panic" postmodernism.

The female body continues to function as the sign of a gendered body opposed to a nonmarked (human) body that is said to be now (in late capitalism) subjugated to discursive systems of power and knowledge. If women have always been postmodern bodies, as Kroker asserts, then what is different about postmodern bodies that hasn't always been the condition of female bodies? The compulsion to theorize the condition of postmodern bodies as something new or even exhausted is due to the novelty the male body experiences coming under this totalizing system for the first time; understandably, panic results.

In Kroker's analysis, female bodies continue to mark gender; thus they announce the deployment of a gendered opposition of bodies in postmodern theory. This is a gendered opposition, whereby the One (recently "invaded" body) is unmarked by gender and the Other (the always postmodern body) is female. Such is the fate of the female body in the postmodern cultural imaginary: an always silent/ silenced conceptual placeholder in hysterical male discourse. As before, her excessiveness threatens the very order of the system.

Is it ironic that the body disappears in postmodern theory just as women and feminists have emerged as an intellectual force within the human disciplines? A similar (ironic?) contradiction emerges with respect to the issue of the body. An organic body marked by certain biological characteristics provided a common identity for women to collectivize as feminists. But the bodily identity of woman proved unstable and unreliable as a source of collective empowerment. Diverse feminist action directs its attention to de-essentializing the biological identity of woman, thus working to deconstruct the organic foundation of feminist thought.

After acknowledging the impossibility of biological essentialism as a foundation for the identity of "woman," feminist thinking proceeds to an analysis of the cultural construction of the body, and is immediately confronted with a discourse that gleefully joins it in deconstructing biological essentialism. In the process, feminists encounter unsolicited assistance in doing away with "the body," which served - at one point, if not now - as the necessary foundation of women's empowerment.

Faced with the prospect of being strategically eclipsed within the modern episteme once again, feminists have a political stake in constructing and critiquing theories of the body within postmodernism. As I have argued elsewhere, it is time for feminism to crash the postmodern party. The final fate of "the body" should not be left entirely to the panic postmodernists - that is, Jean Baudrillard, Deleuze and Guattari, among others. Moreover, we cannot listen obediently while these very same postmodernists delineate for us "the special place of feminist theory today" and lay out for us the proper attitude that feminism should adopt toward the body. But what is a feminist to do?

In her book Gynesis: Configurations of Woman and Modernity, Alice Jardine cautions feminist writers: "The attempt to analyze, to separate ideological and cultural determinations of the 'feminine' from the 'real woman' - seemingly the most logical path for a feminist to follow - may also be the most interminable process, one in which women become not only figuratively but also literally impossible." Jardine describes the paradoxical situation of feminist criticism that on the one hand draws political strength from an essentialist identity of "woman," but on the other has been convinced of the necessity to interrogate such an identity for the differences it obscures:

While proceeding from a "belief" (in women's oppression), we are nevertheless, necessarily, caught up in a permanent whirlwind of reading practices within a universe of fiction and theory written, but for a few official exceptions, by men. Not believing in "Truth," we continue to be fascinated by (elaborate) fictions. This is the profound paradox of the feminist speaking in our contemporary culture: she proceeds from a belief in a world from which - even the philosophers admit - Truth has disappeared. This paradox, it seems to me, can lead to (at least) three possible scenarios: a renewed silence, a form of religion (from mysticism to political orthodoxy), or a continual attention - historical, ideological, and affective - to the place from which we speak.

Another possible solution is to reconstruct our reading practices - which is ultimately what Jardine advocates. She suggests that feminists begin to write new fictions, written through "the continual attention - historical, ideological, and affective - to the place from which we speak". This, to me, perfectly describes Donna Haraway's response to feminism's "profound paradox," and indeed, the founding imperative for her feminist manifesto; in elaborating a new fiction of feminist identity, her "ironic political myth" of cyborg citizenship, she enacts a new reading practice that takes the discursively constructed material body as its starting point and narrates a reconstructed fiction of gender identity.

READING CYBORGS

According to Haraway, in "A Manifesto for Cyborgs," the only bodies that stand a chance in postmodern culture are cyborg bodies. Cyborg bodies are constructed by communication networks and other hybrid discourses such as biotechnology, biopolitics, and female bodybuilding. Variously used as a symbol of antitechnological sentiments or of the possibilities of "better living through chemistry," cyborgs are a product of fears and desires that run deep within our cultural imaginary.

Through the use of technology as the means or context for human hybridization, cyborgs come to represent unfamiliar "otherness," one that challenges the denotative stability of human identity. Andreas Huyssen claims that the crisis of modernism pivots on the problematic of otherness. In this way, cyborgs offer a particularly appropriate emblem of postmodern identity, since cyborg identity is predicated on transgressed boundaries. They fascinate us because they are not like us and yet are just like us. Formed through a radical disruption of otherness, cyborg identity foregrounds the constructedness of otherness. Cyborgs alert us to the way in which identity depends on notions of "the other" that are arbitrary, shifting, and ultimately unstable.

Every cyborg image constructs an implicit opposition between machine and human, at once repressing similarities and highlighting distinctions. In this way it defines the meaning of both the term "human" and the term "artificial." Signs of human-ness and, alternatively, signs of machineness function not only as markers of the "essences" of the dual natures of the hybrid, but also as signs of the inviolable opposition between humans and machines. But because the cyborg embodies both "natures" simultaneously, the resulting hybrid is neither purely human nor purely machine.

The distribution of its dual dispositions is never simply symmetrical, and the proximity of each to the other and the combination of dissimilar parts produces a hybrid often unrecognizable as any familiar personage. By disrupting the stable meanings of the human/machine dualism, other reliable oppositions are also rendered unstable. The cyborg, for Haraway, has the potential to disrupt the persistent dualisms that have been "systemic to the logics and practices of domination of women, people of colour, nature, workers, animals." The most troublesome dualisms include some already mentioned in this chapter: culture/nature, human/artificial, male/female, as well as others such as reality/appearance, truth/illusion, theory/politics.

Cyborg bodies, then, cannot be conceived as belonging wholly to either culture or nature; they are neither wholly technological nor completely organic. In a similar sense, cyborg bodies cannot be completely discursive. Cyborgs are a matter of fiction and a matter of lived experience. They not only subvert the certainty of what counts as nature, but, as Haraway lays out, they also subvert the certainty of the "textualization of everything" by pointing to the lived relations of domination that ground cultural reading(s).

By reasserting a material body, the cyborg rebukes the disappearance of the body within postmodernism. Yet it never contradicts the variety of discursive constructions of the female body. The cyborg connects a discursive body with a historically material body by taking account of the ways in which the body is constructed within different social and cultural formations. Ultimately, the cyborg challenges feminism to search for ways to study the body as it is at once both a cultural construction and a material fact of human life.

The impact of this is decisive: understanding that the body is culturally, not "naturally," constructed means that the body is not solely a matter of materiality; nor can it be reductively a matter of discourse. Its "nature" is culturally determined even when this nature is said to be discursively constructed. To claim that the body is a discursive as well as material construction still leaves everything to say about the particular cultural design of that body within any given historical conjunction.

Haraway explicitly maps the identity of woman onto the image of the cyborg. This foregrounds the ambiguous constitution of the female body - predicated on the blurred boundaries between the individual and the collective, the material and the discursive, the fictive and the real. Both Woman and Cyborg are simultaneously symbolically and biologically produced and reproduced through social interactions. The "self" is one interactional product; the body is another.

The cyborg further displaces the nature-versus-culture opposition since it is clear in this age of body technologies that the given-ness of the female body is a constructed artifact of various systems of meaning. Moreover, as Haraway reminds us, the search for a female "nature" is a utopian quest, which threatens to distract contemporary feminists from more important tasks, such as forming coalitions and alliances with other political groups based not on some natural gender identification, but on the necessity for shared political strategies. This tactical plan of action depends upon feminism's willingness to investigate how women live permanently partial identities, to discover what cultural meanings are taken up, how they are resisted, and in the process, ultimately transformed.

WRITING FEMINISM

Recent feminist scholarship on the construction of cultural systems of power and knowledge question the forms of domination and control that operate in contemporary society. Feminist scholarship by Haraway, Sandra Harding, Ruth Bleier, and Paula Treichler (among others) describe how science, technology, and medicine -as institutionalized domains of socially constructed knowledge - enact practices of domination and oppression based on gender, race, and class distinctions.

Their discussion of issues relating to epistemology, gender, and identity elaborates how the material (gendered) body is discounted as a necessary condition and apparatus of knowledge. Science, medicine, and technology are defined as discursive, social, and symbolic systems in which the female body functions as an ideological marker of "natural sexuality" and "reproduction."

Taken together, these scholars argue that gender is a constructed effect produced at the level of the body. "One important route for reconstructing socialist-feminist politics," Haraway argues, "is through theory and practice addressed to the social relations of science and technology, including crucially the systems of myth and meanings structuring our imaginations."

What this amounts to is the construction of a new reading strategy that is attendant to the historical legacy of the female body as (1) a conceptual placeholder, (2) discursively constructed, and (3) threatening to male systems of knowledge; but also attendant to the way the female body's constructedness organizes the perception of its materiality and the effects of this in women's lives. In this sense the female body is less a singular concept or discoverable unity and more an arrangement of texts, silences, laws, and lines of force. Perhaps the term "articulation" best describes this theoretical configuration of the female body: an articulation among reading effects, writing practices, relations of power, cultural stagings, material bodies, and socially constructed perceptions.

Ruth Bleier has orchestrated one such project, which addresses the shift from biology as clinical practice (a convention of an organic order) to biology as inscription (the reconstituted exercise as part of the informatics of domination). In her book Science and Gender: A Critique of Biology and Its Tbeories on Women, Bleier grounds her analysis of the relationship between gender and science in a consideration of biological determinism. She identifies the "nature versus nurture" debate as a false opposition:

The underlying scientific issue in evaluating any theory of biological determinism is the feasibility of isolating biological from learned influences in the determination of physical characteristics, behaviors, social relationships, and social organization. The effort to separate genetic and environmental influences continues to plague thinking in many [scientific] fields. Yet it represents a false dichotomy that does not reflect biological processes, but like other dualisms may serve reactionary social and political purposes.

Bleier's particular area of interest is neuroanatomy, an increasingly significant area of scientific research in terms of artificial intelligence and the development of brain-imaging technology. The history of scientific research in craniology and neuroanatomy shows that in the early nineteenth century there was considerable interest in demonstrating that the differences between men and women "resided" in the different structures of the male and female brains. Bleier describes how craniology "went out of style" as a scientific field of study as the search for the physiological basis of women's inferiority yielded no significant conclusions.

In her analysis of the history of brain-related science, Bleier demonstrates how science as a specifically cultural institution participates in constructing naturalistic explanations of sexual differences. Bleier demythologizes science by arguing that "it is not the neutral, dispassionate, value-free pursuit of Truth; that scientists are not objective, disinterested, or culturally disengaged from the questions they ask of nature or the methods they use to frame their answers". Furthermore, she argues, it is impossible for science or scientists to do otherwise, since science is a social activity and a cultural process created by persons who live in the world of science as well as in the societies that socialized them.

In constructing this analysis, Bleier decouples "sexual difference" from the study of invariant biological processes by showing how the "meaning" of female physiology has been (and continues to be) constructed by the cultural and social practices of the biological sciences. This contributes to a denaturalizing of woman's subordination, which, as Mary Poovey describes, historically has been supported by biological theories of the female body as defined by its reproductive capacities.

By exposing the position of the female body within neuroanatomy - as one form of scientific discourse -Bleier shows how particular physiological processes come to count as definitive emblems of sexual identity. In this way, Bleier takes a male construct, the female body, inscribed in one discourse, and reinscribes it within another textual/sexual system, one this time informed by feminism, which provides new codes and conventions for "reading" its meaning.

In Bleier's work we see how gender, like the body, is a hybrid construction, belonging both to the order of the material body and the social and discursive systems within which bodies are embedded. So when gender operates as a system of differentiation (in Foucault's terms), it must be considered as both a discursive and material system. As a discourse, gender includes representations, icons, symbols, utterances, signification, and codes. But this discourse is never separate from the bodies that are taken up within it or marked by it.

Paula Treichler essay "AIDS, Homophobia, and Biomedical Discourse: An Epidemic of Signification" directly addresses the way in which discourse constructs the disease and makes it intelligible. Her reading of the biomedical discourse of AIDS demonstrates the ways in which words - more precisely, discourse - enact and reinforce deeply entrenched, pervasive, and often conservative cultural "narratives" about gender; it is also about how words seek, ultimately, to contain and control women's unruly and uncontainable properties.

She argues persuasively that a theoretically informed analysis of AIDS must not reduce it to a matter of attending to the "dual nature" of the body (of AIDS - as both a social and biological entity) but rather must appreciate the extent to which social constructions of the body organize the very way of perceiving and knowing the body: "Our social constructions of AIDS...are based not upon objective, scientifically determined 'reality' but upon what we are told about this reality: that is, upon prior social constructions routinely produced within the discourses of biomedical science".

She goes on to describe the relationship between popular and biomedical discourse as a continuum, not a dichotomy, through which "reality" is constructed and its contradictions played out. This continuum also suggests that the relationship between science and popular discourse is an interaction, not a linear arrangement in which science dictates what popular thought is to think. Language is the arena within which this continuum manifests itself. In a separate article, "AIDS, Gender, and Biomedical Discourse," Treichler demonstrates how gender continues to operate as a submerged discourse within contemporary medical discourse.

In her cultural studies of the AIDS body and her work on the epidemic of signification within the discourse on AIDS, she elaborates how the representation of the female body as inherently pathological and contaminated plays a complex role in the development of medical discourse about AIDS. Given the historical association between the female body and disease, especially sexually transmitted ones, it is surprising to learn that women were explicitly excluded as a targeted risk group of HIV infection for the first four years of the AIDS pandemic. The significance of this exclusion is sobering and illuminates a cultural narrative about the construction of the gendered body. As Treichler explains:

The construction of AIDS as essentially a male-only sexually transmitted disease depends upon the production and reproduction of gendered readings which often require reasoning so outlandish and speculative as to be dizzying. In turn this "knowledge" of AIDS infection and who can "catch it" filters out counter-evidence in a variety of ways, and creates a cycle of invisibility in which women do not believe themselves vulnerable and therefore do not seek medical care or even anonymous testing. The pie-shaped charts standardly include the classic 4 -H "risk groups" - Homosexuals, Heroin addicts, Hemophiliacs, and Haitians - plus their sex partners, gender often unspecified - plus "others."

By focusing on AIDS as something you get because of who you are, not what you do, women were excluded from the list of populations believed to be at risk. "As evidence of AIDS in women mounted," Treichler writes, "speculations were put forward that linked AIDS to prostitutes, IV drug users and women in the third world (primarily Haiti and countries in central Africa)". So as the female body insisted on demonstrating its susceptibility to the variety of afflictions associated with the AIDS syndrome, it became partially visible to the medical community, who used it to mark an opposition between "sexually active males and promiscuous females".

Whereas in previous accounts of AIDS as "a male-only sexually transmitted disease" the female body is literally invisible within medical discourse, the definition of the female body advanced in the recent accounting for AIDS in women suggests that it is merely a container and transmitter of the disease. In her discussion of the relatively recent attempt to address the heterosexual transmission of the HIV virus, Treichler describes its problematic consideration of women:

> First, the women in the risk groups are given their "status" by virtue of their sexual partners - the men they're connected to not by virtue of their own sexual activities. And finally, above all, the purpose of studying women, we are told, is twofold: first, to use incidence in women as a general index to heterosexual spread of the virus, and second, to identify women at risk and prevent "primary" infection in them so that we can prevent the majority of cases of AIDS in children that would result from these maternal risk groups without our intervention.

The female body of this AIDS discourse is identified by its reproductive responsibilities and sexual connections to men. Now that it is established that women can be infected, woman's legacy as an inherently pathological, unruly, uncontainable, but essentially passive vessel returns to haunt her and render her again invisible within medical discourse. Bleier's work in neuroanatomy and Treichler's on AIDS discourse both mark one of the transitions that Haraway identifies as an "informatics of domination": from an order concerned with organic sex role specialization to one that redefines biology as inscription. Central to this transition is the emergence of communication technologies as the premier technologies of culture.

For Haraway, in "A Manifesto for Cyborgs," communication technologies and biotechnologies are the crucial tools recrafting our bodies.... Technologies and scientific discourses can be partially understood as formalizations, i.e., as the frozen moments, of the fluid social interactions constituting them, but they should also be viewed as instruments for enforcing meanings.... Furthermore, communication sciences and modern biologies are constructed by a common move - the translation of the world into a problem of coding, a search for a common language in which all resistance to instrumental control disappears and all heterogeneity can be submitted to disassembly, reassembly, investment, and exchange.

The female body is at the center of this transformation of the social order. As a cyborg, simultaneously discursive and material, the female body is the site at which we can witness the struggle between systems of social order. In the process, new forms of gendered embodiment emerge which on the one hand may display inherited signs of traditional dichotomous gender identity, but which also reinvent gender identity in totally new ways. In postmodern social theory, as was demonstrated in various other historical moments, the female body has been constructed as uncontainable, unruly, and ultimately undecidable. Just as this is woman's legacy, so too is it her promise.

Although the female body is subordinated within institutionalized systems of power and knowledge and crisscrossed by incompatible discourses, it is not fully determined by those systems of meaning; and although woman is technologically constructed, her excesses accumulate, assembling the resources/ techniques to signify/construct herself as transgressive of, if not entirely resistant to, the discourses that seek to contain her. Cyborg bodies pump iron - physically fit, yet unnaturally crafted, they are hyper-built. Cyborg bodies raise the issue of possible new form(s) of gendered embodiment. Their recrafted bodies defy the natural givenness of physical gender identity.

The problem with postmodern body stories is that bodies are never nonmaterial, as these stories suggest. They are never outside history and concrete relations of power and domination. Just as women never speak, write, or act outside of their bodies, cyborgs never leave the meat behind. It is important that feminist approaches to "the body" resist the easy dissolution or dematerialization of the body offered by postmodernist theorists. The cyborg image works well to foreground the radical materiality of the body, which cannot be written out of any feminist account.

Whatever its fate, "the body" in feminist theory has never been simply a blank slate (or screen) upon which or about which to write. From a feminist perspective, attempts to write about the relationship between the contemporary social order and the body are ill-fated endeavors if they do not begin with a consideration of gender, or more explicitly, with a consideration of the gendering of bodies. It seems, at times, that the more "the body" is subjected to theoretical scrutiny, the more resistant it becomes. Just as the disappearance of the body is announced in theory, the material body returns to thwart all attempts to repress it. It remains, for all of the various feminisms, a vital site for the working out of the intersections among feminist politics, theory, and practice in postmodernity.

4

Cosmetic Surgery and New Imaging Technologies

Among the most intriguing new body technologies developed during the 1980s are the techniques of visualization that redefine the range of human perception. New medical imaging technologies such as laparoscopy and computer tomography (CT) make the body visible in such a way that its internal status can be assessed before it is laid bare or opened up surgically. Like the techniques that enable scientists to encode and "read" genetic structures, these new visualization technologies transform the material body into a visual medium.

In the process the body is fractured and fragmented so that isolated parts can be examined visually: the parts can be isolated by function, as in organs or neuron receptors, or by medium, as in fluids, genes, or heat. At the same time, the material body comes to embody the characteristics of technological images. This chapter examines the discourse of cosmetic surgery as it relies upon new technologies of visualization that function similarly to other visualization devices: to fragment the body into isolated parts and pieces and to render it a visual medium.

Cqarole Spitzack suggests that cosmetic surgery actually deploys three overlapping mechanisms of cultural control: inscription, surveillance, and confession. According to Spitzack, the physician's clinical eye functions like Foucault's medical gaze; it is a disciplinary gaze situated within apparatuses of power and knowledge that constructs the female figure as pathological, excessive, unruly, and potentially threatening of the dominant order. This gaze disciplines the unruly female body by first fragmenting it into isolated parts - face, hair, legs, and breasts - and then redefining those parts as inherently flawed and pathological.

When a woman internalizes a fragmented body image and accepts its "flawed" identity, each part of the body then becomes a site for the "fixing" of her physical abnormality. Spitzack characterizes this acceptance as a form of confession:

> In the scenario of the cosmetic surgeon's office, the transformation from illness to health is inscribed on the body of the patient.... The female patient is promised beauty and re-forms in exchange for confession, which is predicated on an admission of a diseased appearance that points to a diseased (powerless) character. A failure to confess, in the clinical setting, is equated with a refusal of health; a preference for disease.

But the cosmetic surgeon's gaze doesn't simply medicalize the female body, it actually redefines it as an object for technological reconstruction. In her reading of the women's films of the 1940s, Mary Ann Doane employs the concept of the "clinical eye" to describe how the technologies of looking represent and situate female film characters as the objects of medical discourse. In Doane's analysis, the medicalization of the female body relies on a surface/depth model of the body, whereby the physician assumes the right and responsibility of divining the truth of the female body - to make visible her invisible depths.

The clinical gaze of the physician reveals the truth of the female body in his act of looking through her to see the "essence" of her illness. According to Doane, the clinical eye marks a shift in the signification of the female body, from a purely surface form of signification to a depth model of signification. She traces this shift through a reading of the difference between mainstream classical cinema and the woman's film of the 1940s. In examining the visualization technologies used in the practice of cosmetic surgery, we can witness the process whereby new imaging technologies are articulated with traditional and ideological beliefs about gender - an articulation that keeps the female body positioned as a privileged object of a normative gaze that is now not simply a medicalized gaze ("the clinical eye") but also a technologized view.

In the application of new visualization technologies, the relationship between the female body and the cultural viewing apparatus has shifted again; in the process, the clinical eye gives way to the deployment of a technological gaze. This application of the gaze does not rely on a surface/depth model of the material body, whereby the body has some sort of structural integrity as a bounded physical object.

In the encounter between women and cosmetic surgeons, it is not so much the inner or essential woman that is visualized; her interior story has no truth of its own. Both her surface and her interiority are flattened and dispersed. Cosmetic surgeons use technological imaging devices to reconstruct the female body as a signifier of ideal feminine beauty. In this sense, surgical techniques literally enact the logic of assembly-line beauty: "difference" is made over into sameness. The technological gaze refashions the material body to reconstruct it in keeping with culturally determined ideals of Western feminine beauty.

THE INSCRIPTION OF CULTURAL STANDARDS OF BEAUTY

Cosmetic surgery enacts a form of cultural signification where we can examine the literal and material reproduction of ideals of beauty. Where visualization technologies bring into focus isolated body parts and pieces, surgical procedures actually carve into the flesh to isolate parts to be manipulated and resculpted. In this way cosmetic surgery literally transforms the material body into a sign of culture.

The discourse of cosmetic surgery offers provocative material for discussing the cultural construction of the gendered body because women are often the intended and preferred subjects of such discourse and men are often the agents performing the surgery. Cosmetic surgery is not simply a discursive site for the "construction of images of women," but a material site at which the physical female body is surgically dissected, stretched, carved, and reconstructed according to cultural and eminently ideological standards of physical appearance.

There are two main fields of plastic surgery. Whereas reconstructive surgery works to repair catastrophic, congenital, or cancer-damage deformities, cosmetic or aesthetic surgery is often an entirely elective endeavor. And whereas reconstructive surgery is associated with the restoration of health, normalcy, and physical function, cosmetic surgery is said to improve self-esteem, social status, and sometimes even professional standing.

All plastic surgery implicitly involves aesthetic judgments of proportion, harmony, and symmetry. In fact, one medical textbook strongly encourages plastic surgeons to acquire some familiarity with classical art theory so that they are better prepared to "judge human form in three dimensions, evaluate all aspects of the deformity, visualize the finished product, and plan the approach that will produce an optimal result." Codifying the aspects of such an "aesthetic sense" seems counterintuitive, but in fact there is a voluminous literature that reports the scientific mea surement of facial proportions in an attempt to accomplish the scientific determination of aesthetic perfection.

According to one surgeon, William Bass, most cosmetic surgeons have some familiarity with the anthropological fields of anthropometry and human osteology. Anthropometry - defined in one source as "a technique for the measurement of men, whether living or dead" is actually a critically important science used by a variety of professional engineers and designers. One example of practical anthropometry is the collection of measurements of infants and children's bodies for use in the design of automobile seat restraints.

Of course it makes a great deal of sense that measurement standards and scales of human proportions are a necessary resource for the design of products for human use; in order to achieve a "fit" with the range of human bodies that will eventually use and inhabit a range of products from office chairs to office buildings, designers must have access to a reliable and standardized set of body measurements. But when the measurement project identifies the "object" being measured as the "American Negro" or the "ideal female face," it is less clear what practical use these measurements serve.

If anthropometry is "a technique for the measurement of men," the fascination of plastic surgeons is the measurement of the ideal. One well cited volume in a series published by the *American Academy of Facial Plastic and Reconstructive Surgery,* titled *Proportions of the Aesthetic Face* (by Nelson Powell and Brian Humphreys), proclaims that it is a "complete sourcebook of information on facial proportion and analysis." In the preface the authors state:

> The face, by its nature, presents itself often for review. We unconsciously evaluate the overall effect each time an acquaintance is made.... This impression is generally related to some scale of beauty or balance.... The harmony and symmetry are compared to a mental, almost magical, ideal subject, which is our basic concept of beauty. Such a concept or complex we shall term the "ideal face."

According to the authors, the purpose of their text is quite simple: to document, objectively, the guidelines for facial symmetry and proportion. Not inconsequentially, the "Ideal Face" depicted throughout this book both in the form of line drawings and in photographs - is of a white woman whose face is perfectly symmetrical in line and profile. The authors claim that although the "male's bone structure is sterner, bolder, and more prominent...the ideals of facial proportion and unified interplay apply to either gender". The only illustration of a male face is contained in the glossary.

This focus on the female body is prevalent in all areas of cosmetic surgery - from the determination of ideal proportions to the marketing of specific cosmetic procedures. The source or history of these idealized drawings is never discussed. But once the facial proportions of these images are codified and measured, they are reproduced by surgeons as they make modifications to their patients' faces. Even though they work with faces that are individually distinct, surgeons use the codified measurements as guidelines for determining treatment goals in the attempt to bring the distinctive face in alignment with artistic ideals of symmetry and proportion.

The treatment of race in this book on "ideal proportions of the aesthetic face" reveals a preference for white, symmetrical faces that heal (apparently) without scarring. On the one hand the authors acknowledge that "bone structure is different in all racial identities" and that "surgeons must acknowledge that racial qualities are appreciated differently in various cultures," but in the end they argue that "the facial form [should be] able to confer harmony and aesthetic appeal regardless of race." It appears that this appreciation for the aesthetic judgment "regardless of race" is not a widely shared assumption among cosmetic surgeons Napoleon N.

Vaughn reports that many cosmetic surgeons, "mindful of keloid formation and hyperpigmented scarring, routinely reject black patients." But the issue of scar tissue formation is entirely ignored in the discussion of the "proportions of the aesthetic face." Powell and Humphreys implicitly argue that black faces can be evaluated in terms of ideal proportions determined by the measurement of Caucasian faces, but they fail to address the issue of postsurgical risks that differentiate black patients from Caucasian ones.

Although it is true that black patients and patients with dark ruddy complexions have a greater propensity to form keloids or hypertrophic scars than do Caucasian patients, many physicians argue that black patients who are shown to be prone to keloid formation in the lower body are not necessarily prone to such formations in the facial area and upper body; therefore a racial propensity for keloid formation should not be a reason to reject a black patient's request for facial cosmetic surgery.

And according to Arthur Sumrail, even though "postoperative dyschromic changes and surgical incision lines are much more visible in many black patients and races of colour than their Caucasian counterparts," these changes and incision lines greatly improve with time and corrective cosmetics. As an abstraction, the "aesthetic face" is designed to assist surgeons in planning surgical goals; but as a cultural artifact, the "aesthetic face" symbolizes a desire for standardized ideals of Caucasian beauty.

It is clear that all plastic surgery invokes standards of physical appearance and functional definitions of the "normal" or "healthy" body. Upon closer investigation we can see how these standards and definitions are culturally determined. In the 1940s and 1950s, women reportedly wanted "pert, upturned noses," but according to one recent survey this shape has gone out of style: "the classic, more natural shape is the ultimate one with which to sniff these days." The obvious question becomes, what condition does the adjective "natural" describe?

In this case we can see how requests for cosmetic reconstructions show the waxing and waning of fashionable desires; in this sense, "fashion surgery" might be a more fitting label for the kind of surgery performed for nonfunctional reasons. But even as high fashion moves toward multiculturalism in the employment of nontraditionally beautiful models, it is striking to learn how great is the demand for cosmetic alterations that are based on Western markers of ideal beauty. In a New York Times Magazine feature, Ann Louise Bardach reports that Asian women often desire surgery to affect a more "Western"shaped eye. Indeed, in some medical articles this surgery is actually referred to as "upper lid westernization," and is reported to be "the most frequently performed cosmetic procedure in the Orient." SurgeonsHall, Webster, and Dubrowski explain:

An upper lid fold is considered a sign of sophistication and refinement to many Orientals across all social strata. It is not quite accurate to say that Orientals undergoing this surgery desire to look Western or American; rather, they desire a more refined Oriental eye.... An upper lid westernization blepharoplasty frequently is given to a young Korean woman on the occasion of her betrothal.

Although other surgeons warn that it is "wise to discuss the Oriental and Occidental eye anatomy in terms of differences not defects, another medical article on this type of surgery was titled "Correction of the Oriental Eyelid." In terms of eyelid shape and design, Hall and his colleagues do not comment on how the "natural" Oriental eye came to be described as having a "poorly defined orbital and periorbital appearance" thus, when their Oriental patients request "larger, wider, less flat, more defined, more awake-appearing eyes and orbital surroundings," these surgeons offer an operative plan for the surgical achievement of what is commonly understood to be a more Westernized appearance.

In discussing the rea sons for the increased demand for this form of blepharoplasty "among the Oriental," Marwali Harahap notes that this technique became popular after World War II; this leads some surgeons to speculate that such a desire for Westernized eyes "stems from the influence of motion pictures and the increasing intermarriage of Asian women and Caucasian men."

THE MARKETING OF YOUTHFULNESS

When a young girl born with "hidden eyes" was scheduled to have massive face reconstruction surgery, surgeons hoped to construct eyelids for her where there were none. The key objectives for her eye surgery were "normalcy" and "functionality," however a review of medical literature on reconstructive surgery reveals that blepharoplasty (eyelid operations) is a common technique of "youth surgery." Because body tissue loses its elasticity in the process of aging, eyelids often begin to sag when a person reaches the early fifties.

Bagginess is caused by fat deposits that build up around the eye and stretch the skin, producing wrinkling and sagging, and is most likely the result of a hernia - the weakening of the tissue around the eye - in which the fat deposits push outward and downward. Although eyestrain and fatigue can result from overworking the muscles around the eyes in an effort to keep eyes looking alert and open, eyelid surgery very rarely involves a "catastrophic" or "cure-based" medical rationale. Yet it is quite common, in both the popular and professional literature, for a plastic surgeon to refer to eye bags as a "deformity."

This is a simple example of the way in which "natural" characteristics of the aging body are redefined as "symptoms," with the consequence that cosmetic surgery is rhetorically constructed as a medical procedure with the power to "cure" or "correct" such physical deformities. Several types of aesthetic surgery have been marketed explicitly for an aging baby-boomer population, with the promise that external symptoms of aging can be put off, taken off, or virtually eliminated.

By the end of the 1980s, the most requested techniques of cosmetic surgery included face lifts, nose reconstructions, tummy tucks, liposuction, skin peels, and hair transplants - surgical techniques that are specifically designed to counteract the effects of gravity and natural body deterioration. More than a few articles have reported that baby boomers are the preferred market for these new medical procedures; as a demographic group they (1) have more money than time to spend on body maintenance, and (2) are just beginning to experience the effects of aging en masse.

Given the size of the baby-boomer population, it is no surprise that as the first wave of baby boomers reach their late forties we should see an increase in advertisements for services such as dental bonding and implants, requests for "revolutionary" new drugs such as Retin-A, and articles about rejuvenation drugs manufactured in Europe from dried fetal extracts. Even though the size of the target market for these produces will continue to increase during the next decade, the competition among plastic surgeons has so intensified that many of them are using image consultants to design advertising campaigns to attract clients.

One campaign that drew a round of criticism from other surgeons displayed a surgically sculpted shapely female body draped over an expensive car. While this is hardly a new combination for U.S. beer advertisers, many cosmetic surgeons claimed that such advertising tarnishes the dignified image of their medical profession. Plastic surgeons are instructed to warn preoperative patients that "this is medicine and not the beauty parlor," but in the same breath, they are also taught that "in our society many cosmetic surgical procedures are not a luxury but are considered necessary."

Apparently this creates a bit of a tension for cosmetic surgeons who on the one hand are keenly aware of the fact that the service they provide is often an entirely elective endeavor, but on the other also realize the potentially serious physical consequences of their medical service. This tension is managed discursively when both physicians and patients construct "curative" justifications for the voluntary submission to surgical treatment. G. Richard Holt and Jean Edwards Holt obliquely refer to the fact that most eyelid operations are done for purely cosmetic reasons and not to increase physical functioning:

Although there are obvious cosmetic advantages to nearly every blepharoplasty, it must be remembered that functional indications are of primary importance. There are several alterations in function that can be improved by a blepharoplasty, and these should be identified preoperatively. They also serve as important diagnoses that are accepted by many third-party insurance carriers as sufficient to warrant payment for the procedure. However, they should be reported as such only if they actually exist.

Apparently, the use of "curative" justifications in a diagnosis not only functions discursively to manage an anxious patient, it also legitimates and authorizes the "elective" surgery for insurance coverage. In the cli mate of a recession, insurance reimbursement is vital to the continuing health of a medical specialty. A more detailed discussion of the economics of medical diagnoses is beyond the scope of this chapter, but it is likely that an investigation into the determining factors of medical reporting would find that economic forces influence the distinction between what can be identified as a "necessary" reconstructive procedure and procedures that are considered purely "elective."

Through the advertising channels of consumer culture, the practices of cosmetic surgery have been transformed into commodities themselves. In one medical report, the surgeon-physicians blatantly claim, "Society's emphasis on a youthful appearance has created a demand for cosmetic plastic surgery." Mary Ruth Wright, a clinical professor of psychology at Baylor University, explains:

> Today medicine encompasses far more than healing, saving, and serving. It has become a commodity, and consumer demands beyond reasonable expectations have emerged. Furthermore, today's concept of medical care goes beyond a physician-patient relationship; it involves society and the community as a whole. Perhaps medicine has overshot its marks; however, little is to be gained by looking back. We are here, practicing medicine in an age where the wonders of technology have put in the hands of physicians what used to be in the hands of fate. The elective surgeon, freed by an exemption from acute medical treatment, is especially affected by the changes that are occurring in the spectrum of modern medicine.

Even though Wright raises the question of whether plastic surgeons are operating beyond the acceptable confines of a medical profession - by performing entirely elective procedures - she dismisses such concerns by refocusing on the biotechnological marvels that "the elective surgeon" can affect. Although her rhetoric sidesteps the question of agency when she states that "elective surgeons are freed from acute medical treatment," her statements implicitly argue that it is the mechanism of the marketplace that "frees" cosmetic surgeons from their duties to provide "acute medical treatment."

One of the consequences of the commodification and, correspondingly, the normalization of cosmetic surgery is that electing not to have cosmetic surgery is sometimes interpreted as a failure to deploy all available resources to maintain a youthful, and therefore socially acceptable and attractive, body appearance. Kathryn Pauly Morgan, in an essay in a special issue of Hypatia on "Feminism and the Body," argues that the normalization of cosmetic surgery - "the inversion of the domains of the deviant and the pathological" - are "catalyzed by the technologizing of women's bodies."

From this point, Morgan goes on to discuss the more philosophical question of why "patients and cosmetic surgeons participate in committing one of the deepest of original philosophical sins, the choice of the apparent over the real". The issue I'd like to consider, drawing on Morgan's analysis of the increasing "naturalization" of cosmetic alteration, is to elaborate the mechanism whereby the apparent is transformed into the real. How are women's bodies technologized? What is the role of cosmetic surgery in the technological reproduction of gendered bodies?

TECHNOLOGY OF THE GENDERED BODY

In recent years, more men are electing cosmetic surgery than in the past, but often in secret. As one article reports, "previously reluctant males are among the booming number of men surreptitiously doing what women have been doing for years: having their eyelids lifted, jowls removed, ears clipped, noses reduced, and chins tightened." One cosmetic surgeon elaborates the reasons why men are beginning to seek elective cosmetic surgery:

> A middle-aged male patient - we'll call him Mr. Dropout - thinks he has a problem. He doesn't think he's too old for the lovely virgins he meets, but he wants to improve things.... When a man consults for aging, generally he is not compulsive about looking younger but he seeks relief from one or more specific defects incidental to aging: male pattern baldness...forehead wrinkling...turkey-gobbler neck. There are many things that can be done to help the aging man look youngeror more virile.

According to yet another cosmetic surgeon, the reason for some me's new concern about appearance is "linked to the increasing competition for top jobs they face at the peak of their careers from women and Baby Boomers. Here the increase in male cosmetic surgery is explained as a shrewd business tactic: "looking good" connotes greater intelligence, competence, and desirability as a colleague. Charges of narcissism, vanity, and self-indulgence are put aside; a man's choice to have cosmetic surgery is explained by appeal to rhetoric of career enhancement: a better looking body is better able to be promoted. In this case, cosmetic surgery is redefined as a body management technique designed to reduce the stress of having to cope with a changing work environment, one that is being threatened by the presence of women and younger people.

While all of these explanations may be true - in the sense that this is how men justify their choice to elect cosmetic surgery - it is clear that other explanations are not even entertained. For example, what about the possibility that men and women are becoming more alike with respect to "the body beautiful," that men are engaging more frequently in female body activities, or even simply that a concern with appearance isn't solely a characteristic of women? What about the possibility that the boundary between genders is eroding? How is it that men avoid the pejorative labels attached to female cosmetic surgery clients?

In their ethnomethodological study of cosmetic surgery, Diana Dull and Candace West examine how surgeons and patients "account" for their decisions to elect cosmetic surgery. They argue that when surgeons divide the patient's body into component parts and pieces, it enables both "surgeons and patients together to establish the problematic status of the part in question and its 'objective' need of 'repair.' " Dull and West go on to argue that this process of fragmentation occurs "in tandem with the accomplishment of gender" which, in relying upon an essentialist view of the female body as always "needing repair," understands women's choice for cosmetic surgery as "natural" and "normal" and as a consequence of their (natural) preoccupation with appearance.

However, because their "essential" natures are defined very differently, men must construct elaborate justifications for their decision to seek cosmetic alterations. This analysis illuminates one of the possible reasons why men and women construct different accounts of their decision to elect cosmetic surgery: the cultural meaning of their gendered bodies already determines the discursive rationale they can invoke to explain bodily practices. Although the bodies and faces of male farmers and construction workers, for example, are excessively "tanned" due to their constant exposure to the sun as part of their work conditions, their ruddy, leathery skin is not considered a liability or deformity of their male bodies.

In contrast, white women who display wrinkled skin due to excessive tanning are sometimes diagnosed with "The Miami Beach Syndrome"; as one surgeon claims, "we find this type of overly tanned, wrinkled skin in women who not only go to Miami every year for three or four months, but lie on the beach with a sun reflector drawing additional rays to their faces." It is no surprise then, that although any body can exhibit the "flaws" that supposedly justify cosmetic surgery, discussion and marketing of such procedures usually constructs the female as the typical patient.

Such differential treatment of gendered bodies illustrates a by now familiar assertion of feminist studies of the body and appearance: the meaning of the presence or absence of any physical quality varies according to the gender of the body upon which it appears. Clearly an apparatus of gender organizes our seemingly most basic, natural, interpretation of human bodies, even when those bodies are technologically refashioned. Thus it appears that although technologies such as those used in cosmetic surgery can reconstruct the "natural" identity of the material body, they do little to disrupt naturalization of feminine corporeal identity.

Wendy Chapkis amplifies this point when she writes: "however much the particulars of the beauty package may change from decade to decade -curves in or out, skin delicate or ruddy, figures fragile or fit - the basic principles remain the same. The body beautiful is woma's responsibility and authority. She will be valued and rewarded on the basis of how close she comes to embodying the ideal". In the popular media (newspapers, magazines), advertisements for surgical services are rarely, if ever, addressed specifically to men. When a man is portrayed as a prospective patient for cosmetic surgery, he is often represented as a serious "business" person for whom a youthful appearance is a necessary business asset.

In a 1988 advertising campaign for The Liposuction Institute in Chicago, each advertisement featured an illustration of a woman's (saddlebag) thighs as the "before" image of liposuction procedures. And of course, many cosmetic alterations are designed especially for women: tattooed eyeliner (marketed as "the ultimate cosmetic"), electrolysis removal of superfluous hair, and face creams.

An advertising representative for DuraSoft explains that the company has begun marketing its coloured contact lenses specifically to black women ostensibly because DuraSoft believes that "black women have fewer cosmetic alternatives," but a more likely reason is that the company wants to create new markets for its cosmetic lenses. The codes that structure cosmetic surgery advertising are gendered in stereotypical ways: being male requires a concern with virility and productivity, whereas being a real woman requires buying beauty products and services.

And yet women who have too many cosmetic alterations are pejoratively labeled "scalpel slaves," to identify them with their obsession for surgical fixes. Women in their late thirties and forties are the most likely candidates for repeat plastic surgery. According to Psychology Today, the typical "plastic surgery junkie" is a woman who uses cosmetic surgery as an opportunity to "indulge in unconscious wishes." Newsweek diagnoses the image problems of "scalpel slaves":

Women in their 40s seem particularly vulnerable to the face-saving appeal of plastic surgery. Many scalpel slaves are older women who are recently divorced or widowed and forced to find jobs or date again. Others are suffering from the empty-nest syndrome. "They're re-entry women," says Dr. Susan Chobanian, a Beverly Hills cosmetic surgeon. "They get insecure about their appearance and show up every six months to get nips and tucks.... Plastic-surgery junkies are in many ways akin to the anorexic or bulimic," according to doctors. "It's a body-image disorder," says one physician. "Junkies don't know what they really look like." Some surgery junkies have a history of anorexia in the late teens, and now, in their late 30s and 40s, they're trying to alter their body image again.

The naturalized identity of the female body as pathological and diseased is culturally reproduced in media discussions and representations of cosmetic surgery services. Moreover, the narrative obsessively recounted is that the female body is flawed in its distinctions and perfect when differences are transformed into sameness.

However, in the case of cosmetic surgery the nature of the "sameness" is deceptive, because the promise is not total identity reconstruction - such that a patient could choose to look like the media star of her choice - but rather the more elusive pledge of "beauty enhancement." When cosmetic surgeons argue that the technological elimination of facial "deformities" will enhance a woman's "natural" beauty, we encounter one of the more persistent contradictions within the discourse of cosmetic surgery: namely, the use of technology to augment "nature."

MORPHING AND THE TECHNO-BODY

Surgeons are taught that the consultation process is actually an incredibly complex social exchange during which patients and surgeons must negotiate highly abstract goals. The accomplishment of goals is said to be directly related to patient satisfaction:

Defining aesthetic goals with patients obviously involve the hazards of perception.... Any practitioner who has recommended and performed orthognathic surgery has most likely encountered patients with unrealistic aesthetic expectations. The surgical team most often accomplishes their functional and aesthetic goals, but, in this situation, the patient is disappointed.... Function, aesthetics, and shaping the patient's expectations into reality must all be addressed while keeping in mind the patient's best interests and desires.

The most commonly used methods of patient facial analysis are radiographic and photographic analysis, where the facial profile is rendered in a two-dimensional medium. The use of photographs and grease pencils is perhaps the simplest method of the surgeon-patient consultation where the task at hand is to suggest the possible benefits of cosmetic surgery at the same time that the patient must be made aware of the surgical plan. Using a Polaroid camera to produce an instantaneous photograph, surgeons often draw lines with markers to indicate the locations of incisions or stretch lines.

"Photograph surgery" is a communication method to negotiate between a patient's expectations and likely surgical outcomes; the reality of those black grease-pencil lines invoke the use of surgical procedures that literally cut into the face and reconstruct it, rendering whatever features nature created obsolete and irrecoverable. The various two-dimensional consultation methods were developed to effect an "objective method of facial analysis," which is understood to be a necessary part of adequate preoperative planning and postoperative evaluation. Since 1989, however, some cosmetic surgeons have been employing new visualization techniques that render the patient's face in three dimensions.

The use of video imaging replaces the use of greasepencil lines and photographic surgery, which some surgeons found to be an inadequate system of consultation because "even when adjustments have been 'drawn on' by the surgeon, it is difficult for most patients to imagine what they might look like postoperatively." Using video imaging, the surgeon can manipulate an actual image of the client's face. Although the cost and skill requirements of these computerized imaging systems represent a sizable investment, using this method of consultation is promoted as a way to manage patient expectations because it provides more information about the results that surgery can accomplish.

More information, in this case, is said to lead to greater patient reassurance. Indeed, one recent study reports that the use of video imaging was well accepted by patients and that most felt that 'video imaging improved communication between patient and surgeon, increased confidence in surgery and surgeon, and enhanced the patient-physician relationship."

The video imaging consultation begins with a series of video shots that must be taken with great precision in terms of camera angle, lighting, face position, make-up, and hair display. Preoperative photograph precision is necessary to ensure that postoperative photographs will objectively record surgical results and not camera special effects. The preoperative video shots are digitally scanned into a computer and then ma nipulated with the use of an imaging processing system. To begin the consultation, the cosmetic surgeon displays two images of the patient's face on the computer screen. The left-hand image remains untouched and unmarked, serving as the prototypical "before" picture of the prospective cosmetic surgery client.

The right-hand image is manipulated by the cosmetic surgeon, using a stylus and pressure-sensitive sketch pad. Using what is really a modified computer "painting" program, the surgeon can manipulate the image in several ways: (1) by picking up a line (a jaw line, for example) and moving it; (2) by reducing a part of the image with an eraser tool (thus eliminating a double chin, for example); or (3) by stretching a part of the face to show what heightened cheekbones might look like.

Throughout the various manipulations, the right-hand image of the patient retains its visual integrity in that it continues to resemble the original, left-hand image save for the artistic manipulations performed by the surgeon. The surgeon can either display multiple procedures on one image or reproduce additional images that illustrate the effects of only one procedure at a time. With the use of a range of rendering tools, which are basically a set of artist's tools (spray can, pencil, eraser), the surgeon can redesign a client's face in the space of a 30-minute consultation.

In an interview with one surgeon who uses this method of patient consultation, he explained that when prospective patients seek surgery they have only a layperson understands of facial anatomy. For example, they might believe that in order to get rid of deep lines around the nose that all they need is to stretch the cheeks and tuck the extra skin behind the ear. But what they really need, he clarified, is to heighten the cheekbones with an implant and bob the nose, which will pull the skin taut over the new cheeks; consequently the lines and folds on either side of the nose will be eliminated and the size of the nose will stay proportionate to cheek width.

In this example, the imaging device would enable the surgeon to educate the patient about the different methods for accomplishing surgical goals. In fact, this surgeon emphasized that the imaging device allows him to visually demonstrate the transformation of the patient's face that he could easily accomplish in surgery, something very difficult to demonstrate in a two-dimensional format. For him, the imaging system is a mechanism whereby his artistic skill can be previewed by prospective patients.

The imaging program can also be used as a surgical planning device. The program can calculate the distance, angle, or surface of the part of the right-hand image that has been modified. In this sense, a manipulated video image is more useful than a photograph in designing the actual surgery, because the comparison between the video image and the cephalometric radiograph "allows for computerized quantification of treatment goals." Thus, if a nose profile line has been redrawn, the imaging program can measure the difference between the redrawn line of the righthand image and the original line on the left-hand image to determine the degree to which the nose needs to be modified during surgery; the surgeon can then use that measurement to plan the surgical procedure.

Some physicians believe that the only way to manage patients' expectations is to assure them of the competency of the physician's skill. Traditionally, physicians have done this by showing prospective patient photographs of previous patients' surgical results. But more recently, the use of new high-tech imaging devices have been employed as a symbol of the quality of the physician's service.

A computer imaging system is a wonderful educational tool in terms of marketing to patients who may not be familiar with the treatments and materials available today.... Marketing the benefits of the system to patients is easy, according to [another physician]; because the "high-tech" equipment lets patients know that they can receive "high-tech" treatment. It gives you the image and identity of being on the cutting edge of dentistry when you can offer the newest and best materials and techniques available.

So in addition to using it as counseling and planning device, the video imaging system can also be employed as a marketing tool. In this case, the expert manipulation of a video file using a computer painting program is translated into a marker of technological expertise in the operating room. But this use of the imaging system as marketing tool is denounced by some surgeons, who believe that its use borders on the unethical because it makes it easier to manipulate patients into having procedures that they do not need or want.

The strongest claim for the use of video imaging is that it provides a realistic image of the aesthetic treatment objective that the patient can visualize. So while some surgeons dismiss it as a possibly unethical marketing device, other physicians argue that it produces "realistic images," "realistic expectations," and a better representation of reality itself.

More telling is the fact that several cosmetic surgeons in the Atlanta metro area have stopped using video imaging as a consultation method because they found that it encouraged patients to form unrealistic expectations about the kind of transformations that can be accomplished through surgical procedures. They report that patients seemed to believe that if a modification could be demonstrated on the video screen, then it could be accomplished in the operating room - that the video transformation guaranteed the physical transformation.

Apparently, the digital transformation of one's own face produces a magical, liquid simulation that is difficult to reject. What some patients fail to understand is that one of the significant difficulties with any kind of cosmetic surgery is that soft tissue changes are impossible to predict accurately. A surgical incision or implantation always disrupts layers of skin, fat, and muscle. How those incised tissues heal is a very idiosyncratic matter - a matter of the irreducible distinctiveness of the material body. After hearing from a number of disappointed patients, members of the American Society of Plastic and Reconstructive Surgeons designed an official "Electronic Imaging Disclaimer" to be used by physicians who employ computerized images in preoperative consultations.

Among the release statements that the patient must sign is one that reads: "I understand that because of the significant differences in how living tissue heals, there may be no relationship between the electronic images and my final surgical result." Where advertising executives play with the possibilities of morphing political candidates, cosmetic surgeons offer patients the promise of permanently "morphed" features. One of the key consequences that some surgeons have discovered is that witnessing video morphing dramatically undermines a patient's ability to distinguish between the real, the possible, and the likely in terms of surgical outcomes.

Through the application of techniques of inscription, surveillance, and confession, cosmetic surgery serves as an ideological site for examining the technological reproduction of the gendered body. A primary effect of these techniques is to produce a gendered identity for the body at hand, techniques that work in different ways for male and female bodies.

In its encounters with the cosmetic surgeon and the discourse of cosmetic surgery, the female body becomes an object of heightened personal surveillance; this scrutiny results in an internalized image of a fractured, fragmented body. The body becomes the vehicle of confession; it is the site at which women, consciously or not, accept the meanings that circulate in popular culture about ideal beauty and, in comparison, devalue the matrial body. In other words, the female body comes to serve as a site of inscription, a billboard for the dominant cultural meanings that the female body is to have in postmodernity.

For some women, and for some feminist scholars, cosmetic surgery illustrates a technological colonization of women's bodies; others see it as a technology women can use for their own ends. Certainly, as I have shown here, in spite of the promise cosmetic surgery offers women for the technological reconstruction of their bodies, in actual application such technologies produce bodies that are very traditionally gendered. Yet I am reluctant to accept as a simple and obvious conclusion that cosmetic surgery is simply one more site where women are passively victimized.

Whether as a form of oppression or a resource of empowerment, it is clear to me that cosmetic surgery is a practice whereby women consciously act to make their bodies mean something to themselves and to others. A different way of looking at this technology might be to take seriously the notion I suggested earlier: to think of cosmetic surgery as "fashion surgery." Like women who get pierced-nose rings, tattoos, and hair sculptures, women who elect cosmetic surgery could be seen to be using their bodies as a vehicle for staging cultural identities.

Even though I have argued that cosmetic surgeons demonstrate an unshakable belief in a Westernized notion of "natural" beauty, and that the discourse of cosmetic surgery is implicated in reproducing such idealization and manipulation of "the natural," other domains of contemporary fashion cannot be so idealized. The anti-aesthetics of cyberpunk and grunge fashion, for example, suggest that feminists, too, might wish to abandon our romantic conceptions of the "natural" body - conceptions that lead us to claim that a surgically refashioned face inevitably marks an oppressed subjectivity. As body piercing and other forms of prosthesis become more common - here I am thinking of Molly Million's implanted mirrorshades and Jael's nail daggers - we may need to adopt a perspective on the bodily performance of gender identity that is not so dogged by neoromantic wistfulness about the natural, unmarked body.

5

The Virtual Body in Cyberspace

This chapter speculates about the body on the electronic frontier. In one sense, this frontier is an imaginary construction that identifies a horizon of contemporary cultural thought. But in another sense it is a real space on the fringe of mainstream culture: the "electronic frontier" names the space of information exchange that already exists in the flow of databases, telephone and fiber-optic networks, computer memory, and other parts of electronic networking services.

The frontier metaphor suggests the possibility of a vast, unexplored territory. Computer enthusiasts, also known as hackers, populate frontier villages; advance scouts/pilgrims include the by now infamous computer viruses, worms, and Trojan horses that were designed very simply to "map" the network into which they were released. In elaborating the Western frontier metaphor, John Perry Barlow explains that in the new small towns, "Main Street is a central minicomputer.... Town Meetings are continuous and discussions range on everything from sexual kinks to depreciation schedules."

In a more material sense, the electronic frontier includes workstations, file servers, networks, and bulletin boards, as well as the code of application programs, information services such as Prodigy and CompuServe, and on-line databases. This frontier functions as the infrastructure of the computer/ information industry and, as such, structures the further development and dissemination of computer technologies and services. One of the most publicized computer applications of the last decade has been the construction of "virtual environments," now more widely known as "virtual reality."

Since 1987, virtual reality (VR) has further evolved into an industry in itself; it is also at the heart of an emergent (sub)culture that includes computer-generated realities, science fiction, fictional sciences, and powerfully evocative new visualization technol ogies. My guiding question for this chapter concerns the role of the body in this formation. To set the stage for a discussion of the body in cyberspace, I offer a reading of the cultural aspects of the virtual reality industry, including its embodiment in a cyberpunk subculture, its media spectacles, and commodities-on-offer.

MARKETING CYBERSPACE

Virtual technologies use graphics programs to create a three-dimensional, computer-generated space that a user/ participant interacts with and manipulates via wired peripherals. In contemporary science fiction, the 3-D, computer-generated space or virtual environment is referred to as "cyberspace," a term first used by William Gibson in his cyberpunk novel Neuromancer and now gaining acceptance among VR technicians to name the interior space of virtual reality programs.

In its fictional form, cyberspace is sometimes referred to as the matrix or "the Net," a shorthand name for the network constructed by the connections between fixed computer consoles and portable computer decks. In cyberpunk novels, "real" geographic urban-suburban space is referred to as "the sprawl," and although hackers often have to hide out or navigate their way through it, the real "action" always occurs in the structured informational space of the matrix.

In its commercial form, cyberspace describes an electronic matrix or virtual environment. It is also listed as a trademark of Autodesk, one of the two better known companies that develop software tools for virtual realities. Standard cyberspace hardware includes a set of wired goggles that track head movement connected to a computer that runs VR software. In 1985, a computer musician named Jaron Lanier founded a company called VPL that prides itself on being a "pioneer in Virtual Reality (VR) and visual programming." Better known than his company's products, Lanier has become a cult figure in the virtual reality subculture, whose members include technological innovators, popular cultural icons, game designers, and computer entrepreneurs. Lanier is often quoted as saying "whatever the physical world has, virtual reality has as well."

Mondo 2000, the preeminent hacker magazine of the 1990s, offers a glimpse into the subculture formed in and around the fictional world of cyberspace. Posing is certainly nothing new to popular subcultures, and indeed, this is part of Mondo's attraction for mainstream readers: it lets us in to the in-crowd. Three features stand out: its glossy, visually dense, techno-art layout; the regularly scheduled iconoclastic reports from the electronic frontier; and mediated interviews with the high priests of street tech, notably William S. Burroughs and Timothy Leary.

It also promotes up-and-coming visionaries such as Lanier and John Perry Barlow, as well as other cultural cybercritics and various rock groups, performance artists, smart drug advocates, and electronic industry movers and shakers. In short, Mondo 2000 publicizes the key features of the new subculture: "founding fathers," mythic narratives of identity, a specialized language, and a lot of new technology. In doing so, Mondo 2000, house organ for the cyberpunk industry, popularizes the worldview of those addicted to the possibilities of life in the microworld.

Topically, Mondo 2000 picks up where McLuhan Mechanical Bride left off, without the rhetorical questions and, for the most part, without the cultural criticism. Where McLuhan fixated on magazine advertisements that hinted at the ominous fusion of sex and technology, Mondo 2000 became the magazine to celebrate the fusion of sex and technology in its advertisements for cyberpunk culture. And yet, in spite of its technolust(er), Mondo 2000 oddly evokes the countercultural rhetoric of the 1960s. In part this reflects the widespread 1990s nostalgia for 1960s fashions and fads; thus, an issue of Mondo might include retro-topics such as "on the road" stories, drug synthesis instructions, mod fashion icons, and reports from the underground.

The difference is that in the 1990s the drugs are intended to make us "smart," hallucinogens are replaced with hallucinogenres, the "Underground" is a band, and the best sex is virtual. In a review of a show curated by Shalom Gorewitz, the Village Voice called the cyberspace artists and hackers "gonzo techno-hippies." Indeed, the juxtaposition of countercultural rhetoric with technological elitism constructs an interesting stage for the promotion of virtual reality technologies.

Mondo 2000 makes no pretense of democracy and no attempt at accessibility, advising readers that unsolicited manuscripts are burned at the full moon and that "unsolicited art work will be electronically scanned and altered and appear uncredited in other magazines." Advertisements plug in-group products: Gibson and Sterling's new novel, reprints of Leary's work, Avital Ronell Telephone Book. But the pleasure of recognition is high.

Articles demonstrate the appropriate attitude to the "New World DisOrder" while they show you who/what you need to know/read/buy to be a member by imitation only. Even though electronically connected cyberpunks are dispersed from coast to coast, it's pretty obvious, according to Mondo, that the happening place to be is on the West Coast. So even though the real story about the development of virtual reality technologies takes shape all over the U.S. - and especially in Britain, Australia, and Italy (among other places) - in keeping with the frontier logic, the best (mythical) cyberspace events have all taken place in our own American wild, wild West.

Of course, the virtual reality industry includes much more than the subculture visualized by Mondo 2000. On the PR front, it includes conferences staged like media events - such as "Cyber Arts International," billed as "the world forum for emerging technologies in the arts, entertainment and education," and "Cyberthon" a multimedia virtual reality fair sponsored by the Whole Earth Institute. Richard Kadrey describes the technology-saturated 24 hours of Cyberthon No.I: "On October 6 and 7 [1990]...the Whole Earth Institute turned the sound stage of San Francisco's Colossal Pictures into the world's biggest virtual-reality fair.

Almost four hundred people got the chance to see and experience a whole range of reality-bending technologies close up. Over three hundred lucky lottery winners got the chance to don goggles and gloves and actually enter virtual worlds created by teams from Autodesk, Sense8, and Jaron Lanier's VPL." Ironically, the conference announcements advertised in Mondo or disseminated through electronic bulletin boards often rely on rhetoric of "reality" to attract conference participants. For example, they offer to make available - for a price, of course - "real" VR programs and equipment.

Registration for the 1991 CyberArts International cost $450 and allowed a participant to visit special exhibits such as the CyberArt Gallery and "Product Expo," where one could "experience" VR live by taking part in interactive music performances (where the audience directs the music) or by trying a "live exercise in producing integrated media."Cyberpunk night at CyberArt, sponsored by Mondo 2000, promised "an evening of elegant entertainment and high tech hallucinations," complete with master of ceremonies Timothy Leary and a "new kind of theatrical entertainment experience."

The exhortations to "experience it live" - the shows and the software systems on display - suggest more than an ironic subtext to the supermediated VR spectacles. They also draw our attention to the process whereby VR technologies are transformed into commodities, through the engagement between people and products. For all the media hype, audience response to VR suggests that, at best, it is at the "Kitty Hawk" stage Gn more PR than VR, as one discussion list participant wrote. "Serious" VR research is another matter, though. It has been reported that some computer scientists do not like the term "virtual reality," originally coined by Jaron Lanier, the VPL maverick.

"The term 'virtual environment' better fits a field of scientific research," claims a professor of computer graphics quoted in a 1991 "Chronicle of Higher Education" article. "Virtual reality is an unattainable goal, like artificial intelligence." Although no official history of VR has been drafted, computer science and computer graphics are its foundation; it draws on Norbert Wiener's work in the 1940s on the science of cybernetics as well as on the early history of calculating machinery.

Other historical contributions include research during the 1960s on two-dimensional and three-dimensional viewing, and work from the 1970s on "visually-coupled" systems. During the 1980s, VR-related research proliferated in the areas of interface design, telerobotics, optical sensors, simulation parameters, and image processing and display. Myron Krueger, sometimes referred to as the father of artificial reality, wrote a very interesting but brief essay on the history of the field, in which he explains that although it took awhile for "the notion of artificial reality to take hold" - due to some common constraints on technological research (few journals and scarce funding for new technologies) and several cultural constraints (such as Senator William Proxmire's Golden Fleece awards and geographical displacement) - "interactive computing is now the norm."

Implicitly he suggests that the biggest constraint inhibiting VR research was the lack of appreciation for its possible wide-scale market applications. Other than NASA's interest in head-mounted displays for reconnaissance and weapon delivery, no one had imagined the consumer market possibilities of human-machine interactive systems. The scene has changed by the mid-1990s. Virtual reality applications in telecommunications, surgical simulation, and computer-aided design are of great interest to current industry planners.

In the electronics industry, VR is touted as an attractive, albeit capital-intensive, business venue; it demands the development of a host of new products, including biotechnical apparatuses such as datagloves, wired bodysuits, head-mounted tracking devices, goggles, headphones, miniaturized LCD screens, and digitizing cameras. These devices and programs are incredibly expensive, not only to develop, but also to purchase. A cyberspace system marketed by VPL, called "A Reality Built for Two" or RB2, retailed for $250,000 in 1991; it comes with two headsets, two sets of DataGloves, and a powerful minicomputer.

One of the main purposes of the splashy VR demonstrations and conventions is to create investment interest as well as a market for VR applications. Members of the cyberpunk subculture - who are also the programmers, designers, and technicians - seem to take for granted the economic imperative to create a market for their products. In his description of the design of a cyberspace playhouse for sports and fitness, Randal Walser, then manager of the Autodesk Cyberspace Project, explains:

The critical thing to realize about the design of cyberspaces for sports is that sporting decks will generally have sophisticated props, like recombinant bicycles and inclined treadmills, and that sporting houses will make money by renting time on those decks. The purpose of a cyberspace for sports is not just to help people have fun and stay fit. It is also to help keep sporting houses in business, by keeping their decks full of players.

Other industry futurists envision large-scale VR installations primarily for entertainment and leisure services and would love to attract the backing of Disney or Universal - who have theme parks that currently use robotics - to invest in the development of "Dream Parks" that are based on "interactive role-playing environments." These speculations about the future of VR contribute to a "bottom-line" message about its potential: there is a lot of money to be made in the development and marketing of cyberspace.

In summary, the key features of this new subculture include popular cultural artifacts (e.g., Mondo 2000 and the films Lawnmower Man and Johnny Mnemonic), a mythic set of founding fathers, a specialized language that draws on the science of computer technology and computer programming, and the promise of new hightech commodities. Oddly, at the same time that it promotes the sexiness of new technology and is unabashedly elitist, it also evokes a countercultural belief in the possibility of resistance within a corporate culture. Such juxtapositions - of technology and the counterculture, of "reality effects" and real demonstrations, of the science and the PR - suggest that cyberpunk subculture is actively engaged in the work of processing cultural meanings.

As it plays itself out, the future of virtual reality is intimately tied to the capitalist structure of the information technology industry. Now that various cultural visionaries have turned their attention to the work of imagining the future of VR, they ensure that it will be fully articulated to a commodity structure. The staged subcultural events draw our attention to the process whereby technologies are transformed into technological commodities.

As "countercultural" as members of this subculture want to be, the virtual reality industry actually disseminates a certain mythology and a set of metaphors and concepts that cannot help but reproduce the anxieties and preoccupations of contemporary culture. As Jack Zipes claims, "the inevitable outcome of most mass-mediated fairy tales is a happy reconfirmation of the system which produces them." More than once, the popular press have commented that simulated experiences "offer opportunities for safe activity in a risky world."

Called "electronic LSD," or an "electronic out-of-body experience," VR in its celebrated media form seems little more than an escape from conventional reality, a way out for those who confront the severe limitations reality imposes in the form of corporate ideology, determining social structures, and the physical body itself. A more traditional ideological critique of the VR industry probably would begin by elaborating its participation in postindustrial capitalist modes of production and would go on to expose the way that the "oppositional" subculture actually promotes bourgeois notions such as creative genius, hyperindividualism, and transcendent subjectivity.

In his essay "Hacking Away at the Counterculture," Andrew Ross elaborates how the story "told by the critical left about new cultural technologies is that of monolithic, panoptical social control, effortlessly achieved through a smooth, endlessly interlocking system of networks of surveillance." But, as he goes on to write, this "is not always the best story to tell."

I agree that this ideological critique may be too totalizing. When discussing new technologies, it is important to try to avoid the trap of technological determinism that argues that these technologies necessarily and unilaterally expand the hegemonic control by a techno-elite. Technologies have limited agency. Having said that though, it does appear that virtual reality technologies are implicated in the production of a certain set of cultural narratives that reproduce dominant relations of power. Perhaps a better approach for evaluating the meaning of these new technologies is to try to elaborate the ways in which such technologies and, more importantly, the use of such technologies, are determined by broader social and cultural forces.

One of the most often-repeated claims about virtual reality is that it provides the technological means to construct personal realities free from the determination of body-based ("real") identities. Whereas VR promoters have focused primarily on the subjective and expressive dimensions of VR in public relations campaigns for VR games, users are also told that the physical body is of no consequence in virtual worlds. Even though some games may soon allow players to design personal avatars or puppets -simulations of oneself - more frequently VR is promoted as a body-free environment, a place of escape from the corporeal embodiment of gender and race.

Upon analyzing the "lived" experience of virtual reality, I discovered that this conceptual denial of the body is accomplished through the material repression of the physical body. The phenomenological experience of cyberspace depends upon and in fact requires the willful repression of the material body. In saying this, I am implicitly arguing that we need to extend the ideological critique of virtual reality technologies.

From a feminist perspective it is clear that the repression of the material body belies a gender bias in the supposedly disembodied (and gender-free) world of virtual reality. In arguing that this repression is a technological phenomenon claiming that it is entirely determined by the technology. On the contrary, how VR technologies articulate cultural narratives about the techno-body so that these technologies have the effect of naturalizing a gendered body phenomenon.

A TRIP THROUGH CYBERSPACE

In contrast to a 2-D database, VR applications allow users to interact with three-dimensional representations of information. So instead of searching a database for lexical indicators or parts of computer code, a VR patron can interact with a data storage environment and browse through information that is represented graphically. According to one article in "Industry Week", with VR "you can imagine CAD models that, in effect, come alive.... You can enter them. You can make them any scale. They could be models of molecules, for example, and you could move about within these molecules with your whole body to examine their structures." In this way, the cyberspacial matrix serves as an abstract environment within which computer patrons can navigate.

All VR systems involve the interface of the body and technology in the use of some kind of bio-apparatus; three of the more common ones are the Nintendo PowerGlove; a headmount that includes LCD screens; and a "hotsuit," which is a set of wired overalls. Although my first trip through VR (with goggles and a track ball) was uneventful.

The point of contact with the interior spaces of VR - the way that this scene makes sense - is through an eye-level perspective that shifts as the user/patron turns her head; the changes in the scene projected on the small screens corresponds roughly with the real-time perspectival changes one would expect as one normally turns the head. Although other VR users have reported a noticeable time lag in the change of scene as the head turns, I notice no significant lag.

In most VR programs, a user experiences VR through a disembodied gaze - a floating, moving "perspective" - that mimes the movement of a disembodied camera "eye." This is a familiar aspect of what may be called a filmic phenomenology, where the camera simulates the movement of perspective that rarely includes a self-referential visual inspection of the body as the vehicle of that perspective. The disembodiment of the eye is accomplished through the manipulation of the camera to approximate the height and angle of the point of view of an eye; the body of that eye is repressed, in that it is rarely shown (revealed) and never felt.

The naturalization of the filmic gaze is one of the foundational planks of psychoanalytic film criticism and certainly not a new discovery. But what is of interest to me in my encounter with virtual reality is the way that the repression of the body is technologically naturalized. I think this happens because we have internalized the technological gaze to such an extent that "perspective" is a naturalized organizing locus of sense knowledge. As a consequence, the body, as a sense apparatus, is nothing more than excess baggage for the cyberspace traveler.

THE BIOPOLITICS OF VIRTUAL BODIES

What is becoming increasingly clear in encounters with virtual reality applications is that visualization technologies no longer simply mimic or represent reality - they virtually recreate it. But the difference between the reality constructed in VR worlds and the reality constructed in the everyday world is a matter of epistemology, not ontology. They are both cultural as well as technological constructions, fully saturated by the media and other forms of everyday technologies.

With respect to VR, it no longer makes sense to ask whose reality/perspective is represented in the various VR worlds, the industry, or the subculture; rather we should ask what reality is created therein, and how this reality articulates relationships between technologies, bodies, and cultural narratives. Where the first line of questioning assumes that "perspective" and "point of view" are the main channels of knowledge, the second line of questioning asserts that there is no singular reality to virtual reality, and that the "realities" constructed therein embody the desires of those who program them.

Another critical framework, one informed by feminist epistemology, asks a slightly different set of questions about the realities of cyberspace; given this formation of an industry and now a subculture based on the use of virtual technologies, what are the biopolitics of virtual bodies in cyberspace? Which is to say, how do virtual reality technologies engage socially and culturally marked bodies? This set of questions begins with the material body and opens onto institutional and social issues.

What is the rela tion of the material body to the "sensory" simulation provided by virtual technologies? What are the phenomenological dimensions of the technologically mediated body? Does VR transform body-based subjectivities? How do various interfaces negotiate the split between the material body of the user and the locus of perception that either free-floats in a virtual world or is connected in some fashion to a virtual puppet? Demographically, what kinds of bodies reside in cyberspace: humanoid?

More specifically, how is the disembodied technological gaze marked by the signs or logic of gender and race? What kind of "reality surplus" is produced? When virtual "realities" are bought and sold, who will profit? What kinds of bodies are cybernetically employed in the production of computer components? At one level, VR enables the willing suspension of disbelief whereby a participant adjusts the way that sensory information is processed; certain senses are realigned (vision without gravity) to process the simulated experience, while other registers of reality are repressed.

The fact that a floating point of view is intelligible attests to the flexibility of embodied sense organs. So although the body may disappear representationally in virtual worlds - indeed, we may go to great lengths to repress it and erase its referential traces - it does not disappear materially in the interface with the VR apparatus or, for that matter, in the phenomenological frame of the user. In VR discourse, where knowledge is operationalized as "data interconnectedness," there is little consensus on the main problematic of virtual reality, let alone on the particulars of a cultural critique of it.

For Michael Spring, the major conceptual problem is developing a robust model to visualize data interconnectedness. Virtual reality researchers, in reflecting on its significance, struggle to articulate an adequate understanding of the process of reality construction; almost intuitively, they understand the necessity of specifying the relationship between visual representations and meaning, but they often fall back on mechanistic models of the process of communication.

In delineating the difference between film and cyberspace, for example, Randal Walser writes: "whereas film depicts a reality to an audience, cyberspace grants a virtual body and a role, to everyone in the audience." In this account Walser offers an extremely simplistic understanding of the relationships among film, representation, and the viewing situation. Although this is gradually changing as artists become involved in the design of virtual worlds, virtual reality applications for the most part show little understanding of the dynamics of visual representation, let alone spectatorship, subjectivity, or phenome nological embodiment. In the end, though, as Jaron Lanier reminds us, "whatever the physical world has, virtual reality has as well." So the question emerges, what exactly does it offer?

In short, what these VR encounters really provide is an illusion of control over reality, nature, and especially over the unruly, genderand race-marked, essentially mortal body. It is not a coincidence that VR emerges in the 1980s, during a decade when the body is understood to be increasingly vulnerable (literally, as well as discursively) to infection as well as to gender, race, ethnicity, and ability critiques. With virtual reality we are offered the vision of a body-free universe.

Despite the rhetorical disclaimers that this was not a Nintendo war, media coverage of the Persian Gulf spectacle provided numerous examples of the deployment of a disembodied technological gaze; the bomb's-eye view was perhaps the most fascinating and therefore most disturbing example of the seductive power of a disembodied gaze to mask the violence of reality. The critical point here is that these new technological applications - VR, Nintendo, or bomb-cam - do not create disembodied citizens. Rather, they are themselves consequences of social changes already in place.

If "the frontier" functions as a metaphor to describe the social and economic context for the development of new computer/information technologies, "cyberspace" functions metaphorically to describe the space of the disembodied "social" in a hypertechnological informational society. Cyberspace - as a popular cultural construct - shows us what can happen when popular culture "talks back" to cultural theory (to borrow a phrase from Fred Pfeil); cyberspace offers a way to think about the location of the social in postindustrial capitalism.

Although this space is structured, it is impossible to map; there is no Archimedian point from which to construct a totalizing vision of the scene. At best you can wander through it, reading/writing as you walk, and maybe stumble upon something that was not programmed for you. Rich in information, if you know what you are looking for, the experience of cyberspace is always conjunctural: an effect of intersecting practices - economic, technological, bodily, political, and cultural.

In her "Esquire" article on virtual reality, Sallie Tisdale notes a "curious absence of narrative at Cyberthon, both in and out of the virtual worlds. It was an absence of plot - there is no story yet, no cosmology." In part, this is true; virtual reality promoters are computer scientists and system hackers, not cultural critics, and, for the most part, they recognize this fact - which in part accounts for their willingness, and indeed, enthusi asm to engage the work of artists and other cultural visionaries.

On the other hand, these new technologies are implicated in the reproduction of at least one very traditional cultural narrative: the possibility of transcendence, whereby the physical body and its social meanings can be technologically neutralized. If the applications that utilize a disembodied gaze as the locus of perspective do away with the body altogether, the applications that include a representation of the body project a utopian desire for control over the form of personal embodiment. The promises of VR-connected bodies are described by Scott Fisher in his article "Virtual Environments":

The two users will participate and interact in a shared virtual environment but each will view it from their relative, spatially disparate viewpoint. The objective is to provide a collaborative worldspace in which remotely located participants can virtually interact with some of the nuances of face-to-face meetings while also having access to their personal dataspace facilities.... With full-body tracking capability, it will also be possible for each user to be represented in this space by his or her life-size virtual representation in any chosen form - a kind of electronic persona....these virtual forms might range from fantasy figures to inanimate objects or from different figures to different people.

In the speculative discourse of VR, we are promised whatever body we want, which doesn't say anything about the body. What forms of embodiment would people choose if they could design their virtual bodies without the pain or cost of physical restructuring? If we look to those who are already participating in body reconstruction programs - for instance, cosmetic surgery and bodybuilding - we would find that their reconstructed bodies display very traditional gender and race markers of beauty, strength, and sexuality.

There is plenty of evidence to suggest that a reconstructed body does not guarantee a reconstructed cultural identity. Nor does "freedom from a body," imply that people will exercise the "freedom to be" any other kind of body than the one they already enjoy or desire. Fictional accounts of cyberspace play out the fantasy of casting off the body as an obsolete piece of meat, but, not surprisingly, these fictions do not eradicate body-based systems of differentiation and domination.

In fact, Fred Pfeil demonstrates "several ways in which much of the new SF written by men, for all the boundary erosions and breakdowns it dramatizes, remains stuck in a masculinist frame." In the course of Gibson Neuromancer trilogy, for example, not only is the hero's body eventually reconstructed from fragments of skin, so is his macho-male identity. It is true that in cyberpunk narratives individual male and female bodies may be coded slightly differently than they are in prevailing cultural norms.

For example, Gibson's main female character in Neuromancer, Molly, has been technologically modified with implanted weaponry that on the one hand makes her a powerful embodiment of female identity, no longer constrained by norms of passivity and proper femininity. On the other hand, Molly's body implants more fully literalize the characteristically threatening nature of her female body. Early in his adventures, Gibson's hero, Case, must negotiate a cyberspace invasion where he is plugged in to Molly's body. Molly gets a rider, and Case gets to find out "just how tight those jeans really are".

Then he keyed the new switch. The abrupt jolt into other flesh.... For a few minutes he fought helplessly to control her body. Then he willed himself into passivity, became the passenger behind her eyes.... Her body language was disorienting, her style foreign. She seemed continually on the verge of colliding with someone, but people melted out of her way, stepped sideways, made room. Once "inside" Molly, Case finds the "passivity of the situation irritating."

This passivity refers to his lack of control over Molly's body, so in a sense Case does experience, with the help of VR technology, a bodily state more traditionally feminine. But his simstim "experience" makes no lasting impression. Nor does it provide the occasion for the development of some insight into the politics of gendered bodies. His passivity is easily sexualized. To tease him, Molly reaches into her jacket, "a finger circling a nipple under warm silk. The sensation made [Case] catches his breath". This cybernetic penetration, we discover, follows a sexual encounter between Case and Molly when he recalls "their mutual grunt of unity when he'd entered her". Inside of cyberspace, or out, the relations between these cybernetically connected bodies often recreate traditional heterosexual gender identities.

Probably no collection so effectively betrays the masculinist values of the new cyberpunk writers as the science fiction anthology titled Semiotext(e) SF. In their attempt to "jolt" the commercial SF publishing industry, guest editors Rudy

Rucker and Peter Lamborn Wilson invited contri butions that had been rejected by other, more mainstream magazines. As they explained, "we hoped to tap a deep and almost-inarticulate groundswell of resentment against the ever-increasing stodginess, neoconservatism, big-bucks mania and wretched taste of most SF publishers".

Although they clearly collected a range of formerly rejected material, they also produced a volume that loudly announces the gender conservatism of cyberpunk writers. Penetrating penises figure prominently on every page in the form of a flip-book illustration of the "High Performance Waldo", a penis that is modeled on "the Biomorph human penis rarely seen beyond the best sex professionals". Indeed, the sexualization of the female body is a common theme in the various cyberpunk short stories.

On this point, Andrew Ross argues that cyberpunk fiction offers the "most fully delineated urban fantasies of white male folklore." In saying this, he also describes the logic behind the techno-fantasies embodied in VR applications where chic French women are made available as flirting partners to help you, the ideal male audience member, perfect your French language skills. In contemporary cyberpunk narratives, as in VR applications, cyberspace heroes are usually men, whose racial identity, although rarely described explicitly, is contextually white.

Cyberspace playmates are usually beautiful, sexualized, albeit sometimes violently powerful women. Cyberspace offers white men an enticing retreat from the burdens of their cultural identities. In this sense, it is apparent that although cyberspace seems to represent a territory free from the burdens of history, it will, in effect, serve as another site for the technological and no less conventional inscription of the gendered, race-marked body. So despite the fact that VR technologies offer a new stage for the construction and performance of body-based identities, it is likely that old identities will continue to be more comfortable, and thus more frequently reproduced.

THE REARTICULATION OF OLD IDENTITIES TO NEW TECHNOLOGIES

The virtual body is neither simply a surface upon which are written the dominant narratives of Western culture, nor a representation of cultural ideals of beauty or of sexual desire. It has been transformed into the very medium of cultural expression itself, manipulated, digitalized, and technologically constructed in virtual environments. Enhanced visualization technologies make it difficult to continue to think about the material body as a bounded entity, or to continue to distinguish its inside from its outside, its surface from its depth, its aura from its projection.

As the virtual body is deployed as a medium of information and of encryption, the structural integrity of the material body as a bounded physical object is technologically deconstructed. If we think of the body not as a product, but rather as a process - and embodiment as an effect - we can begin to ask questions about how the body is staged differently in different realities. Virtual environments offer a new arena for the staging of the body -what dramas will be played out in these virtual worlds?

Even though the fetishistic nature of such technological devices (especially of the splashy demo tapes) fuels the fantasies of VR technicians (for ultimate world control), the possibilities for realizing these fantasies are probably determined more by the socioeconomic context of corporate sponsorship than by the libidinal promise of virtually safe sex - which is to say that VR research and development cannot continue without commercial investment. But this isn't the whole story.

Interspersed throughout the pages of Mondo 2000 and conference announcements, a tension of sorts emerges in the attempt to discursively negotiate a corporate com modity system while upholding oppositional notions of countercultural iconoclasm, individual genius, and artistic creativity. The result is the formation of a postmodern schizo-culture that is unselfconsciously elitist and often disingenuous in offering its hacker's version of the American Dream.

As Donna Haraway argues, we must be able to get beyond the rhetoric produced by both the techno-advocates and the cultural critics, because both of them inadvertently construct a demonology of technology. The issues we need to investigate concern the way that VR technologies produce simultaneous effects that are not easily judged to be "good" or "bad," or moral or immoral.

For example, virtual reality applications, in an ideal form, involve a network of individual-machine interfaces located at remote outposts. In this sense, VR promotes both technological access and decentralization. But then, does it promote the further instrumental rationalization of everyday life or a new epistemological pluralism? Even as VR technology promises a new form of intersubjectivity, it contributes to a heretofore unknown epidemic of cultural autism. Intimacy is now redefined as a quality of interaction between the human body and the machine.

What about notions of privacy and hygiene? Who will have access to virtual reality applications and, more broadly, to the networks that serve as the infrastructure of the emerging information society? Sensory processing is a fertile field for scientific research. In fact, we are fascinated by the possibility that we may be able to technologically monitor brain functioning. Several sophisticated new visualization technologies - such as PET (positron emission tomography), MRI (magnetic resonance imaging), and MEG (magnetoencephalogy) - offer ways to visualize brain activity.

In the best light, this is done in hopes of constructing a map of brain processing patterns; but even as these technologies promise new vistas for scientific research, the possibility for establishing new "biologically based" standards of body functioning - for example, defining what is "normal" according to neural firing patterns - suggests that this is not a politically neutral technology.

The fact that new imaging technologies produce "better" images of human anatomy does not guarantee that doctors are using the images to produce "better" diagnoses and/or treatment programs for patients. By analogy, the fact that virtual realities offer new information environments does not guarantee that people will use the information in better ways. It is just as likely that these new technologies will be used primarily to tell old stories - stories that reproduce, in hightech guise, traditional narratives about the gendered, race-marked body.

CYBERPUNK AS A FEMINIST IMAGINARY

Teresa de Lauretis anticipated the critical response that cyberpunk science fiction enjoys from postmodern readers when she provisionally suggested (in 1980) that in "every historical period, certain art forms (or certain literary forms...), have become central to the episteme or historical vision of a given society.... If we compare it with traditional or postmodern fiction, we see that SF might, just might, be crucial from now on."

In one of the first reports on cyberpunk as a new science fiction subgenre, Darko Suvin, quoting Raymond Williams, argues for its cultural significance by claiming that cyberpunk novels (especially those by William Gibson) articulate a new structure of feeling: "a particular quality of social experience and relationship...which gives the sense of a generation or of a period." Several critics have discussed the details of the relationship between cyberpunk and a postmodern sensibility.

For example, in her essay "Cybernetic Deconstructions: Cyberpunk and Postmodernism," Veronica Hollinger reads cyberpunk through a poststructuralist antihumanism to claim that cyberpunk is "an analysis of the postmodern identification of human and machine." Her main point is that cyberpunk participates in the (postmodern) deconstruction of human subjectivity. According to her reading, cyberpunk narratives "radically decenter the human body, the sacred icon of essential self in the same way that the virtual reality of cyberspace works to decenter conventional humanist notions of an unproblematic 'real.' "By the end of her analysis, though, we discover that the antihumanist critique of cyberpunk doesn't hold.

Cyberpunk collapses under the weight of its own genre determinations. It is still, Hollinger argues, about the "reinsertion of the human into the reality which its technology is in the process of shaping." In support of Hollinger's conclusion, it is more useful to think of cyberpunk as offering a vision of posthuman existence where "technology" and the "human" are understood in contiguous rather than oppositional terms. This notion suggests a continuum between the terms "human" and "technology" that considers the relationship between them not a dichotomy but rather a relationship of degree; human identity, according to this schema, is understood as a value somewhere between the two (idealized) ends.

As an example of the cyberpunk meditation on the posthuman condition, Synners posits a world populated by "Homo datum," people whose natural habitat is "the net," synners for whom disconnection from the information economy is not an option. This leads one character to speculate that there are three species of technological humans: "synthe sizing humans, synthe sized humans," and the "bastard offspring of both" - artificial intelligences. The original syn, in this case, is neither an act nor a transgression, but rather the human condition of being "incur ably informed." Death, according to this logic, is defined as a brain-scan flatline.

To the extent that we read cyberpunk through postmodern social theory, one of the most obvious thematic connections between the two is the way in which each discourse configures the space of the social as a landscape structured by the network of relations among multinational capitalist corporations. As Fredric Jameson suggests, the generic structure of cyberpunk science fiction represents an attempt to "think the impossible totality of the contemporary world system." This space of "the decentered global network," metaphorically known as cyberspace, is a bewildering place for the individual/subject who is left to his/her own devices to construct a map of the relationship between a corporeal locale and the totality of "transnational corporate realities."

The focal tension in Synners concerns the multinational Diversifications' takeover of two small companies: Eye-Traxx, an independent music-video production company, and Hall Galen Enterprises, a company that employs the medical researcher who invented and patented the procedures for brain socket implants. As a result of the takeover, two of the four main characters, Gina and Visual Mark, become Diversifications' corporate property. Visual Mark was one of Eye-Traxx's original synners, a human synthesizer who is now nearing the age of 50: "It was as if he had a pipeline to some primal dream spot, where music and image created each other, the pictures suggesting the music, the music generating the pictures, in a synesthetic frenzy."

Diversifications intend to market its new brain sockets by offering virtual reality rock videos: Visual Mark is the best music-video synner in the business. Diversifications' brain sockets not only allow music videos to be fed into a receiving brain; they also provide a direct interface between a brain and a computer. This type of brain-to-computer connection proves to have dire consequences. While Diversifications tries to corner the market on a lucrative new form of electronic addiction - by providing the sockets and what is fed into the sockets - their socket clients encounter a fatal side effect: "inter-cranial meltdown" in the form of cerebral stroke.

In elaborating the distinctions between cyberpunk science fiction and its generic antecedents, namely New Wave and feminist science fiction from the late 1960s and 1970s, Fred Pfeil writes: "I am tempted to say [cyberpunk novels] have no 'political unconscious": [but are rather] a kind of writing in which, instead of delving and probing for neurotic symptoms, we are invited to witness and evaluate a relatively open acting out." That a cyberpunk work's neurotic symptoms are easily identified does not disqualify it as an interesting cultural text; on the contrary, Pfeil argues that this is a productive, creative mutation:

This new SF hardly requires the literary analyst's ingenuity in order for us to find or fathom its real social content; the collective anxieties and desires that fuel it are relatively openly evoked and worked through. And the shift from formal and aesthetic experimentation back to experiments in social thought itself suggests that in at least some senses and sectors we have indeed moved on from that earlier humanist debate on freedom, power and order to some new or at least mutated social and ideological ground, which is once again open and fresh enough to be explicitly tried on and explored.

In the case of Synners, the "real social content," according to Pfeil's formulation, is not simply the plottings of a hostile corporate takeover, but also what we can read off its textual surface about the technological configuration of human life in multinational capitalism.

Several topics nominate themselves as experiments in thinking through the social consequences of new technologies, any one of which could serve as the organizing perspective for elaborating an interpretive map of Cadigan's cos mology: the capitalist production of electronic addictions, the recording practices of video vigilantes, or the multiplication of television channels devoted to new forms of pornography: disasterporn, medporn, foodporn. In addition to speculating about the dynamics of new communication technologies, Synners also offers a critical account of the commodification of information.

Truth is cheap, but information costs.... "Besides being rich," Fez said, "you have to be extra sharp these days to pick up any real information. You have to know what you're looking for, and you have to know how it's filed. Browsers need not apply. Broke ones, anyway. I miss the newspaper." This subtext also includes a political critique of the availability of information and of the difficulty of determining relevance in the midst of the "Instant Information Revolution."

"Good guess, but the real title is Need to Know," said the same voice close to his ear. "It's an indictment of our present system of information dispersal. You're allowed to know only those things the information czars decide that you need to know. They call it 'market research' and 'efficient use of resources' and 'no-waste,' but it's the same old shit they've been doing to us for more than one-hundred years - keep 'em confused and in the dark. You gotta be a stone-ham super-Renaissance person to find out what's really going on."

Pfeil is right when he says that isolating passages such as these hardly requires literary ingenuity to identify expressions of collective anxieties. Indeed, such skeptical statements about information overload and information manipulation resonate strongly with Baudrillard's reading of the postmodern scene: "We are in a universe where there is more and more information, and less and less meaning."

And yet, in contrast to the reading Baudrillard offers, Carolyn Marvin argues that "information cannot be said to exist at all unless it has meaning, and meaning is established only in social relationships with cultural reference and value." In her critique of the dominant notion of information-as-commodity (a notion that is at the heart of the ideology of the information age), Marvin redefines information, not as a quantifiable entity but rather as a "state of knowing," which reasserts a knowing body as its necessary materialist foundation.

This embodied notion of information is at the heart of Synners. Moving around a postmodernist reading of cyberpunk science fic tion that would focus on its figuration of multinational capitalism and the technological deconstruction of human identity, I would like to elaborate an alternative reading of Synners that focuses on the relation of the material body to cyberspace. In the course of developing an ideological critique of a capitalist information economy, Cadigan focuses attention on an often repressed dimension of the information age: the constitution of the informed body.

The problem is not just that information "costs," or even that it replicates exponentially, but rather that information is never merely discursive. What we encounter in the Cadigan novel is the narrativization of four different versions of cyberpunk embodiment: the marked body, the disappearing body, the laboring body, and the repressed body. In this sense, the four central characters symbolize the different embodied relations one can have, in theory and in fiction, to a nonmaterial space of information access and exchange. Where

Sam hacks the net through a terminal powered by her own body, Visual Mark actually inhabits the network as he mutates into a disembodied, sentient artificial intelligence (AI).

Although both Gina and Gabe travel through cyberspace on their way to someplace else, Gabe is addicted to cyberspace simulations and Gina endures them. Each character plays a significant role in the novel's climactic confrontation in cyberspace: a role determined in part by their individual relationships to Diversifications and in part by their bodily identities. Sam, Gabe's daughter and the only real hacker among the four, is a virtuoso at gaining access to the net.

She is the character who best describes the labour of computer hacking and the virtual acrobatics of cyberspace travel: "If you couldn't walk on the floor, you walked on the ceiling. If you couldn't walk on the ceiling, you walked on the walls, and if you couldn't walk on the walls, you walked in them, encrypted. Pure hacking." As competent as she is in negotiating the cyberspatial landscape of the net, Sam tries to live her embodied life outside of any institutional structure. Her only affiliations are to other punks and hackers, who form a community of sorts and who live out on "the Manhattan-Hermosa strip, what the kids called the Mimosa, part of the old postquake land of the lost."

Sam trades encrypted data and hacking talents for stray pieces of equipment and living necessities. In what proves to be a critically important "information commodity" acquisition, Sam hacks the specifications for an insulin-pump chip reader that runs off of body energy. When every terminal connected to "the System" is infected by a debilitating virus, Sam's insulin-pump chip reader is the only noninfected access point to the net. Connected by thin needles inserted into her abdomen, the chip reader draws its power from Sam's body. Seventeen-year-old Sam is a cyberspace hacker of considerable talent who shuns the heroic cowboy role. And for the most part, she is content to provide the power while others, namely Gina and Gabe, go in for the final showdown.

Recoiling from a real-time wife who despises him for his failure to live up to his artistic potential, Gabe spends most of his working time, when he should be designing advertising campaigns, playing the role (Hotwire) of a film noir leading man in a computer simulation built from pieces of an old movie thriller; his two female cyberspace sidekicks are "templates [that] had been assembled from two real, living people." Where Visual Mark cleaves to cyberspace because the world isn't big enough for his expansive visual mind, Gabe becomes addicted to cyberspace because the world is just too big for him. He retreats to the simulation pit for the safety and familiarity it offers.

"He'd been running around in simulation for so long, he'd forgotten how to run a realife, real-time routine; he'd forgotten that if he made mistakes, there was no safety-net program to jump in and correct for him." Throughout the novel, Gabe moves in and out of a real-time life and his simulated fantasy world. In real time, his body is continually brought to life, through pain, intoxication, and desire caused by Gina, first when she punches him in the face with a misplaced stab intended for Mark, then later when he gets toxed after she feeds him two LotusLands (a "mildly hallucinogenic beverage").

After they make love for the first time, Gina wonders if Gabe has ever felt desire before: "She didn't think Gabe Ludovic had ever jumped the fast train in his life. Standing at the end of fifteen years of marriage, he'd wanted a lot more than sex. The wanting had been all but tangible, a heat that surprised both of them." After a climactic cyberspace struggle, his repressed body reawakens; Gabe learns to feel his body again (or for the first time) with Gina's help.

Like Visual Mark, Gina is a synner who synthesizes images, sound, and special effects to produce virtual reality music videos. For all her disdain and outright hostility toward other people and institutions, "Badass Gina Aiesi" has an intense emotional connection to Mark, her partner of 20 years, which she romanticizes in an odd way:

They weren't smooch-faces; it didn't work that way, for her or for him.... One time, though...one time, three-four-five years into the madness, there'd been a place where they'd come together one night, and it had been different.... He'd been reaching, and she'd been reaching, and for a little while there, they'd gotten through. Maybe that had been the night when the little overlapping space called their life had come into existence.

Gina's body, marked by its colour, "wild forest hardwood," and her dreadlocks, figures prominently in the narrative description of her sexual encounters, first with Visual Mark and then with Gabe. After both she and Visual Mark have brain sockets implanted by Diversifications' surgeonon-contract, they jack in together and experience a visual replay of shared memories: "The pov was excruciatingly slow as it moved across Mark's face to her own, lingering on the texture of her dreadlocks next to his pale, drawn flesh, finally moving on to the contrast of her deep brown skin." The characteristics that mark Gina are her anger, her exasperated love for Mark, and the colour of her skin.

Like others who bought sockets for jacking in, Visual Mark begins to spend less and less time off-line and more and more time plugged in to the global network known as "the System." This leads him to reflect on the metaphysical nature of his physical body: "he lost all awareness of the meat that had been his prison for close to fifty years, and the relief he felt at having laid his burden down was as great as himself." After suffering a small stroke (one of the unpleasant side effects of brain sockets) while he was jacked in, Visual Mark prepares for "the big one" - a stroke that will release his consciousness into the system and allow him to leave his meat behind.

He was already accustomed to the idea of having multiple awarenesses and a single concentrated core that were both the essence of self. The old meat organ would not have been able to cope with that kind of reality, but out here he appropriated more capacity the way he once might have exchanged a smaller shirt for a larger one. And sure enough, while his body is jacked in, Mark strokes out. He tries to get Gina to pull his plugs, but she is too late. As his meat dies, both his consciousness and his stroke enter "the System." In the process, his stroke is transformed into a deadly virus (or spike) that initiates a worldwide network crash.

Like the dramatic climax in recent cyberpunk films such as Circuitry Man, Lawnmower Man, and Mindwarp, the final showdown in Synners takes place in cyberspace. Working together, a small community of domestic exiles, hackers, and punks assemble a workstation (powered by Sam's insulin-pump chip reader) that enables Gina and Gabe to go on-line to fight the virus/stroke - an intelligent entity of some dubious ontological status that now threatens the integrity of the entire networked world. Like a cyberspace Terminator, the virus/stroke is rationally determined to infect/destroy whoever comes looking for it. In the course of their cyberspace brawl, Gabe and Gina confront the virus's simulation of their individual worse fears.

A "reluctant hero" till the very end, Gabe's cyberspace enemy is a simple construct: the fear of embodiment. "I can't remember what it feels like to have a body," he repeats obsessively during his final confrontation in cyberspace. What he learns through the encounter is that his whole body is a hotsuit; that is, he learns to feel the body that he has technologically repressed. Gina's cyberspace struggle is with an embodiment of her own deepest fears about missed chances, lost love, and suffocating commitment. Her cyberspace showdown replays her obsessive 20-year-long search for Mark: "Old habits, they do die hard, don't they.

That's yours, ain't it -looking for Mark." "Why do you still want to love?" she is asked by the omniscient virus. In one sense her struggle is to confront the fact that she loves an addict and still wants to save him. The crucial decision Gina faces is whether to stay with Mark in cyberspace - where there is no pain, no separation - or to renounce him and return to the real world where such love is impossible. In the end, Gabe and Gina defeat the virus and the global network shortly reestablishes connections. But when Gina finally wakes to reunite with Gabe, we find out that although they have changed for the machines, the machines didn't change for them. "The door only swings one way. Once it's out of the box, it's always too big to get back in.

Can't bury that technology.... Every technology has its original sin.... And we still got to live with what we made." Darko Suvin asks two additional questions about the shape of a cyberpunk sensibility: whose structure of feeling? and to what ideological horizons or consequences does it apply? As if in response, Fred Pfeil suggests that most cyberpunk science fiction "remains stuck in a masculinist frame," in that cyberpunk dramas, like most video game narratives, remain "focused on the struggle of the male protagonist...to wend his lonely way through the worlds."

Andrew Ross concurs with Pfeil's assessment and adds: "One barely needs to scratch the surface of the cyberpunk genre, no matter how maturely sketched out, to expose a baroque edifice of adolescent male fantasies." In reading Synners as a feminist imaginary, I would argue that it offers an alternative narrative of cyberpunk identity that begins with the assumption that bodies are always gendered and always marked by race. In one sense, Cadigan's novel is implicitly informed by Donna Haraway's cyborg politics: the gendered distinctions among characters hold true to a cyborgian figuration of gender differences, whereby the female body is coded as a body-in-connection and the male body as a body-in-isolation.

Synners illuminates the gendered differences in the way that the characters relate to the technological space of information. Sam and Gina, the two female hackers, actively manipulate the dimensions of cybernetic space in order to communicate with other people. Gabe and Visual Mark, on the other hand, are addicted to cyberspace for the release it offers from the loneliness of their material bodies.

The racial distinctions between characters are revealed through the novel's representation of sexual desire. Gina is the only character to be identified by skin colour. She is also the focal object and subject of heterosexual desire, for a moment by Mark and more frequently by Gabe; and we know both men's racial identities by their marked differences from Gina's. In this way, the unmarked characters are marked by the absence of identifying marks.

Although we are never directly told their racial identities, both Visual Mark and Gabe are contextually identified as white in contrast to Gina, whose skin colour and hair texture is explicitly described. In different ways and with different political connotations, Synners reasserts that gender and race are defining elements of posthuman identity. So even as Synners discursively represents different forms of technological embodiment, it also reasserts the critical importance of the materiality of bodies in any analysis of the information age.

Maybe Pfeil is right in his claim that cyberpunk novels have no political unconscious, in that their symbolic preoccupations are relatively easy to access. But in constructing this reading of Synners, not to emphasize its cyberpunk characteristics but rather to point to its feminist preoccupations, that it expresses some form of allegorical narrative; as a work of the feminist imagination, it narrativizes certain tensions and obsessions that animate feminist thinking across cultural discourses.

The male body, in contrast, is repressed or disappearing. This reading suggests a slight revision of Arthur Kroker's theory of the postmodern body, where he argues that the signal form of postmodern embodiment is the "disappearing body." In this matrix (a modified semiotic square), each of Cadigan's characters represents a different form of technological embodiment endemic to postmodernity. These fictional characters suggest the other kinds of bodies (in contrast to Kroker's claim) that populate the (technological) postmodern scene.

Other bodies require additional investigation by cultural critics. For example, what are the biopolitics surrounding the multicultural bodies used as mannequins for high-fashion messages? Who will determine who will receive the artificial body parts engineered to replace failing organic ones? To this end, this matrix suggests new body projects that are likely to occupy feminist scholars in the near future.

In offering gendered descriptions of multiple forms of postmodern embodiment, Synners sets the stage for the elaboration of a feminist theory of the relationship of material bodies to cyberspace and of the construction of agency in technological encounters. But even in saying this, I must assert that the final horizon of this reading is not Cadigan's novel, but rather the insights it offers for a feminist analysis of the politics of new information technologies. To this end, Synners suggests a beginning point in the elaboration of a map of contemporary cyberculture, where technology serves as a site for the reinscription of cultural narratives of gender and race identities.

THE BIOPOLITICS OF NEW INFORMATION TECHNOLOGY

This reading of Synners also implies that a political judgment of any technology is difficult to render in the abstract. Technologies always have multiple effects. Determining the meaning of those effects is not a simple process. For example, several news articles about the phenomenon of virtual reality boldly assert that VR applications, such as "Virtual Valerie" and 900-number phone sex services, are technologies of safe (fluidless) sex.

One Atlanta-based sex expert goes so far as to say that VR will be a mainstream sex aid by the end of the decade, stimulating yet pathogenically prudent. And yet I notice how the very same phenomenon enables new forms of social and cultural autism. Brenda Laurel, a VR researcher and designer, reports: "'ve had men tell me that one of the reasons they got into this business was to escape the social aspects of being a male in America - to escape women in particular."

Sandy Stone studies electronic communities and the bodies that labour in cyberspace - including VR systems engineers as well as phone sex workers. In her analysis of the virtual body, she concludes that cyberspace both disembodies and re-embodies in a gendered fashion: "the desire to cross the human/machine boundary, to penetrate and merge, which is part of the evocation of cyberspace...shares certain conceptual and affective characteristics with numerous fictional evocations of the inarticulate longing of the male for the female." But, as she goes on to argue, "to enter cyberspace is to physically put on cyberspace.

To become the cyborg, to put on the seductive and dangerous cybernetic space like a garment, is to put on the female." Even as she elaborates the gendered dimensions of cyberspace connection, Stone sees an inherent ambiguity in cyberspace technologies that is tied to the facticity of the material body. For as much as they offer the opportunity for new forms of virtual engagement, Stone rightly asserts that "no refigured virtual body, no matter how beautiful, will slow the death of a cyberpunk with AIDS. Even in the age of the technosubject, life is lived through bodies."

If on the one hand new communication technologies such as VR create new contexts for knowing/talking/signing/fucking bodies, they also enable new forms of repression of the material body. Studies of the new modes of electronic communication, for example, indicate that the anonymity offered by the computer screen empowers antisocial behaviors such as "flaming" and borderline illegal behaviors such as trespassing, E-mail snooping, and MUD-rape. And yet, for all the anonymity they offer, many computer communications reproduce stereotypically gendered patterns of conversation.

In the Jargon File, the entry "Gender and Ethnicity" claims that although "hackerdom is still predominantly male," hackers are genderand colour-blind in their interactions with other hackers due to the fact that they communicate (primarily) through text-based network channels. This assertion rests on the assumption that "text-based channels" represent a gender-neutral medium of exchange, that language itself is free from any form of gender, race, or ethnic determinations.

Both of these assumptions are called into question not only by feminist research on electronic communication and interpretive theory, but also by female network users who participate in cyberpunk's virtual subculture. This was dramatically, or rather textually, illustrated in an exchange that occurred on FutureCulture, an electronic discussion list devoted to cyberpunk subculture. The thread of discussion concerned a floating utopia called "Autopia." The exchange about women in "Autopia" began innocently from the cyberdeck of a student:

It may just be my imagination, but it seems that the bulk of the people participating in Autopia discussions are men. And hasn't anyone else noticed that most people on FutureCulture are men? Not to mention the over-all population of the net generally speaking. I'd like to get women into this discussion but I'm not even sure if there are any women on FC. Are there?

In response, a male participant pointed out:

If you haven't noticed, the bulk of the people on these networks are men. It is about 80% male with higher percentages in some places.

Yeah. Clearly the Internet is dominated by men. It just seems that some outreach to women might be in order. Hanging out on a ship with hundreds of male computer jocks isn't exactly my idea of utopia.

A female participant wrote back:

Now, this is a loaded question. A lot of women will not open themselves to possible net harassment by admitting they are listening. Of course, if they've come this far, they are likely to be the more bold/brave/stupid type.

Which leaves me where? Cuz, yes, I am a woman & I hang out on the Internet, read cyberpunk, do interesting things with locks and computers. I don't program, I don't MU*/D/SH. I do technical work/repair. I write. I read. I'm a relatively bright individual. This posting was followed by a self-acknowledged sexist statement from a male participant who asked others if they too found that women on the net were extremely unattractive. After being flamed from several other men in the discussion, one reply rebuked the original poster:

Concepts of physical beauty are hold overs from 'MEAT' space. On the net they don't apply. We are all just bits and bytes blowing in the phospor stream. Concepts of physical beauty might be a "meat thing," but gender identity persists in the "phospor stream" whether we like it or not. Eventually the thread returned to the question of what a woman might say about "Autopia," the floating utopia idea. Several postings later, the same female participant responded:

And, would you like to know why, overall, I am uninterested in the idea of Autopia? Because I'm a responsible person. (Over-responsible, if you want to get into the nit-picky psychological semantics, but that's another point.) As a responsible person, I end up doing/am expected to do all the shit work. All the little details that others don't think of; like setting up laundry duty, dishes, cooking, building, re pairs, handling garbage. This is not to say that I fall into the typical "FEMALE" role, because both women and men have left these duties to fall in my lap.

And, it's not a case that if I leave it, it will eventually get done either - you'd be amazed at how long people will ignore garbage or dishes; at how many people can't use a screw driver or hold a hammer correctly. Plus, how about security? There is a kind of assumption that goes on, especially on the net that folks on whatever computer network are a higher intelligence, above craven acts of violence. If you end up with 50 men for every woman, how are you going to insure her safety? So, talk about security issues, waste disposal, cooking and cleaning duties, the actual wiring of whatever ship for onboard computers, how you're planning on securing hard drives for rough seas, how you're going to eat, in what shifts are you going to sleep, who's going to steer, how you are going to get navigators.

Where will you get the money for the endeavor? If you decide against a ship, and go for an island, how are you going to deal with the overrunning the natural habitat? What are you going to do if you cause some species that only lived on *that* island to become extinct? What are you going to do with refugees from the worlds of hurt on this planet, which are looking for someplace to escape to?

As one other (male) participant in the discussion pointed out, these are imminently practical concerns, but not ones that were raised until the female participant emerged from the silence she was lurking in. Her original point was passed over quickly, even as it was enacted in the course of the subsequent discussion: electronic discussion lists are governed by gendered codes of discursive interchange that often are not hospitable to female participants. This suggests that on-line communication is structured similarly to communication in other settings, and is overtly subjected to forms of gender, status, age, and race determinations.

Hoai-An Truong, a member of Bay Area Women in Telecommunications (BAWIT), writes:

Despite the fact that computer networking systems obscure physical characteristics, many women find that gender follows them into the on-line community, and sets a tone for their public and private interactions there - to such an extent that some women purposefully choose gender neutral identities, or refrain from expressing their opinions.

Thus we see an interesting paradox in action. Cyberspace is a place where bodies aren't suppose to matter, but many women discover that they do matter. The false denial of the body (mainly by male users) requires the defensive denial of the body (mainly by female users) so that communication can occur. For some women, this denial of the body is simply not worth the effort. Most men apparently never notice.

GENDERED GEOGRAPHIES OF CYBERSPACE LANDSCAPES

In Landscape for a Good Woman, a genre-bending theoretical critique of psychoanalysis and working-class social history, Carolyn Steedman asserts that autobiography is useful for the production of cultural criticism because "[p]ersonal interpretations of past time - the stories that people tell themselves in order to explain how they got to the place they currently inhabit - are often in deep and ambiguous conflict with the official interpretive devices of a culture." Steedman describes the conflict she experiences when she takes cultural theory personally:

The structures of class analysis and schools of cultural criticism... cannot deal with everything there is to say about my mother's life.... The usefulness of the biographical and autobiographical core of the book lies in the challenge it may offer to much of our conventional understanding of childhood, working-class childhood, and littlegirlhood.

In writing stories that aren't central to a dominant culture, specifically the story of her working-class childhood and a deauthorized father -Steedman simultaneously revises the insights of psychoanalytic theory and the discursive conventions of cultural criticism. More specifically, she links an autobiographical account of her working-class childhood with a biographical account of her mother's class determinations to serve as the context for a narrative critique of a classic psychoanalytical case study; Steedman's intent is to articulate the relationship between narratives of the self and narratives of history.

Her broader point is to demonstrate that working-class histories, in whatever form they are found, as case studies or autobiographical narratives, often contradict the official "interpretive devices" of a dominant culture. Im plicit in Steedman's work is the argument that provoking such a conflict creates the opportunity to interfere with the ongoing codification of official interpretations. Although different accounts of this conflict could be written, I suggest that the "ambiguous conflict" between the autobiographical notes which opened this chapter and the dominant, if not exactly official, interpretive theory of our era - postmodernism - concerns the penchant to celebrate the perpetual present.

Steve Best and Doug Kellner identify this tendency as "radical presentism" and argue that "the erasure of depth also flattens out history and experience, for lost in a postmodern present, one is cut off from those sedimented traditions, those continuities and historical memories which nurture historical consciousness and provide a rich, textured, multidimensional present." Presentism augments two ideological projects of the information age: the construction of social theories narrated by disembodied virtual minds, and the construction of technological histories written without women, without workers, and without politics.

I would like to conclude by discussing the gendered aspects of the development of those technologies that have been identified as central to the New Edge and the age of information: microelectronics, telecommunications networks, and other forms of computer technologies. To read accounts of the development of information technologies, for example, one might conclude that women have only just begun to show an interest in and aptitude for technological knowledge, innovation, and employment. This signals yet another pervasive myth of the information age: namely that everything that is important to know is transparently accessible with the right access codes. Feminist thinkers know differently.

THE GENDERING OF TECHNOLOGICAL HISTORIES

Gathering even basic biographical material about the women who participated in traditionally male-dominated technical and professional fields -including the physical and natural sciences, engineering, mathematics, military science, and astronomy - is not an easy project. The historical material that is available illuminates the daunting structural barriers that many women had to overcome in order to pursue their interests and research in scientific and technological fields.

The structural barriers range from formal prohibition against women's education to legal restrictions of women's property rights, which caused many women inventors to patent their inventions under brothers' or husbands' names. In reporting on the treatment of gender and women's subjects in the 24-year history of the journal Technology and Culture (the journal of the Society for the History of Technology), Joan Rothschild asserts that one of the reasons for the lack of discussion about gender in the historiography of technology is a consequence of a "literal identification of the male with technology."

This association has been seriously challenged by recent feminist studies that seek not only to recover women's contribution to the historical development of different technologies, but also to rethink the history of technology from a feminist perspective. Autumn Stanley, for one, argues that the history of technology omits women in part because of a categorical exclusion of the technologies that women were specifically instrumental in developing as not "proper" technologies: here she lists food preparation, nursing and infant care, and menstruation technologies.

Other feminists investigate social arrangements that reproduce the masculinist identification with technologies that intimately affect women's lives, such as domestic technologies, as well as studies of specific domains that are still dominated by male scientists, engineers, and medical researchers, such as the new reproductive technologies. As I implied in the opening remarks about my mother's computer employment history, women's relationship to the technology of the workplace has been a troubled one.

The expansion of clerical occupations after World War I resulted in the feminization of such occupations; women were preferentially hired over men because they were less expensive to employ. This kept the costs of expansion contained. After World War II, many forms of female office work were subjected to the analysis of scientific management. Tasks were routinized and rationalized; bookkeepers and other office workers became "machine attendants who performed standardized repetitive calculating operations."

This repetitive work was the perfect material for automated calculators. Although some labour historians assert that the introduction of electronic calculators and computers occurred during a time of economic expansion, and thus had the effect of actually increasing the number of clerical jobs available for displaced workers, the new jobs were often sex-stratified such that better paying data-processing positions were staffed by men.

These technologies had contradictory effects on women's employment, increasing the opportunity for new jobs, but at the same time downgrading the skill level of office workers who were employed to attend the new machines. In forming a judgment about the impact of these technologies on women's lives, it is also important to remember that it is likely that the women who were displaced from their bookkeeping positions in the 1950s by the introduction of electronic technology did not necessarily experience this as an employment failure. No doubt some of them, like my mother, were eager to get on with the real business of their lives, which was getting married, having children, and raising families.

In the 10 years since the personal computer became widely available as a mass-produced consumer item, it has become an entirely naturalized fixture in the workplace, either at home or at the business office. It is also becoming common to criticize the claims that computers increase office worker productivity - the primary marketing line for the sale of personal computers to businesses and industries. Some critics protest that the real impact of computers and word-processing systems has been to increase the quantity of time spent producing documents, while others argue that the computerized office decreases the quality of work life due to physical discomfort and information overload.

Sociological studies of the gendered aspects of computer employment focus on the de-skilling and displacement of female clerical workers in different industries. While these studies on women as laborers are vital for an understanding of the social and economic impact of computers, there is less research available about women's creative or educational use of information technologies or their role in the history of computing. But there is also a class bias reflected in these investigations: by focusing on women's computer use in the workplace, such studies restrict their critical investigation to those women who have access to what remains a costly technology that is beyond the reach and skill level of many women in the United States today.

The question of women's employment and computer technology can be asked another way. For example, Les Levidow studies the women who make the tiny silicon chips that serve as the electronic guts for cheap computer gadgets. Both in affluent (until recently) Silicon Valley and in a relatively poor Malaysian state (Penang), the large majority of chip makers are poorly paid immigrant women.

Yet another way to approach the question of women and technological histories, one more sensitive to class-related issue, is to ask "Who counts?" This leads to the investigation of both those who determine who counts as instances of what identities, and also those who are treated as numbers or cases in the construction of a database. The politics of databases will be a critical agenda item for the 1990s as an increasing number of businesses, services, and state agencies go "on-line."

Determining who has access to data and how to gain access to data that is supposedly available to the "public" is a multidimensional project that involves the use of computers, skill at network access, and education in locating and negotiating access to government-supported databases. Even a chief data coordinator with the U.S. Geological Survey asserts that "data markets, data access, and data dissemination are complicated, fuzzy, emotional topics right now." She "predicts that they likely will be the major issues of the decade."

Questions of public access and the status of information in the computer age are just now attracting public attention. As Kenneth B. Allen argues, the same technologies that enable us to "create, manipulate, and disseminate information" also, ironically, "threaten to diminish public access to government information." The issue of citizens' rights to information needs to be monitored by computer-savvy citizen advocates. The question becomes, where will such advocates come from? Two immediate answers come to the fore: they will be either educated or elected.

Feminist scholars and teachers can contribute to both by encouraging women students to address information policy issues in their research projects and by supporting women candidates who will serve on the federal and state boards that govern information access. These candidates and policy students will certainly face several difficult issues involving bodies, information, and criminal charges. The Council for State Governments describes one item of state legislation proposed in 1993: the Prenatal Exposure to Controlled Substances Act.

This act would require "substance abuse treatment personnel to report to the state department of children and family services any pregnant woman who is addicted to drugs or alcohol." The positive consequence of such an act would require states to "bring treatment services to alcohol and/or substance abusing pregnant women." Negative consequences, such as the criminalization of pregnant women for delivering a controlled substance to a minor, are not mentioned. This act could, as Jennifer Terry suggests, serve as a "technology of surveillance," whereby the unborn fetus is guaranteed certain rights denied to the pregnant woman: "[for] poor women, interventions into daily life through social welfare and the criminal justice system render recourse to the right to privacy somewhat moot."

THE CULTURAL FORMATION OF THE NEW EDGE

In synthesizing this account of an emergent cultural formation, with its emphasis on signifying practices and forms of embodiment, it becomes clear that there is much work to be done to elaborate its connections to dominant cultural forms of production, consumption, communication, and control. I've tried to show how ongoing ideological projects such as the repression of history, of the body, of feminist foremothers are rearticulated through the use of new information technologies.

Certainly an investigation of the broader cultural formation suggests new subjects for feminism now and in the future: global workers, homeworkers, knowledge engineers, corporate scientists, brain police, and permanent temporary workers. In telling the cyberpunk story of the coordination between technology and technical expertise and how it becomes subject to corporate control, Synners offers a countermythology of the information age - not that information wants to be free, but rather that access to information is going to cost, and cost a lot.

Through its postfeminist portrayal of empowered female bodies who play off and against repressed or hysterical male bodies, Synners offers an alternative vision of technological embodiment that is consistent with a gendered history of technology: where technology isn't the means of escape from or transcendence of the body, but rather the means of communication and connection with other bodies. Synners also raises questions about the meaning of race in a technological age.

How is technological disembodiment also a comment on the desire to transcend racial identities? How are material bodies race-marked through technological encounters? How are racial identities articulated to myths of technological progress? Despite our condition of being incurably informed, we don't have enough information about the embodied aspects of new information technologies. Simply put, we need a great deal more in order to construct analyses of the information age that can serve as a foundation for critical political interventions.

Synners also suggests the importance of a cyberpunk mythology for the construction of feminist cultural studies of scientific and technological formations. Gina and Sam make interesting subjects for feminist theory in that their technological competencies and synner talents emphasize the need for feminist activists to encourage women to develop technological skills and for feminist teachers to promote educational efforts to increase technological literacy.

The challenge is how to harness the power of technological knowledge to a feminist agenda while struggling against an increasing industrial imperialism that eagerly assimilates new technoworkers to labour in the interests of private enterprise. The question is how to empower technological agents so that they work on behalf of the right kind of social change.

FEMINISM AND TECHNOLOGY FROM A COMMUNICATION PERSPECTIVE

Across disciplines, studies of technology offer fertile ground for understanding women's experience and for engaging the world through feminist critique. Women's studies research, in turn, contributes distinctly to understanding issues central to living in an increasingly technological world. The goal of this special issue is to emphasize the contribution of communication research in exploring the relationship between gender, feminism, and technology.

The collection of articles presented here reminds us of how technology is simultaneously both rapidly changing and yet stubbornly intractable. Consider, we live in a time when technological artifacts are highly mutable (think of how quickly cell phones change, or of the frequency of software updates), but yet 25 years of research into the study of culture in dozens of technological contexts consistently reveals the dominance of masculinist ideologies of mastery and control. The always-connected communication reality of 2007 is almost inconceivably different from that of the land-line world of

1987, yet our research finds that identity, interaction, and communication consistently exhibit clearly gendered characteristics and present familiar concerns of women's access, voice, and empowerment.

A common theme among these four essays is a caution to look beyond the veneer of the technological artifact to underlying, enduring elements of communication and social interaction. To introduce the essays, I suggest two deeper concerns they speak to. The first is the fallacy of "add women and stir." The second is the fallacy of technological determinism.

AVOIDING THE FALLACY OF ADD WOMEN AND STIR

A number of recent reports warn that the United States will likely face a serious shortage of scientists, engineers, and other technical professionals in the near future. One strategy for addressing this shortage is to increase the representation of women and girls in STEM fields (science, technology, engineering, and medicine). Typically referred to as "pipeline" solutions, these efforts are gaining steady momentum at all levels of education, from elementary school through post-graduate training.

Historically, technical disciplines have not attracted many women. As many scholars (and women scientists and engineers) attest, a main problem is that these disciplines have not been very attractive to women. In response, a growing number of initiatives examine ways to make STEM subjects more interesting and more engaging to women. For example, recently Bryn Mawr and Georgia Tech both introduced courses that teach computer science by assigning students to program robots. Industry-academic consortia, such as the National Center for Women in Technology attempt to raise awareness of the situation and to support change initiatives, particularly those aimed at curriculum reform.

These efforts are significant and important for addressing the problem of women's absence. However, the voices and contributions of communication scholars are essential in these efforts in order to avoid the fallacy of "add women and stir." Lasting change requires more than the addition of female bodies. It requires a careful examination of the complex issues embedded (and often taken for granted) in technological contexts. For example, an instructor who revises a course to make the content more relevant and engaging to women, and yet maintains a traditional pedagogy emphasizing competition and individual accomplishment, has not recognized the importance of reforming the experience of women in these disciplines.

This critical stance is particularly relevant as computer science begins to incorporate a new area of study: the design and development of digital games. Game design is an interesting domain because it not only utilizes standard elements of computer science (such as programming and graphics), it is also immediately relevant to students who have either grown up playing computer games or who hope to work in the burgeoning game industry (or both). Games do not need to be solely for entertainment.

Potentially, students can bring their expertise to bear in socially relevant contexts such as education, or even social and political activism. Educational institutions envision games studies as an emphasis that will attract more people into computer science and information technology. Two of the papers here suggest some important issues for institutions to consider as they look to game studies as ways to attract women to computer science and engineering. Charles Soukup's essay, "Mastering the Game: Gender and the Entelechial Motivational System of Video Games," makes a persuasive argument that mastery, control, and domination are not only pervasive within contemporary digital games but also possibly intrinsic to their success.

Drawing on Burke's conception of human motivation, Soukup examines the discourse of the gaming community to identify a key characteristic that makes games engaging: the possibility of achieving perfection. The ability to do such things as "beat the game" or attaining the top possible score, Soukup argues, is what drives players to continue playing. The growing popularity of tournament play of video games, including the early video game classic PacMan, and the crowning of "top scorers" is testament to this. Digital games are, indeed for some, possibly more engaging (and even addictive) than other aspects of life, because perfection is attainable.

Though there are games that do not fit this genre (e.g., Sims, Animal Crossing), because they do not have an equally strong motivational stance, they are less likely to be engaging (and, therefore, less likely to be commercially successful). Soukup's piece directs us to consider and critique not only the content of games (which are often violent and sometimes misogynistic), but also the gendered qualities of those things that might be taken for granted (and therefore invisible) in the deeper structure underlying game play.

If educational institutions pause to examine and take seriously how the attractiveness of games is gendered at the level of game structure, then one question that arises is whether there are viable alternatives. One avenue for exploration calls us to move one step back from the artifact of the "game," to instead understand the more general notion of fun and its relationship to "play". In "Not just Fun and Games: Digital Play, Gender and Attitudes Towards Technology," Elena Bertozzi and Seungwhan Lee survey ordinary folks to understand how people experience "play" through various online activities.

Their findings are a significant contribution to the larger discourse about the relationship between women and technology. Stereotypes often portray women as less interested in technology or as finding less pleasure in it. But Bertozzi and Lee's findings suggest that the masculine mystique surrounding digital gameplay may be due more to appearance than reality. They report that overall, there was no significant difference between men and women in terms of amount of digital play, or in feelings of guilt over engaging in digital play.

However, men tended to engage more in "mental rotation" games for play (games requiring alteration of identity or perception, such as role-playing games), and women tended to engage in communication activities as play (particularly instant messaging). I see evidence of this in my own household, where my son enjoys devoting hours to any number of console games and my daughter will spend an entire evening updating her "profile" (website) and chatting online with friends she could just as easily go and see in person. Both of my children are engaged in play, yet most discussions of games do not explore communication and social activities as gameplay.

Working from these results, one implication for game design might be to introduce earlier in a game more opportunities for rich interaction with game characters, or (in the case of online games) with other players. In most games, such interaction is possible (or needed in the gameplay) only after achieving higher levels of "technical" skills (i.e., the ability to defeat many enemies through combat). Indeed, it would be interesting to see a subgenre of digital games that require increasingly sophisticated communication skills to succeed, rather than better aim or dexterity.

Bertozzi and Lee also report a positive correlation between digital play (inclusive of all types of activity) and both technophilia (positive attitudes toward technology) and perceived levels of technical self-efficacy. Providing girls with positive experiences online, regardless of whether or not these activities are preparation for computer science or engineering, can set the foundation for them to shape the future of those fields because they can perceive themselves as actors, and as legitimate stakeholders, rather than as outsiders of the club.

AVOIDING THE FALLACY OF TECHNOLOGICAL DETERMINISM

Technological determinism is a discourse with great rhetorical force. As Smith (1994) summarizes it:

The gist of technological determinism is heartbreaking in its simplicity: the belief that social progress is driven by technological innovation, which in turn follows an "inevitable" course.

Technological determinism, as a discourse, is incessently performative, as it envisions new possibilities and promises change. The desire to see technologies as liberating, as enabling progress and ameliorating social problems is not itself undesirable. Indeed, technologies, including communication technologies, have made possible new avenues for important social and political change. Danger arises when we forget that technological determinism is a belief and a discourse, rather than an accurate empirical account of the world.

Feminist scholarship has long documented the way in which technologies and technological development is used in pursuit of control, mastery, and the value of progress. An important role for communication scholarship is to persist in interrogating the discourse surrounding technological development. Communication technologies in particular frequently are identified as creating new opportunities for women's empowerment by providing access to information and knowledge and by expanding women's networks. Yet it is important that we do not become enraptured with these possibilities and fall once again into a deterministic stance.

Our research must continue to interrogate technology use, to recognize the ways in which social forces remain stubbornly intractable, and thereby to understand the more complicated and more subtle effects of technologies. Pauline Hope Cheong explores the complicated nature of the digital divide in her article "Gender and Perceived Internet Efficacy: Examining Secondary Digital Divide Issues in Singapore." Generally, the digital divide is a reference to the gap between those who have access to technology and those who do not. The secondary digital divide is more subtle and, therefore, more difficult to identify and to ameliorate. Decreasing the access gap, for instance, may have the unintended consequence of deepening other divides.

Cheong demonstrates this effect with regard to the gender divide in Singapore. Using a survey of over 700 respondents, well distributed over several demographic characteristics, she reports that despite the extraordinarily high penetration of communication technology in Singapore, women continue to exhibit the same patterns of low perceptions of internet efficacy as are found in countries with much lower rates of diffusion. This study calls on us as researchers to beware of our assumption that all digital divides are due to (and are measured by) access to technological artifacts such as cell phones or the Internet.

We should carefully consider other types and causes of secondary divides, such as the social and cultural norms that reinforce the secondary divide of gender. Alternatively, technologies often present opportunities for us to interrogate our own assumptions about traditional constructs, even exposing possibilities for critique of our own positioning. For example, an excellent exploration of the relationship between culture, society, and technology is offered by Meredith Anderson and Wesley Shrum in their essay "Circumvention and Social Change: ICTs and the Discourse of Empowerment."

Based on extensive interviews and participant observation with women scientists in Kerala, India, the study tells a compelling story of how the introduction of communication technology changes the lives of women not by challenging and changing social codes and norms, but instead by allowing women to circumvent them. The authors point out that women are not denied access to professions or to salary due to gender, as has been (and arguably still is) common in Western countries.

But, according to social custom, women do not have freedom of movement, whether professional or physical. Sustained or unsupervised contact between women and unrelated men is a serious violation of norms. A married woman's mobility is granted by permission of her husband. In this context, Internet access provides a means for women to interact with others, to gain access to knowledge and to professional networks, and to be active and productive scientists without violating gender roles.

As the authors point out, the notion of circumvention as a form of empowerment sits rather uncomfortably with Western sensibilities, especially given the strong emphasis on individualism and individual freedom. Yet, for the participants, it was not that they desired independence, but settled for circumvention. Circumvention was empowering because it allowed them to achieve greater professional success while remaining connected to family and culture in ways that they found important and valuable.

Each of these studies provides important new empirical data of women's experience with technology in non-Western contexts. Further, they each caution us to beware of deterministic assumptions that may be taken for granted in our own research. Gender studies and technology studies face a similar challenge: how to theorize, critique, and ultimately understand an artifact that is both deeply social and self-evidently material. This is the tension Haraway plays at with the cyborg and with FemaleMan and oncomouse.

Unresolvable, it is therefore productive, creating opportunities for us to engage the discourse surrounding technology use, technological development, and policy making. As the presence of communication technologies continues to shape (and be shaped by) our social world, the voice of communication scholars becomes ever more important. The essays in this issue offer valuable contributions to that discourse.

6

Third Wave Feminism

"Third wave" feminism is a phrase commonly used among feminist scholars today to distinguish among earlier periods of feminist activism. As an emerging feminist movement, the third wave is still in the process of defining itself and acknowledges that it is both similar to and different from previous waves of feminist thought and activity. For example, consciousness-raising, a rhetorical strategy utilized extensively by feminists in the 1970s to give voice to women's experiences, remains an important part of developing feminist awareness today. For many feminists and other social critics, consciousness-raising is central to the process of creating a critical awareness of our culture.

Although some studies have addressed the rhetorical functions of consciousness-raising, little attention has been paid to the ways in which the process of consciousness-raising has evolved and been adapted by contemporary feminists. Kathie Sarachild is credited with developing feminist consciousness-raising as a small group process in the early 1970s. Although "second wave" feminists did not invent consciousness-raising, it was a rhetorical strategy that they deliberately cultivated to enable women to share personal experiences of gender discrimination in conversations and meetings designed specifically for these purposes.

Sarachild's original conception of consciousness-raising entailed women who met in small groups to share their experiences through personal testimony in order to relate to one another and generalize experiences. Consciousness-raising, although conducted in these informal groups, included organizers who encouraged each woman to contribute her own experiences. The groups then discussed forms of resisting oppression, actions, and organizing new consciousness-raisings groups. The Redstockings Collective argued that this process was a way to unite women so that they could understand that their individual experiences were not isolated events and to eliminate self-blame.

Kamen describes second wave consciousness-raising as a process where women "learned to ask new questions about themselves, built self-esteem and a sense of entitlement to opportunity, gave names to their common experiences and discovered that they were not alone. Consciousness-raising was a foundation for change ..." Consciousness-raising for women was rooted in recognizing personal oppression.

Karlyn Kohrs Campbell's 1973 groundbreaking article, "The Rhetoric of Women's Liberation: An Oxymoron," describes a consciousness-raising process designed to address affirmation "of the affective, of the validity of personal experience, of the necessity for self-exposure and self-criticism, of the value of dialogue, and of the goal of autonomous, individual decision making".

Although consciousness-raising usually occurred in small groups, other forms of sharing individual experiences such as essays, articles, and lectures also contributed to the process of consciousness-raising. Consciousness-raising allowed women to bridge their separation or address the fact that their lives were often under the control of their husbands, fathers, or male employers. Women often had negative self-images, in part because of their lack of voice and subordination to men. Furthermore, Campbell contends "Because oppressed groups tend to develop passive personality traits, consciousness-raising is an attractive communication style to people working for social change".

In most accounts, the rhetorical strategy of consciousness-raising has been defined as a small group process. For instance,

Cheseboro, Cragan, and McCullough define consciousness-raising as "a personal, face-to-face interaction which appears to create new psychological orientations for those involved in the process.... the personal face-to-face interaction technique is selected because it is consistent with the radical revolutionary's belief that shared personal experience should generate political theory and action".

They explain that the process of consciousness-raising results in a group identity where "members often perceive other group members as 'sisters' and 'brothers' of a new 'cultural family' and 'community'". This group identity for feminists is often referred to as sisterhood. The concept of sisterhood, however, is not without its flaws. Campbell observes that the notion of sisterhood has not appealed to all women, and has "proved false for many and has been attacked by those who felt excluded from much of its talk, action, and organization".

In this chapter, we argue that third wave feminist consciousness-raising has evolved in style, substance, and function in comparison to previous conceptions of consciousness-raising. Consciousness-raising experiences and practices have been called the foundation for social activism and movements. Examining how consciousness-raising as a rhetorical option has changed is important for understanding how individuals develop a critical consciousness in contemporary contexts. This study of the evolution of consciousness-raising offers new insight into the process of social awareness and how individuals acquire and enact critical perspectives.

Our research centers on the rhetoric of third wave feminists and seeks to expand communication scholars' understanding of the rhetorical function and stylistic elements of contemporary feminist consciousness-raising. While third wave feminism continues to be an ambiguous concept, it can be generally understood as an area of emerging feminist thought, often embraced by young women and men, that is informed by predecessor feminisms as well as changing cultural conditions and expectations.

Heywood and Drake argue that, for them, third wave feminism is "a generational perspective, gathering the voices of young activists struggling to come to terms with the historical specificity of our feminisms and with the times in which we came of age (the late 1970s through the late 1980s)". Heywood and Drake also explain that third wave feminism is concerned with:

> The development of modes of thinking that can come to terms with the multiple, constantly shifting bases of oppression in relation to the multiple, interpenetrating axes of identity, and the creation of a coalition politics based on these understandings-understandings that acknowledge the existence of oppression, even though it is not fashionable to say so.

Dicker and Piepmeier further illustrate what third wave feminism means to them: "We argue that the third wave has less to do with a neat generational divide than with a cultural context: the third wave consists of those of us who have developed our sense of identity in a world shaped by technology, global capitalism, multiple models of sexuality, changing national demographics, and declining economic vitality".

To illustrate the process of third wave consciousness-raising, we examine the rhetoric of third wave feminist discourse. For our purposes here, we have selected excerpts from six influential feminist works. The first text, Manifesta: Young Women, Feminism, and the Future, was written by Jennifer Baumgardner and Amy Richards. The other five sources that we have used are collections of personal essays and critical reflections on third wave feminism.

These anthologies include: To Be Real: Telling the Truth and Changing the Face of Feminism (1995) edited by Rebecca Walker, Men Doing Feminism edited by Tom Digby, Listen Up: Voices from the Next Feminist Generation, New Expanded Edition edited by Barbara Findlen, Colonize This!: Young Women of Colour on Today's Feminism edited by Daisy Hernandez and Bushra Rehman, and Catching a Wave: Reclaiming Feminism for the 21st Century edited by Rory Dicker and Alison Piepmeier. These texts represent an emerging genre of feminist thinking in which the writers identify themselves as third wave feminists or as members of a new generation of feminist thinkers.

Furthermore, these texts are commonly recognized as constitutive of third wave feminist thinking. These works were also selected because their writers employ a number of different consciousnessraising approaches and represent the ideas of a diverse group of women and men about the nature, scope, and functions of feminism in the twenty-first century. As the rhetorical problems surrounding feminism have shifted over the last forty years, feminists have adapted the process of consciousness-raising to address the current rhetorical situation more adequately.

Our study of the rhetoric of third wave consciousness-raising begins with a discussion of how third wave feminists define their version of feminism. We then proceed with our examination in two sections: 1) the rhetorical problem and cultural context for third wave feminists and 2) the evolution of consciousness-raising as a response to current rhetorical exigencies. Specifically, we aim to show how third wave feminist consciousness-raising instills a critical perspective that focuses on personal and social injustices.

We argue that these rhetorical responses function as consciousness-raising in the public sphere, through mass media, popular culture, and college classrooms, fostering both public and private dialogue about gender inequities and aiming at self-persuasion. We conclude that this rhetoric seeks to increase understanding and to embrace diverse feminist perspectives. Thus, from a communication perspective it provides a new framework in which to understand the rhetorical functions of consciousness-raising.

FEMINISM IN TRANSITION

Third wave feminists are in the process of creating a body of work that speaks to a new generation of feminists. Third wave feminists have benefited substantially from the work of their feminist predecessors, but these successes have also created a high level of expectation. Astrid Henry, in Catching a Wave, explains how young women today seem to have a more tenuous relationship with feminism:

To understand feminism as something we inherit rather than create on our own has significant consequences for the ways in which we take on the cause of feminism and identify ourselves as feminists. Because women of my generation often do not experience feminism as a process-that is, as something we actively choose or help to create-we have a much more ambivalent identification with it. Even for those of us who see ourselves as aligned with second wave feminism, our sense of "owning" feminism can still feel tenuous.

We own feminism in the sense that it is our birthright, yet in other ways it is not ours. It belongs to another generation, another group of women: second wave feminists. They were the ones who went through the heady experience of creating feminism; we just get to reap the benefits. Third wave feminism, then, can be understood as an attempt by emerging feminists to make the movement their own. However, there appears to be no universal consensus about how that should happen.

Third wave feminism is an ambiguous and amorphous concept, likely because as an emerging movement, it has yet to develop any sense of collective identity. Third wave feminist texts demonstrate the wide experiences that both unite and divide young women and men. Although some third wave feminists actively attempt to distance themselves from previous feminist waves, it is more often the case that third wave feminists see themselves as building on the legacy of feminism. Dicker and Piepmeier explain that, "Typically, the third wave is thought of as a younger generation's feminism, one that rejects traditional-or stereotypical-understandings of feminism and as such is antithetical or oppositional to its supposed predecessor, the second wave. The feminism we claim, however, aligns itself with second wave strategies for recognizing and addressing structural inequalities".

In fact, many third wave feminists do not define their ideology as a distinct, new brand of feminism, but rather, they acknowledge their indebtedness and connections to second wave thinking. Roxanne Harde observes "I think you would be hard-pressed to find any idea among third wave thinkers that is wholly unique and distinct from the second wave".

Third wave feminists, then, draw on the experiences of their predecessors and then adapt their rhetorical strategies to new situations and cultural contexts.

OBSTACLES IN CONTEMPORARY CONSCIOUSNESS-RAISING

Consciousness-raising was initiated by many second wave feminist groups as a way to address women's negative self-concepts, divisions between women, and counter-persuasive social forces, such as fathers and husbands resistant to ideas of feminism and women's rights. For third wave feminists today, the rhetorical obstacles of second wave feminist consciousness-raising still exist, but many young feminists have a different sense of self-concept, are no longer divided significantly from other women, and have more supportive feminist-minded women and men in their lives.

The rhetorical problem for third wave feminists, then, is how to address the cultural context of a society that has afforded young women new opportunities, but at the same time, created new barriers. Some of the rhetorical obstacles that third wave feminists encounter in consciousness-raising include a perception that feminist successes have rectified most, if not all, gender inequities, a lack of recognition of contemporary and covert gender inequities, feminist backlash and negative stereotypes of feminism, and a historical understanding of feminism as an exclusive movement.

These barriers mean that feminist rhetoric has to address and prove that gender inequities still exist, refute stereotypes and feminist backlash, and create greater identification among those who call themselves feminists. Legal and political changes have created a different cultural context for feminist thinking and activism. Legal changes, such as the legalization of abortion, more effective birth control methods, laws against sexual harassment and workplace discrimination, and Title IX have created greater protections for women.

Children are raised with a sense of entitlement and empowerment because of legal, economic, political, and social protections and changing attitudes that are both different and similar to women who were raised before second wave feminist thought was widespread. For example, Whitney Walker, in Listen Up, explains that she was raised in an atmosphere of equality: "I was raised on feminist children's books like Free to Be ... You and Me, and I knew boys weren't better than girls. I also refused to believe they were stronger. When bullies picked on me or my friends, I hit them in the knees with my Holly Hobby lunch pail and that was that".

In numerous accounts, third wave feminists note that they grew up exposed to feminist ideas and actions, but came to realize later in their lives that gender inequities still persisted. The pervasive rhetoric of equality that these contemporary feminists encountered growing up means that consciousness-raising rhetoric has to address how and why gender inequities continue, a theme that third wave feminists expound on continually in their work.

Gender discrimination and exclusion have, in many cases, become more difficult to recognize, especially because of this unquestioned belief in the success of the women's movement and the presence of gender equality. The failure to realize that not everyone has this same set of assumptions about equality may leave some people ill-equipped to deal with discrimination when confronted with it. Ellen Neuborne, in Listen Up, illustrates how her feminist upbringing left her unable to recognize or address forms of gender inequity that she had been programmed to ignore:

I am a daughter of the movement. How did I fall for this? I thought the battle had been won. I thought that sexism was a remote experience, like the Depression. Gloria had taken care of all that in the seventies. Imagine my surprise. And while I was blissfully unaware, the perpetrators were getting smarter. What my mother taught me to look for-pats on the butt, honey, sweetie, and cupcake, make me some coffee-are not the methods of choice for today's sexists. Those were just the fringes of what they were really up to. Sadly, enough of them have figured out how to mouth the words of equality while still behaving like pigs. They're harder to spot.

These more subtle forms of discrimination lure some people into thinking that there is no longer a need for feminism or feminist consciousness-raising. This masking ultimately undermines a collective understanding of discrimination at all levels. The successes of feminism have also led some people to conclude that feminism is no longer necessary. For example, in a 1998 survey, 48% of women surveyed answered that feminism is relevant to most women, but only 28% of women answered that feminism today is relevant to them personally.

Furthermore, media portrayals have led women to regard feminists negatively. In the same 1998 survey, only 32% of women answered that they view feminists favorably, while 43% answered that they had an unfavorable impression. This negative perception appears to be a relatively recent phenomenon since earlier surveys do not reflect the same level of disdain. For instance, a 1986 Newsweek survey indicated that, "56 per cent of women consider themselves feminists; 71 per cent say that the movement has improved their lives; only 4 per cent describe themselves as antifeminist".

Although these surveys are only limited samples of the population, the difference in women's perceptions about feminism between 1986 and 1998 is alarmingly clear. The backlash and perpetuation of stereotypes of feminists undoubtedly contribute to this contrast. Perhaps the most prominent negative stereotypes of feminists are based on physical appearance and radical personas. Societal stereotypes cast feminists as hairy, man-hating, lesbian, ugly, radical, and bra-burning, despite that such characteristics may challenge normative thinking. Erica Gilbert-Levin, in Listen Up, explains her experiences with publicly declaring herself a feminist, "Students joked about it during classes, calling me a man-hater and warning that radical, hairy-legged feminists were going to take over the school and make all the boys their slaves".

Although these stereotypes are not new, contemporary feminists must grapple with the fact that these stereotypes have been prevalent for so long that they have become the standard conception of feminists. Additionally, ad hominem attacks, red herrings, and hyperbole such as the media caricature of the "feminazi" construct a rhetorical barrier for consciousness-raising in contemporary American society. Consciousness-raising as a rhetorical strategy must address these images in order to build a space where audiences are willing to try out feminism as an ideological construct.

As Barbara Findlen, the editor of the Listen Up anthology, observes, third wave feminists are aware of this rhetorical need to address these stereotypes: "Some young women do fear the feminist label, largely because of the stereotypes and distortions that still abound. If something or someone is appealing, fun or popular, it or she can't be feminist. Feminists are often assumed to be strident, man-hating, unattractive-and lesbian". Another rhetorical problem that third wave feminists address in their consciousness-raising efforts concerns the perceived exclusivity in second wave feminism. Second wave feminism has been critiqued as a predominately white, middle-class phenomenon that failed to speak to the experiences of women of colour, the working class, and other marginalized individuals.

Third wave feminist texts such as *To Be Real, Listen Up, and Colonize* focus on diversity as a primary issue often observing how feminism has failed to include women of colour and other diverse aspects of women. For example, Paula Austin explains her perception of what feminism has meant and why she has felt excluded: "I have felt left out of feminism mostly because it leaves out women who looked like my mother-traditionally feminine, of colour, poor, powerful despite the impacts of oppression on her psyche. It leaves no room for women who find their power through a perceived powerlessness". In a similar vein, Susan Muaddi Darraj explains how her experiences with second wave feminism created a sense of exclusion:

I realized then that most of the women in the class were upper-middle and middle-class white women-and I felt like a complete outsider. Perhaps they could understand Friedan because her brand of feminism spoke directly to their experience. But it didn't speak to mine. I didn't view housework as a mark of oppression. There was a certain sense of pride placed on a clean, welcoming home, and both my parents had always placed value on it.

Although there is certainly debate about how second wave feminism excluded some and included others, these writers demonstrate that how they learn about feminism and their sense of cultural memory is marked by this sense of exclusion. These rhetorical obstacles, in many ways, are similar to those that second wave feminists faced; they undoubtedly encountered negative stereotypes, backlash, and a variety of other obstacles.

However, these rhetorical exigencies in conjunction with changes in contemporary society, work together to create a set of rhetorical problems that are different than what previous feminists encountered. The evolution of these rhetorical problems over time demands a rhetorical response that is adapted to this contemporary situation. The rhetorical features of traditional small-group conscious raising were designed to overcome a distinct set of barriers, and as these barriers have evolved so must the consciousness-raising designed to address them.

FEATURES OF CONSCIOUSNESS-RAISING IN THIRD WAVE FEMINISM

Third wave feminist consciousness-raising draws heavily from the practice of consciousness-raising developed during the second wave. Campbell argues that the stylistic features of second wave consciousness-raising are the result of strategic adaptation to an acute rhetorical problem. She claims that consciousness-raising is "characterized by rhetorical interactions that emphasize affective proofs and personal testimony, participation and dialogue, self-revelation and self-criticism, the goal of autonomous decision making through self-persuasion, and the strategic use of techniques for 'violating the reality structure'".

These features persist in third wave consciousness-raising, but additional features have become apparent as feminists adapt their rhetorical responses to a changing set of problems and cultural conditions. In this section, we illustrate the rhetorical features, both stylistic and substantive, of third wave consciousness-raising which include sharing personal stories in public venues like books and magazines, sharing experiences and reading feminist theory in classrooms, consuming popular culture, exploring issues of diversity and new audiences, and creating new options for self-expression.

In the 1970s, personal testimony in small groups was a key feature of second wave consciousness-raising since it allowed women to recognize the connected nature of their personal experiences. Although third wave feminists tend not to utilize the small group format for consciousness-raising, personal stories continue to play an important role in helping people recognize that their experiences of oppression or discrimination are not isolated. In the third wave, these stories are still very much a part of consciousness-raising, except that these personal stories tend to appear in public venues like anthologies, books, and feminist magazines such as Bitch and Bust.

Furthermore, these stories function as a major rhetorical component of consciousness-raising due to the diversity of texts available. Women may engage in conscious-raising with their female friends and colleagues, but these books allow their readers to engage with a number of ideas they may not encounter in their personal or professional lives. For example, third wave feminist anthologies contain a number of stories about issues such as relationships with one's mother or father, first experiences with sex, the reflections of a feminist fitness instructor, testing positive for HIV, generational differences within families, being a feminist super model, having an abortion, and choosing to become a parent.

These stories rely heavily on personal experience that often center on a moment when the writers needed feminism, when they came to a feminist consciousness, or when they were able to overcome some personal obstacle. For example, Aisha Hakim-Dyce shares her decision to become a seminude go-go dancer:

I had never thought that my underemployed status would lead me to seriously consider a stint that would require me to shake my breasts and gyrate my hips to the catcalls, whistles, and sexually explicit suggestions of men. I believed that my identity as a politically astute and active woman would somehow protect me from exploitative situations that having a politically correct worldview would somehow translate into tangible economic benefits. Reality check, anyone? ... The more depressed I became because of my economic situation, the less manipulative such work seemed. After all, I began to reason, if silly men want to give away their money in order to watch my breasts and hips jiggle, why not?

This story illustrates how personal testimony can connect the lives of individuals who share the same set of circumstances or reveal personal thoughts and secretive moments to others. Similar stories allow readers to explore diverse feminist perspectives that may not be available to them within their immediate circle of friends and family. These stories often function as a cathartic mechanism for the writers who can share the private thoughts that may have caused them anguish and agony in the course of determining how to resist oppression, objectification, and exclusion.

These stories also function to expose their readers to new ideas and situations and raise consciousness about the diversity of women's experiences in the world. These stories and personal narratives are similar to those in earlier feminist anthologies, such as This Bridge Called My Back, but focus on contemporary experiences of life for young women in the 21st century.

As Angela Davis (1995) explains in the afterward of To Be Real, "in seeking to dismantle this status quo and break free of its strictures, many of these writers attempt to work through their often complex relationships with the notion of social activism as responsibility by recalling embarrassing childhood experiences with radical mothers, or by rejecting the concept of "political correctness," which so often is assumed to be an activist posture". Sharing personal stories, then, becomes an avenue of consciousness-raising not only for the audience, but also for the individuals who share their personal experiences of oppression and discrimination.

For third wave feminists, private sphere consciousness-raising may include unorganized and informal conversations that take place among family, friends, and colleagues. However, consciousness-raising is not limited to the private sphere and is now much more likely to be a public experience. For example, women's studies classes and other classes that include feminist components are responsible for creating a generation well-versed in feminist theory, ideas, and activism.

Third wave feminists are exposed to feminist critique and philosophy in college, graduate school, or even sexual harassment seminars in the work place. This theme of feminist consciousness-raising in institutional and educational settings appears repeatedly in third wave rhetoric. One woman explains how the college classroom fostered a critical perspective for her:

But during my first year of college, nothing upside downed my world as much as Women's Studies 101. I learned that maybe I wasn't so odd after all, because maybe, just maybe, patriarchal social constructions had caused the various forms of discrimination I'd experienced all my life, both as a woman and as a person of colour. The other women in the class connected with me; we had a shared understanding. I was overjoyed. I embraced my new friend feminism.

Learning feminism and participating in consciousness-raising in the classroom are unique experiences and a direct result of the legacy of feminist successes in the United States, since women's studies classes and topics were not common in the 1960s and 1970s.

College and high school teachers and students also have a much wider array of feminist texts to choose from, so that individuals can find texts that speak to their experience, expose them to new ideas, challenge their notions of what feminism means, and create new ground for feminist theory. For example, Susan Muaddi Darraj (2002) explains this diversity of rhetorical possibilities:

I had started reading the work of Black feminists, such as bell hooks, who took on Betty Friedan full force. She challenged the relevance of Friedan's ideas about housewives to Black women, who have always had to work. Her work led me to

Gloria Anzaldua, who led me to Barbara Smith, and the list grew. I was heartened by the fact that Black women and other women of colour had the courage to carve a feminism of their own out of the monolithic block that was generally accepted as "feminism."

Similarly, Cristina Tzintzun in Colonize This! explains how she personally connected with feminist texts: "I read all of the feminist literature that I could get my hands on. They gave me the support I needed. They made me feel less alone. They made me proud to call myself feminist and queer. Those books taught me more than my [high] school ever could".

These texts create the possibility of defining feminism for oneself, since an individual must decide which theories explain and resonate with her own experiences, but also bridge experiences and connect women together. The wide diversity of feminist texts creates more opportunities for identification and helps build on the idea that there are many different kinds of feminism and that many different kinds of people are feminists. In today's cultural context of diversity, economic and social pressure, and individualism, this flexibility is an extremely appealing rhetorical feature of consciousness-raising.

Popular culture has also become a viable forum for third wave feminist consciousness-raising. Women are increasingly visible in television, film, music, and other media outlets. There are growing numbers of feminist role models and cultural icons that girls and women admire and respect. Kristina Sheryl Wong (2003), in Catching a Wave, explains how popular culture functions for young feminists:

"The concept of feminism has become so academic that only a select few understand its new meaning. In spite of this, feminist politics can be shared with the world if it is carefully disguised in the mass media. Popular culture provides an effective vehicle to carry the self-celebrating concepts of third wave feminism".

As Wong observes, popular culture female icons may speak to young women in ways that academic feminism cannot. Many of these female icons represent strong, independent women with whom young women identify. Some television shows have inspired third wave feminists through the use of empowered female characters; audiences come to believe that women are capable of the same kinds of action packed adventures as men. For instance, Michele Byers explains how Buffy the Vampire Slayer functions as a vehicle for feminist consciousness-raising for its audiences:

> Buffy's redefinition of girlhood and womanhood intersects with the question of feminism. The most explicit link I see between Buffy and feminism as a political ideology and practice is that both espouse a belief in the rights of women and, significantly, the right to equality in all things. The series dramatizes the struggle that many young women face to be strong, independent, articulate, ambitious, and powerful. And this is done without erasing women's desire for connection. The feminist inclination of this show also appears in its refusal to make its female characters masculine.

Television shows and movies that include characters like Buffy expose viewers to new ideas of female empowerment, and such shows are increasingly common and popular among female (and sometimes male) audiences. Popular music is another form of popular culture that can serve as an avenue for feminist consciousness-raising. Gwendolyn Pough states that "My development as a Black woman and a Black feminist is deeply tied to my love of hip hop". She further explains that "Another way that hip hop helped me to develop a feminist consciousness was the exposure it gave me to sexual harassment and the attitude it gave me to deal with it".

Although Pough acknowledges that hip-hop and rap can have gendered and heterosexist tendencies, her ability to simultaneously enjoy and critically evaluate such music instilled a sense of consciousness. Similarly, other third wave feminists cite Ani DiFranco, Madonna, Courtney Love, or Alanis Morissette as key feminist influences. Erin Harde explains that "For me, some women in music present the most accessible, and therefore influential, feminist agenda of the third wave. Consider the lyrics of Alanis Morissette, who was probably one of the first women rockers to make me consider oppression and emancipation".

Popular culture icons have long influenced how young women and others involved in social consciousness become aware of social injustices and their own sense of oppression, yet most academic literature has failed to address the power and influence of popular culture in consciousness-raising. However, this examination of third wave feminist texts reveals that many young women are empowered by female role models and become aware of their own oppression and the possibilities for emancipation through the consumption of popular culture. More importantly, young female audiences take away messages of empowerment from popular television shows and music, even though these texts may be problematic from other feminist perspectives.

DIVERSE EXPERIENCES AND AUDIENCES

Many third wave feminist texts deliberately seek to include diverse ethnic, social, and economic perspectives to create a sense of inclusiveness. This practice encourages many third wave feminists to read and know diverse perspectives that extend beyond their own. Furthermore, much third wave literature focuses on traditionally marginalized perspectives rather than more dominant or mainstream feminist perspectives. As Jee Yeun Lee explains:

"I want to emphasize that the feminism that I and other young women come to today is one that is at least sensitive to issues of exclusion. If perhaps twenty years ago charges of racism, classism, and homophobia were not taken seriously, today they are the cause of extreme anguish and soul-searching. I am profoundly grateful to older feminists of colour and their white allies who struggled to bring U.S. feminist movements to this point".

Rory Dicker and Alison Piepmeier, the editors of Catching a Wave, also explain that "Many of the goals of the third wave are similar to those of the second wave, though some, such as its insistence on women's diversity, are new". The third wave anthologies, Colonize This!, Listen Up, and To Be Real are predominantly about the experiences of women of colour and have made explicit efforts to include a number of diverse perspectives. Third wave feminists also seek to extend their consciousness-raising efforts to audiences that include men. Hopkins suggests that feminism would be better understood as a critical strategy made up of a set of beliefs, actions, goals, and positions concerning gender oppression in our culture rather than a movement for and about women.

A group of third wave feminists offers a similar definition, "A third wave feminist politics is more properly a politics of gender, which involves critiquing and reevaluating both male and female social roles so that both genders may live in peace with one another". These definitions of feminism shift the focus from women's oppression to the harm that patriarchal oppression does to all people. For many third wave feminists, these inclusive definitions of feminism more closely resonate with their personal experience in a patriarchal culture, the importance of their relationships with men, and the desire to create more inclusive feminisms.

Although consciousness-raising is a difficult process, young men are increasingly joining the feminist ranks. Katz laments that there is very little consciousness-raising leadership among men since speaking out against other men's sexism or violence toward women is contrary to the traditional socialization of men. Two feminist texts, *Men Doing Feminism* and *To Be Real*, where men share their personal experiences with feminism, seek to expand the realm of feminism.

Schmitt explains that an important rhetorical barrier to feminist consciousness for men is the aversion to relationships that men are taught throughout their lives. Their quest to appear independent and self-sufficient inhibits their ability to share the kinds of personal experiences that lead to a consciousness shift. Like third wave women, some men indicate that they came to consciousness as an undergraduate or graduate student in women's studies classes or other classes that utilized feminist perspectives.

Additionally, feminism increasingly plays an important role in their intellectual formation. Young men are also more likely to have been raised in a feminist household. Men who have a feminist consciousness, or who identify themselves as feminists, are then in a position to encourage other men to rethink their habits and behaviors. Julia Wood suggests that "one rhetorical strategy used by profeminist men is performing a traitorous identity, in which a member of a group criticizes particular attitudes and actions that are common and accepted among members of that group". In fact, this support network is critical since social change happens and feminist consciousness develops when men are challenged by a caring, compassionate community.

OPTIONS FOR SELF EXPRESSION

Consciousness-raising creates numerous options for self-expression. Elements of consciousness-raising found in popular culture, the classroom, or books and magazines allow individuals to take what they want from the emerging feminist theory and leave what is not useful. These rhetorical functions of consciousness-raising also create new possibilities for voice.

Lee explains that her experiences with consciousness-raising allowed her to express herself in new ways: "For the first time I found people who articulated those murky half-formed feelings that I could previously only express incoherently as 'But that's not fair!' ... So to come to a class that addressed these issues directly and gave me the words for all those pent-up feelings and frustrations were a tremendously affirming and empowering experience". In a more specific example, Kiini Ibura Salaam explains how feminism influenced her consciousness:

"Today I can identify exactly what catcalling is and how it functions in women's lives. At its most basic level catcalling is sexual harassment. Verbal assaults, invitations and compliments are opportunities for men to demonstrate who is predator and who is prey. One catcall yanks a woman out of the category of human being and places her firmly in the position of sexual object".

These women observe that a feminist consciousness enabled them to build a new set of vocabularies that originated from their critical consciousness that then fostered consciousness or critical thought in other areas. Lisa Weiner-Mahfuz similarly explains her connection to consciousness and expression: "I did not have the language to articulate why these feelings were so personal to me until I started exploring feminism. Feminism awakened my commitment to fighting injustice. Feminism challenged me to see how deeply I had internalized my own assimilation".

Not only does feminist consciousness-raising provide women and men with a vocabulary to describe their experiences, but it also helps illuminate the interconnected nature of oppression and inculcate a more critical perspective on the world. Lourdes-marie Prophete describes this kind of experience:

I get a lot of the "aha" factor when I think about how gender roles and sexism framed my life and my mom's. The "aha" factor is when you have always felt something but couldn't articulate it until someone gives you a naming system that allows you to point at all the pieces. While in Gambia a couple of years after college, I was criticized at a market by a female merchant for being too aggressive when I negotiated the price. She said I acted like a man and I should remember that I am just a girl. I felt horrible and wondered if I had been rude when I realized her criticism that "I wasn't acting like a girl" came from her acceptance of gender roles and male privilege. By analyzing the incident this way, I was also creating a mental world where things can be different.

Critical consciousness, then, not only leads to more avenues of self-expression but may also spur personal activism because once something has been named and described; it can become the target of social change. In this chapter, we argue that third wave feminists have employed consciousness-raising in ways both similar and different to the feminist consciousness-raising groups of the 1960s and 1970s. In essence, third wave feminists still use consciousness-raising for the same reasons that Campbell and Cheseboro, Cragan, and McCullough have identified, yet third wave feminists have also used consciousness-raising to address new demands and have employed different rhetorical features of consciousness-raising, both in terms of style and substance.

While third wave feminists may encounter a different set of rhetorical problems, it remains to be seen if their use of stories, popular culture, and version of feminism will successfully address these rhetorical problems. As an emerging movement, third wave feminism is still in the process of determining its rhetorical character and its rhetorical needs. Third wave feminist consciousness-raising, then, provides an expanding framework for understanding the functions of consciousness-raising as a rhetorical option. Third wave consciousness-raising rarely occurs in the organized, small group setting that was often the hallmark of consciousness-raising groups in the 1960s and 1970s that Campbell describes.

Instead, consciousness-raising has changed, expanded, and adapted to new social contexts. One of the ways in which third wave consciousness-raising has adapted to the changing cultural climate is that it seeks to address larger and more public audiences. In addition to traditional private sphere settings, consciousness-raising now occurs in semi-public settings, such as classrooms, or in mass media venues, such as anthologies and books that are widely available.

Third wave feminists have responded to the rhetorical exigencies of their time through writing and story telling, as a way to explain how feminism has succeeded in creating greater opportunities for women, but also observing that gender inequities still exist. They also have used these public venues and mass media outlets to address diversity issues within feminism, which would not be possible in the same way within a small group of people who share a particular geographic proximity. In a small group consciousness-raising session, a limited number of people participate in consciousness-raising activities for a limited amount of time.

However, consciousness-raising in books and popular culture can provide a wider array of perspectives than any one small group. The books and anthologies that we examined in this chapter contain essays from writers who differ across a range of identity categories including social and economic class, ethnicity, geographical location, sexual orientation, and gender. Third wave consciousness-raising also resists the demands of a structured time for consciousness-raising, and instead allows individuals to read stories, watch movies, or participates in popular culture whenever and wherever it is convenient for them. This increases the flexibility of consciousness-raising and emphasizes the individual nature of consciousness shifts.

The expanding forms of third wave feminist consciousness-raising also create new avenues to an individual's own consciousness-raising because a person may engage in self-dialogue and persuasion to a greater extent than if she were participating in a small group consciousness-raising session. In small group consciousness-raising, individuals share their experiences interactively with personal revelations, questions, answers, and group discussion.

When individuals read third wave anthologies or consume popular culture, consciousness-raising is produced via internal dialogue rather than a small group interaction. For example, reading essays is a process of conversing with the writers of those texts, but the writers cannot actively respond to the reader's questions and ideas. Instead, readers must engage in their own self-dialogue and self-persuasion that may lead to building one's self-esteem, recognizing gender inequities, or developing a critical perspective. Similarly, in consuming popular culture, a viewer may converse with other audience members while watching a show or listening to music, but ultimately must engage in internal dialogues that may be either subconscious or conscious forms of self-persuasion.

For instance, an individual might watch Buffy the Vampire Slayer and have a conscious internal dialogue about Buffy's strength and independence or women's empowerment. Conversely, this same individual may seek to emulate the characters in the show without ever consciously deciding that there are certain characteristics she wants to embrace for feminist reasons. Third wave feminism enacted in popular culture and through the mass media serves to raise consciousness by allowing individuals to engage in moments of identification and private reflection, even when these texts are consumed in public settings.

Furthermore, many of these feminist-minded audiences are able to focus on messages of empowerment, while simultaneously rejecting messages of sexualization or objectification. Consciousness-raising, then, provides a critical framework where audiences problematize texts rather than passively accept their messages. A better understanding of third wave feminist consciousness-raising rhetoric also contributes to research on rhetorical movements because this third wave rhetoric is both self- and other-directed. Richard Gregg discusses how the ego-function of social protest rhetoric revolves around the self-directed need to affirm one's ego and sense of self.

Charles Stewart identifies several features of this self-directed rhetoric, where individuals realize oppression, establish self-esteem, search for new identities, and locate social standing and status. Sharing and relating to experiences found in third wave anthologies or in women's studies classrooms create space for individuals to develop self-esteem and fulfill this ego-function of rhetoric. Third wave texts are self-directed in that they are cathartic for the writers, but they are also other-directed because readers learn about new experiences or relate to the writers' experiences.

Stewart, using animal rights activists as an example, observes that other-directed rhetoric that addresses disenfranchised groups is also possible. According to Stewart, these individuals seek self-affirmation, location of status, and development of self-identity, but these goals are part of helping others rather than helping themselves; these individuals are not marked by despair or a sense of inferiority. Third wave feminist rhetoric also reflects this other-directed focus because these feminists are focused on the oppression of all people, as their emphasis on diverse audiences indicates. Their rhetoric employs both self and other-directed motives. In essence, the rhetorical practices of third wave feminist consciousness-raising blur the distinctions between the self and other-directed ego functions that Gregg and Stewart outline.

A final implication of third wave consciousness-raising rhetoric is that it does not directly seek to generate social activism, protest, sisterhood, confrontation, or movement. Third wave feminist consciousness-raising may have this effect, but that is not the primary goal. Rather, third wave feminists share their stories, listen to others' stories, consume popular culture in ways that they find empowering, and create new vocabularies to enhance their own lives, but these activities do not necessarily lead to social activism in its traditional forms. While many third wave feminists openly embrace various forms of activism, they do not want to force individuals to take an activist stance or assume that certain forms of activism are appropriate for all people.

In contrast to Cheseboro, Cragan, and McCullough's definition of consciousness-raising and Campbell's description of second wave consciousness-raising, third wave feminists offer their stories and experiences, but do not necessarily expect a social movement to develop as a result. This offering of perspectives without the demand of audience action or change embodies what Foss and Griffin term "invitational rhetoric." In fact, this feature of third wave feminist rhetoric may be precisely what is so confounding to those attempting to understand the third wave by measuring it against traditional notions of feminism and feminist consciousness-raising.

The absence of a shared feminist agenda set of goals or well-defined purposes makes interpreting third wave feminist rhetoric all the more difficult. Yet, in many ways, this is precisely their objective. The writers present their ideas and let the audience decide what to do with them, rather than overtly building a platform for social movement. In essence, third wave feminist rhetoric creates space for sharing experiences, reading stories, and developing a critical perspective. Third wave consciousness-raising rhetoric simultaneously reaches a large, public audience, but also sparks private, internal dialogue and self-persuasion.

Campbell suggests that second wave feminism employed oxymoronic rhetoric in that it was "a genre without a rhetor, a rhetoric in search of an audience, that transforms traditional argumentation into confrontation, that 'persuades' by 'violating the reality structure' but that presumes a consubstantiality so radical that it permits the most intimate of identifications". Third wave feminist rhetoric can also be described as oxymoronic for many of the same reasons, but new oxymorons continue to emerge as consciousness-raising rhetoric is adapted over time to respond to shifting rhetorical situations.

For instance, new oxymorons might include public rhetoric that is designed for private reflection rather than public movement, and a growing number of individuals who are united in name but who do not have a shared agenda for change. Third wave consciousness-raising rhetoric, like the second wave rhetoric that Campbell describes, resists explanation by traditional rhetorical standards because it is persuasive, but it is not aimed at any particular outcome. Rhetorical scholars should strive to better understand the ways in which rhetorical problems and situations both persist and shift over time.

Many of the aspects of the rhetorical problem of feminist advocacy that Campbell identified over thirty years ago are still present today, but there have also been substantial changes in that rhetorical situation as it currently exists. We have examined some of the ways that third wave feminists have adapted traditional consciousness-raising techniques to reach a wider, more public and more diverse audience.

Other social movements that have rhetoric designed to overcome a particular set of exigencies may be well served by a careful examination of the ways that these exigencies have changed in light of emerging cultural conditions. Consciousness-raising that takes into account the evolving nature of rhetorical problems and the audience it is designed to reach will certainly be more effective than strategies that have become outdated or obsolete.

7

Feminism and Mainstream Science Studies

In the 'science wars,' a few natural scientists and other 'defenders' of science have argued that a scientifically ignorant and political subversive movement, bent on destroying science, has arisen within the 'academic left'. This charge has been brought against both contemporary mainstream science and technology studies (STS) scholars such as Harry Collins and Bruno Latour, and many prominent feminist epistemologists and analysts of science, such as Sandra Harding, Donna Haraway, and Evelyn Fox Keller.

It may seem ironic that mainstream STSers and feminists are charged as co-conspirators, and that feminist authors have attracted so much attention (however negative) from the defenders of science: several prominent feminist scholars have been arguing for some time that mainstream STSers show comparatively little interest in feminist work, or in any kind of sustained political attack on science. In her latest book, Donna Haraway wishes "that the 'left' were really so unified!" and complains (not for the first time) about the dearth of references to "oppositional" STS in mainstream accounts:

Either critical scholars in antiracist, feminist cultural studies of science and technology have not been clear enough about racial formation, gender-in-the-making, the forging of class, and the discursive production of sexuality through the constitutive practices of technoscience production themselves, or the science studies scholars aren't reading or listening - or both.... It is past time to end the failure of mainstream and oppositional science studies scholars to engage each other's work. Not everyone agrees. In introducing a volume of essays on gender and technology, one which draws on both feminist and mainstream STS, Rosalind Gill and Keith Grint claim that "We no longer need to argue the case that the relations between gender and technology deserve attention; that argument has been won".

Has the point of feminist work been taken by mainstream STS, as Gill and Grint (and the 'defenders of science') suggest, or is Haraway's diagnosis more accurate? I provide a response to this question by reviewing some recent works in feminist and mainstream STS. My contentions are that feminist STS has begun to integrate the insights of mainstream STS, particularly the branch known as actor-network theory (ANT); that feminist STS, while increasingly recognized by mainstream STSers, is still cast as a separate field of enquiry within mainstream STS; that boundary-work efforts create important differences between these two fields which account in part for the limited dialogue between them; and that further dialogue could substantially improve work in both fields.

Gill and Grint point to the "danger of reifying the idea of a strong mainstream tradition in relation to which feminist researchers see themselves as marginal"; and they suggest that streams of STS viewed as mainstream by feminists may themselves be marginalized in academia in various ways. I think they are quite right. My use of the term 'mainstream STS' posits not a hegemonic influence in academia generally, but a constructed relation to more explicitly politically-radical perspectives, especially feminism. The boundaries between feminist and mainstream STS are not given, but made. But, as constructivists keep pointing out, the fact that something is made does not make it any less 'real.' While I risk reifying a Great Divide between feminism and mainstream STS by talking about the way the Divide is made, ignoring conflicts and boundary-work may be more risky for those of us who want to move beyond simplistic divides.

Bruno Latour contends that "we have never been modern": the modern distinction between nature and society, science and politics, cannot hold. "Science ... is politics by other means". Yet some mainstream STSers seem to suggest that their work is immune from this charge - that they are politically disinterested investigators of science, while feminists are 'just' politicos. To an extent, some feminists have gone along with this, responding that mainstream STS should be more politically engaged.

The politically engaged/politically neutral dichotomy in STS is itself a deeply political boundary-work device that justifies each field's lack of engagement with the other. In combination, the fields can contribute to more sophisticated understandings of both the internal workings of scientific practice and broader social and political relations - moving beyond the internalist/externalist dichotomy as well as the engaged/neutral divide.

Inevitably, my introductions reflect my research interests, reading choices, and personal interactions with mainstream and feminist STS, which lead to particular understandings of the fields and their interrelations. I have a broader and more long-standing interest in feminist work. But it is not just in this sense that my introductions are not disinterested summaries; they also provide a backdrop to the particular arguments I want to make.

They trouble each field's representations of the other. One way to deconstruct these representations and pave the way to greater cross-fertilization is to provide alternative readings. My introductions also reflect each field's self-representations. I leave to others the task of evaluating the validity of these, though it seems to me that feminists' and mainstreamers' representations of their communities have a hearing on the evolution of debates between and within the fields.

FEMINIST SCIENCE AND TECHNOLOGY STUDIES

In the past twenty years, feminist theorists and researchers have been among the most prolific contributors to debates about science, technology, and knowledge in the social sciences and humanities. Feminist scholarship is, of course, united by a focus on questions of gender. But, despite frequent assumptions to the contrary, such a focus is anything but narrow. It allows for very diverse approaches to studying science and technology and produces many insights into issues intimately bound up with, but not limited to, questions of gender: issues of power and inequality, varieties of knowing and knowers, discourse and materiality, subjectivity and objectivity, embodiment, representation, work, resistance, and the lay/expert divide, for example.

Reviews of feminist work tend to address diverse areas of scholarship simultaneously. They point to progressions and new streams, but tend to present them as complementing earlier feminist inquiries. This is not to suggest that feminist work is monolithic or that an orthodox consensus has developed - quite the contrary. Rather, there is an acknowledgment of old debts and, despite suggestions of fruitful new directions; only rarely is there explicit disparagement of the ones the foremothers took.

As in feminism generally, there is a preoccupation with tensions between the need to respect differences while strategically forging bases for solidarity. Thus, there is a shared goal of providing insights into the diversely articulated interactions of science and axes of difference and equality (primarily gender, but also race, ethnicity, sexuality, class, and ability). Feminist analyses pertinent to this discussion can be roughly categorized into four areas: the experiences of women in science and technology; the effects of science and technology on women; cultural constructions of gender in science and technology; and feminist theories of scientific knowledge.

First, the experiences of women and other marginalized groups in scientific and technological education work, and research has generated a great deal of feminist scholarship. Feminist scholars have documented practices of exclusion that effectively discourage women from participating in many scientific disciplines. Much of this work discusses explicit forms of discrimination, such as differentials in pay and employment status, sexual harassment, and the failure of scientific communities to acknowledge important work by women scientists; other sources focus on more subtle barriers, such as the effects of chilly climates, gender roles, the masculine cultures of science and technology, and female under-representati on on women's interest in pursuing scientific and technical careers.

But feminist scholars have also documented that, despite these obstacles, some women have developed strong interests in, and made important (though often unacknowledged) contributions to, scientific and technological development, as professional scientists and technologists and as amateur scientists and popularizers of science. Some feminist literature has pointed to the possibility of doing science differently and has argued that differing familial responsibilities of male and female scientists affect the nature of their work.

Finally, feminist scholarship addresses the exclusion of women's concerns in science and technology and ways in which this might be rectified through new pedagogical, research, and assessment approaches. Second, the effects of science and technology on women's lives are explored. Many of the earlier works explore how genetic and reproductive technologies affect women, often in highly negative ways. The implications of domestic and computer technologies and chemicals on women's work and health have been analysed also.

Some early feminist work presented almost uniformly negative depictions of the effects of science and technology on women, and implied that certain technologies are intrinsically sexist. Recently, more nuanced approaches have become the norm. For example, Jennifer Terry and Melodie Calvert argue that, although men and women are "situated differently" regarding technology, particular technologies do not oppress all women in the same ways, nor do they n ecessarily oppress all women. Terry and Calvert destabilize the notion of gender - it "is not a property of the body existing to it, but an effect of shifting boundaries" - and argue that outright rejection of technology not only isn't an option, but that critical engagement may provide opportunities to transform, invent, and make decisions about technology.

A third theme in feminist science studies is the cultural construction of gender - and its interaction with other axes of difference, particularly race - in science and technology. An earlier distinction in feminism between sex and gender has given way to analyses of the ways in which both sex and gender are constructed - analyses which are not anti-materialist but are focussed upon the meanings made of the material, and the ways in which these meanings change over time and across disciplines. Notable contributions include analyses of the connections between the Church and the masculinist cultures of science and technology and of ideologies of dominance and control in science which construct women and nature in similar ways.

Feminists have argued that gendered assumptions and metaphors configure technology and scientific theories and models, both in disciplines that are explicitly concerned with sex and gender and in those for which sexual difference is not a primary focus of investigation. These works assert that gender is not peripheral but integral to the doing of science, and not merely in the senses that most scientists are male, that women scientists have been marginalized, or that individual scientists have sexist biases that affect their work. Rather, cultural notions about gender and race are embedded in - used as an unacknowledged resource in the development of- technology and scientific methods, theories, models, and research problems; and technology and science help to configure gender and race in ways that vary historically.

The hope is that understanding these embeddings and configurations can enable progressive reworking of technologies. The biological and medical sciences have been the most frequent targets of this kind of feminist analysis. These sciences have obvious and concrete effects on women's lives, have made pejorative claims about women's nature, and have been the subject of much grassroots feminist activism. Also, many prominent feminist critics of science - Lynda Birke, Ruth Bleier, Donna Haraway, Ruth Hubbard, Anne Fausto-Sterling, Evelyn Fox Keller, Pat Spallone - were trained in biological and related sciences.

Few analyses of gendered metaphors in physics, mathematics, chemistry has been undertaken, presumably because the influence of cultural constructions of gender seems to be less obvious in these fields and they seem more 'gender-neutral' in their effects. However, Donna Hughes and Margaret Wertheim have argued that statistics and physics contain profoundly gendered assumptions. Other feminist analyses of the 'hard' sciences and mathematics surely will follow.

Finally, within feminist epistemology, lively and engaging debates rage about the nature of scientific knowledge (hegemonic, universalistic, objectivistic, and/or androcentric), the possibilities (or lack thereof) of distinctively women's knowledges that can contest scientific knowledge, the relations between scientific and non-scientific knowledge, and the correspondence (or lack thereof) between knowledge and reality in both scientific and experiential knowledges. Sandra Harding defines three prototypical positions: feminist empiricism, feminist standpoint theory, and feminist postmodernism. According to Harding, feminist empiricism advocates the scientific method and merely seeks to eradicate the biases (such as sexism and racism) that may intrude upon 'good' or unbiased scientific work.

This was a beginning position for feminist critique, often promoted by feminists who were practicing scientists. However, it is rarely espoused by contemporary feminist theorists. The term 'feminist empiricism' has been appropriated by Lynn Hankinson Nelson and Helen Longino, but their position bears little resemblance to what Harding has in mind. While they accept the notion that knowledge claims should be evidence-based, they emphasize that evidence standards are not self-evident nor defined exclusively by the scientific method-they are set by epistemological communities, only some of which are scientific.

In this emphasis on local and communal knowledge practices, their perspective has more in common with standpoint theory and feminist postmodernism than the feminist empiricism that Harding describes. In fact, Longino has argued that "Harding's feminist empiricist is a straw woman - designed to give way to feminist standpoint theory". Standpoint theory has been enormously influential. Its various incarnations emphasize the social locatedness of all knowers and call into question the fundamental premise that science presents a transcendent objectivity or 'view from nowhere.' Instead, standpoint theorists argue that the experience of oppression gives women and other marginalized groups a privileged view of social reality which, while not necessarily reflective of The Truth, is less distorted than that of dominant groups (especially white, middle-class men, who comprise the majority of scientists).

Theorists that have been associated with this perspective include Patricia Hill Collins, Nancy Hartsock, Hilary Rose, and Dorothy Smith. In the 1990s, feminist postmodernist critiques of epistemology have gained sway, the result of two developments: the impact of poststructuralist (especially Foucauldian) critiques of epistemology; and the critiques of lesbian feminists and women of colour regarding the unitary white, heterosexual subject of feminist theory. Feminist scholars connected with this category include Judith Butler, Jane Flax, Nancy Fraser and Linda Nicholson, and Susan Hekman.

Feminist postmodernism troubles many feminists, both because of its 'malestream' roots and because it calls into question the foundations of feminist politics and the very notion of truth. It attacks as essentialist the notion of coherent identities (such as 'woman') upon which the notion of social location is based; emphasizes the discursive production of knowledges, identities and their associated social locations; argues for a fragmented conception of identity and social location; and seems to promote a radical version of relativism.

Relativism comes in many forms, of course. Both standpoint theory and Longino's and Nelson's feminist empiricism emphasize that truths and standards for evaluating them vary across social groups. This form of relativism, one which most feminist and mainstream STSers would accept, resembles what mainstream STSers Knorr-Cetina and Mulkay call "epistemic relativism": the assertion "that knowledge is rooted in a particular time and culture ... and does not just mimic nature." But such a position does not entail "judgmental relativism," the position "that all forms of knowledge are 'equally valid' [or invalid], and that we cannot compare different forms of knowledge and discriminate among them".

Since standpoint theorists and feminist empiricists suggest that we can adjudicate among knowledge claims, they are not judgmental relativists. Feminist postmodernists more closely approach judgmental relativism by suggesting that any standard of adjudication is an artefact of discursiv e formations and power/knowledge relations, and that the 'reality' to which any claim refers is itself the product of these formations and relations. But ultimately these suggestions rely upon realism too (e.g. discursive formations exist and they in fact promote the making of some claims and not others).

So feminist empiricism, standpoint theory, and postmodernism all raise methodological, political, and theoretical questions which the long-standing debates have failed to resolve: How do we justify women's knowledge claims about the world, without reverting to the untenable view from nowhere promoted by scientific rationality? Is it possible to talk about 'women's ways of knowing' without invoking essentialism, which has been attributed to feminist standpoint theory? How do we deal with versions of feminist postmodernism that seem to suggest that all claims, women's included, are 'mere' power plays, with no way to adjudicate among competing accounts, and is feminist postmodernism a form of discursive determinism?

How do we interpret postmodernist critiques of knowing subjects and identity politics, given they seemed to arise just as non-pale, non-male subjects were contesting the model of the pale male knower with their own claims to privileged standpoints? In summary, feminist analyses of science, technology, and knowledge have posited "the gendered and sexualized structure, the ideologies, and the symbolism that characterize the institution, the practices, the methodologies, and the theories of science".

The 'problems with science' cannot can be eliminated through affirmative action or the elimination of 'bias' - they are constitutive of science and technology themselves. The scientific method and scientific rationality are called into question as positing an untenable view from nowhere; knowledge, the knowing subject, and scientific and technological practices and products are themselves products of their social, material, and discursive contexts.

MAINSTREAM STS

In contrast to feminism, reviewers of mainstream STS frequently define their immediate intellectual communities rather narrowly, claiming a series of radical schisms from earlier approaches and devoting a great deal of attention to conflicts within the field. The resulting landscape is difficult to describe briefly; even eighteen years ago, when things were considerably more simple, Knorr-Cetina and Mulkay described six science studies streams, arguing that it was "impossible to identify a single set of characteristics" that united them, and noting the "the major divides which separate the ... perspectives from each other."

Nevertheless, many reviews of mainstream STS trace the development of contemporary mainstream STS in several stages: from a focus upon how social factors may intrude upon science (while scientific knowledge, done properly, is 'society-free'); to a sociology of scientific knowledge which focusses on the products of science, its truth-claims, which are constitutively social in character; to a focus upon the process of doing scientific work itself. Accounts of the intellectual foundations of mainstream STS vary quite widely, but virtually all emphasize a radical departure from Mertonian sociology of science.

Mertonians sought to identify the social organization of science as an institution like any other; but they avoided analysis of the methods, metaphysics, and most of the claims of natural science - an understandable concession, since Merton's claims for a scientific sociology required hitching the discipline's wagon to the natural sciences. Passing, usually disparaging references are made to Mertonian approaches in contemporary STS. Trevor Pinch, for example, characterizes a contemporary "sociology of the scientific community" that eschews Mertonian foci on "traditional aspects of the scientific community such as scientists' career structures, the reward system and norms of scientific behaviour" and attends instead to "the very content of scientific knowledge". Bruno Latour even contests the notion of a nature distinct from society, undermining the very disciplinary divisions that defined the Mertonian project.

Usually, contemporary mainstream STS is traced to the sociology of scientific knowledge (SSK) of the 1970s, especially the 'strong program' of David Bloor. Bloor advocated an epistemological agnosticism based upon a symmetry principle: 'true' (accepted) and 'false' (discredited) knowledge should be analysed in the same fashion; 'good' science does not merely reflect nature while 'bad' science is the outcome of social factors, 'biases,' and so on; both 'good' and 'bad' science reflect social factors.

Bloor and his colleagues in the Edinburgh school - notably Barry Barnes, Steve Shapin, and Donald MacKenzie - studied the substantive content and outcome of scientific controversies, usually explaining them via reference to the interests of powerful groups. The Bath school, with Harry Collins as its chief proponent, focussed more heavily on the settling of controversies within the scientific community, but implicitly accepted the Edinburgh school's interests model regarding society-science relations.

Following a debate in STS circles, the interests model came to be seen as naive - a development which, according to David Hess, signalled the death of macrostructural analysis in mainstream STS. After this, the influence of SSK and its social realism declined somewhat. Various new 'turns' have been described. For example, Knorr-Cetina and Mulkay describe a "linguistic turn"; Steve Woolgar describes a "turn to technology". I take up Pickering's description of a turn to "scientific practice and culture" - microsocial, ethnographically-oriented studies of scientific work and the material, linguistic, and interactional elements of scientific cultures - since this is a particularly inclusive characterization of the turn.

Early examples of such studies are Knorr-Cetina and Latour and Woolgar. Even within this new focus, there are authors and schools with diverse theoretical and methodological approaches: the discourse analysis of Michael Mulkay and his students, the reflexive program of Steve Woolgar and Malcolm Ashmore, the social construction of technology (SCOT) program of Wiebe Bijker and Trevor Pinch, the ethnomethodological approach of Michael Lynch, the interactionist 'social worlds' approach elaborated by Anselm Strauss' students, and the ANT approach of Latour, Michel Callon and John Law.

While I focus most upon ANT, all of these schools share a concern to delineate the mundane practices by which scientific claims and technologies are produced. They focus on science as an achievement that develops through local, contingent, negotiated, consensus-building, collective claimsmaking practices. The collective and eclectic nature of scientific fact-building can be discerned in three sites: the laboratory, where initial claims get constructed; the scientific community, where the claims get debated and established; and the larger community, where non-scientists (both human and non-human) must be enlisted to make the claims and to make them true.

In this literature, the laboratory is defined broadly, as any locale in which the work of producing scientific claims (which may or may not become facts) is done. While other approaches emphasize scientific theory, materiality is the focus of studies of scientific practice; hence the shift from abstract knowledge to concrete practices. Material constraints include the local availability of equipment and materials, the preferences of funding agencies, and the skills of available personnel.

Moreover, laboratory work cannot be done without the collection of objects that Hacking, in a suitably mundane way, calls 'things': substances, populations, and samples that are the targets of investigation, instruments that interfere with the target, detectors that measure the interference, and data generators. The target is not simply observed; nature is chaotic and must be interfered with to produce analyzable phenomena. But targets, instruments, and other materials may not cooperate, despite efforts to make elements of nature as controlled as possible. Thus a conception of material, non-human agency is an important element, particularly in ANT.

Instruments and scientists in the laboratory produce reams of inscriptions, which are "not so much a method of transferring information as a material operation of creating order ... Objects appear because of the constant process of sorting". The inscriptions themselves become the objects of study, replacing the original target; their profusion is itself a possible source of disorder, so they are combined and ordered until one stands "out of and for" the masses that have been produced. Interpreting and clarifying inscriptions to make them meaningful and usable is no easy task, but must be negotiated among laboratory workers.

Through various conversational devices, evidence-fixation is accomplished: a working conclusion upon which to proceed, rather than a definitive account of what is seen, is produced. The point is to not to make the data fit a given theory, but to establish them as analyzable via reference to local interpretations, rules, and decision criteria. Once the meaning of data has been set in the lab, they must be converted into evidence suitable for publication if the fact is to be stabilized in the wider scientific community. The fixed-upon meaning must be made to stand out and the viability of alternate explanations of the data must be reduced.

Illustrations in scientific publications help to accomplish this. Images may be cut and pasted together to create the most salient signal; pointers may be added to highlight some features and minimize others; graphing an image identifies it with the analytic resources of mathematics, making it more durable, invariant, universal, and measurable. Textual devices, too, make the journal article more persuasive. An "audiovisual display" combines text and illustration, directing the reader to see the illustration in a particular way.

Citation makes a claim more persuasive; other texts and their authors become allies which, in supporting the statement made by the author, raise the costs of dissension. Latour and Woolgar identify five statement types used in journal articles, which are differentiated by the extent to which they include 'modalities' - statements about statements - and the types of modalities employed (they may question or enhance the facticity of the statement). Once a statement becomes an established fact, or 'blackbox,' modalities disappear and the context of the statement's creation is erased. Content and context are separated. Reuniting them is a tactic for casting aspersions on the validity of the claim.

Once a strong network has been formed around a claim, it can only be contested by insiders who have the requisite material resources and allies. However, studies of scientific practice suggest the great extent to which the success of a claim depends upon the manipulation of the world outside the lab and the forging of alliances with non-scientists. Science works not because it is true to the world but because the world is tinkered with to make science work. Infrastructural work, such as the development of metrological constants, the cooperation of state agencies and local residents, and the enlistment of communications media, is required to get the claim to work in the wider world.

Scientific facts must be consistently applied in order to work; they do not work in just any reality, but only in a particularly constituted one. This particularly constituted reality requires the cooperation of a great many non-scientists to extend scientific claims across time and space. Actor-network theorists especially extend agency to non-human 'actants'. Both humans and non-humans must be 'enrolled' into the scientific network through 'translation,' defined by Gallon and Law as "a process in which sets of relations between projects, interests, goals, and naturally-occurring entities - objects which might otherwise be quite separate from one another - are proposed and brought into being."

Scientists define a problem, and define the actors involved so as to fit the defined problem and proposed solution. The scientists must establish themselves as 'obligatory passage points' through which the actors must work to solve the problem. They must keep competitors away from the actors they want to enrol. They cannot enrol all of the actors at once, so they focus on (what they hope is) a representative sample of the population, adjusting their projects to get the sample to cooperate. Even if they succeed in enrolling the representatives, the general population may refuse to be enrolled en masse.

The seeds of a useful theory of power exist here:

> Understanding what sociologists generally call power relationships means describing the way in which actors are defined, associated and simultaneously obliged to remain faithful to their alliances ... It also permits an explanation of how a few obtain the right to express and to represent the many silent actors of the social and natural worlds they have mobilized.

Callon acknowledges that violence, seduction, transaction, and consent without discussion are possible techniques of enrolment. But it must be said that ANT generally emphasizes scientists' tactics of persuasion in the enrolment of allies. If they are successful, the scientists become the general representatives of the populations involved and can speak for and about them in a 'discourse of certainty.' The populations have been 'displaced'-moved from their original state to one more in line with the scientists' project. The end result is a 'sociotechnical network' composed of links between different and previously unconnected entities, both human and non-human.

Networks may be extended across various communities, both scientific and non-scientific, for example through the use of 'standardized packages' - techniques, tools, concepts, and theories that are used in various disciplines and therefore yield commensurable projects, data, and knowledge claims. Sociotechnical networks are stronger because of their heterogeneity; to destroy them, many diverse actors have to be persuaded or forced to change their alliances, interests, and identities. So, non-scientist 'outsiders' are integral to the process of network extension. Without their cooperation, the network will not get made, nor will it extend very far.

EPISTEMOLOGICAL AND POLITICAL CONTROVERSIES IN STS

Epistemological matters are as hotly debated in this literature as they are within feminism. The emphasis on the constructed nature of scientific claims has frequently been misunderstood as judgmental relativism. But the authors upon whom I have focussed are neither simple realists, because 'reality' must be worked upon in order for us to know it, nor judgmental relativists, because some claims really are stronger than others. Perhaps Ian Hacking comes closest to the spirit of the approach when he argues for a distinction between realism about entities and realism about theories.

He asserts that an established entity, one which can be manipulated predictably to create other entities, is real (at least in terms of scientific practice) - "if you can spray them, then they are real," he says of electrons. Moreover, scientific practice requires material resources and has material, not merely discursive, effects: it is world-changing; it kills rats and gets people to change their behaviour. For Latour, both realism and relativism are symptoms of scientific practice, inappropriately distinguishing between natural 'facts' and social 'factors'; one takes out-there-ness as given while the other denies it.

The very category of out-there-ness is a consequence of scientific practice, but parts of scientific knowledge about out-there-ness work, even if they cannot jump out of the network in which they exist. The realist/relativist controversy is displaced; the important issue is how some claims become more credible than others. Reality is measured by effectivity rather than truth-correspondence. Within mainstream STS, criticisms of the ANT approach centre around two principles made explicit by Michel Gallon and supported by Latour: the principles of generalized symmetry and generalized agnosticism.

Symmetry principles have been advanced in science studies for many years; Merton contended that science should be studied in the same way as other social institutions, and we have seen that Bloor advocated symmetrical analysis of true and false claims. Actor-network theorists go a step further;

arguing that non-human ('natural') and human ('social') actants should be described using the same vocabulary and explanatory principles.

Gallon and Latour argue that the natural and social sciences assign ontological statuses to humans and non-humans to create the nature/society divide; that the intentionality and identity of non-humans are variable in scientists' usage; a nd that traditional approaches cannot come to terms with hybrids that cross the nature/culture divide or with technology that, although non-human, embodies human intention (thereby contesting the dichotomy between purposeful action and mindless behaviour). The actornetwork approach, Gallon and Latour argue, allows the investigator to examine how ontological statuses are allocated, modified, and contested within science, rather than taking these statuses as inherent.

They do not deny that there are differences between humans and non-humans, but ask how these differences are defined in science. The principle of generalized agnosticism holds that the investigator should not take sides in the technical or social aspects of the controversy being studied; the interests and identities of the actors involved should not be fixed in advance. The implications of this statement (and comparable ones by other STSers) generated an entire special issue of Social Studies of Science regarding the politics of STS. The principle of generalized agnosticism is tied to debates about the Bloorian principle of symmetry because (many argue) politics and judgments about truth and falsity cannot be neatly separated.

Dick Pels contends that proponents of symmetry and agnosticism are not disinterested parties, but arc engaging in "knowledge-political actions," attempts to reconfigure and thereby to rule over the field Pels points out that agnostic methodological approaches in effect make previously accepted claims seem more dubious and dismissed claims more prob able, and are "often a cool and detached way of siding with the oppressed" - a tactic which mimics the professed value-neutrality of science even as it attacks it.

As Vicky Singleton notes, the actor-network approach can be viewed as an effort to extend democracy to non-humans, and Latour's advocacy of a "Parliament of Things" is an explicitly political statement: "It is time to do for these new masses what our forebears did for humans.'No innovation without representation' or 'no pollution without representation' could be among the mot d'ordres". But there are other senses in which ANT and other varieties of mainstream STS are politically engaged; we see this in their depictions of feminism.

COMMON THEMES IN FEMINIST AND MAINSTREAM STS

Both feminist and mainstream STS challenge the notions that science is a purely rational activity and that science done right is unbiased. Both emphasize the role of social context in scientific practice. Part of that context is the knowledge community in which scientific practice takes place: studies of scientific practice share with many varieties of feminism, particularly the feminist empiricism of Helen Longino and Lynn Hankinson Nelson, a view of knowledge as a communal holding rooted in local conditions and standards. This contrasts sharply with individualist accounts of knowledge, in which the knower's observations and reasoning are supposedly independent from the communities to which s/he belongs.

Moreover, both feminists and science studies scholars demonstrate an interest in critically examining blackboxes, or well-established scientific facts. The mainstream STS principle of generalized symmetry demands that established scientific 'truths' should be analysed in the same way as claims that have been discredited; and for feminists, the analysis of 'truths' is a more pressing matter than the analysis of claims which, having been discredited, are likely to affect women and other marginalized groups less. Another shared theme is the examination of multiple viewpoints in scientific knowledge-making.

The actions of scientists who create knowledge claims are only one facet of such studies. Feminists have focussed on the work of women as activists, consumers, and critics of science and technology, and on the role of corporate and professional communities in advancing scientific claims and technologies, many of which have had harmful effects on women. Studies of scientific practice have demonstrated the effects of cooperation and resistance by funding agencies, government, business, other members of the scientific community, social movements, and the non-human subjects of research on nascent knowledge claims and scientific research, and an entire subfield of STS is devoted to analysing the public's role in science.

Traditional epistemological approaches are challenged in both fields; both provide important critiques of positivism, empiricism, and naive realism. Both fields adopt a broadly constructivist position. In recent feminist work, social and discursive constructivism has been emphasized although material objects and elements of nature are frequently described as active parts of scientific knowledge creation.

In some varieties of mainstream STS, particularly ANT, the role of the material and natural are more explicitly factored into a constructivism that can no longer, be called social constructivism because of ANT's objections to nature/society dichotomies. Both fields have been influenced by postmodernism and poststructuralism and, like these approaches, they exhibit a penchant for deconstructing dualisms such as nature/culture and human/nonhuman; feminism deconstructs male/female and masculine/feminine as well. However, many feminists and mainstream STSers alike reject the discursi ve determinist and relativist implications of some postmodernist and post-structuralist theory.

EVIDENCE OF CROSS-FERTILIZATION

There is no doubt that the boundary between feminism and mainstream STS is increasingly permeable. In recent years, David Hess has published an introductory text on science studies and an article reviewing the field, both of which devote considerable attention to feminist and other 'critical' versions of STS. An edited volume discusses gender and technology debates among feminists and social constructivists. The papers included in this collection had their origins in a conference on gender and technology at Brunel University (one of the major STS centres in the UK).

Work from this conference was also published in a special issue of Science, Technology, & Human Values, and at least two other special issues of mainstream STS journals have published special issues on feminism and science studies. Donna Haraway's work, of course, has had an enormous impact on mainstream STS, and two other American feminists, Adele Clarke and Susan Leigh Star, are prominent in mainstream STS. In recent years, the Society for Social Studies of Science has awarded the annual Fleck Prize for best STS book to three feminists.

Also, the landmark Handbook of Science and Technology Studies devotes to feminist scholarship and women in science, and these are authored by prominent feminist scholars Evelyn Fox Keller, Judy Wajcman, and Mary Frank Fox, who are situated much more firmly in feminist than in mainstream STS. Seven other articles in the collection explicitly discuss feminist activism and/or feminist science studies. A recent science studies reader contains several feminist contributions, including authors not often cited in the mainstream literature.

Even Hilary Rose, a staunch critic of mainstream STS, acknowledges that the "masculine culture" of science studies is changing due to pressure from feminist graduate students and the hiring of feminists in some STS departments. The situation has changed since Sara Delamont pointed fourteen years ago to mainstream STS's "blind spot" regarding gender and feminist scholarship. But while feminism and gender tend to be discussed in special issues of mainstream STS journals or restricted to specific articles in STS books, the effects of mainstream STS are more diffused throughout feminist work. Thus, it is rare now to find a recent feminist STS work that does not incorporate the insights of mainstream STSers. More positively, though, I can say that when mainstream STS do engage with feminist work, it is in a sustained way that recognizes the marginalization of feminist authors in the field and that attempts to grapple with the issues they raise.

AREAS OF CONTENTION

So feminist STS and some varieties of mainstream STS, particularly ANT, have much in common, and some dialogue is occurring between them. But much of that dialogue concerns the differences and tensions between feminist and mainstream STS. Feminists have published more on this issue, whereas fewer published mainstream critiques of feminist work-at least explicit ones-exist, a function probably of feminism's 'separate area' status in mainstream STS. As a result, this section contains more feminist critiques of mainstream STS than vice versa. I begin with two misconceptions.

First, in personal exchanges with mainstream STSers, I have noted a tendency to reduce feminist STS to an effort to 'get more women into science and technology.' Obviously, this is an important part of (especially early) feminist STS, but it is not the thrust of most recent feminist work in the field. Alison Adam obviously has had similar experiences:

Indeed, it is not surprising to find that many people uninitiated with feminist theory will take the 'women into' problem as encompassing the entire scope of the gender and science/technology enterprise and will assume that studies such as the present one are primarily aimed at getting more women into science and technology. Those with a more theoretically informed interest will have to find ways of living with the labels that they will inevitably acquire, whether or not those labels are appropriate.

The second misconception, common among feminists, is that ANT is antirealist and a radical form of "social constructivism". I would argue with David Hess that, while ANT is constructivist, it is inappropriate to call it a form of social constructivism; Latour is in fact at great pains to point out that material, discursive, and social elements are all crucial parts of scientific practice, and that the outcomes of science can not be explained merely by preexisting 'social factors,' as social constructivism would suggest. Rose also argues that Latourian constructivism is equivalent to "total relativism" and "gives us no way of judging between competing and plausible accounts". Latour's position is not equivalent to judgmental relativism, as he is quite clear that some claims are stronger than others.

Donna Haraway notes the machismo and use of militaristic metaphors in some science studies works. So we have charges of "epistemological chicken" and "failures of nerve"; Steve Shapin describes the modern STSer as an irreverent daredevil who, because of his audacity, may make dangerous and powerful scientist-enemies - but, hey, "he [sic] who rides on the back of the tiger may wind up inside". The machismo appears not merely in mainstream STSers' depictions of their work, but also in their depictions of scientists. Emily Martin suggests a connection here to capitalist ideology:

... the Latourian scientist who bursts upon the scene is an accumulating, aggressive individual born of capitalism, forming his networks and gathering his allies everywhere, resembling all too closely a Western businessman. We may wonder whether all scientists have, or ever bad, such a monadic, agonistic, competitive approach to the world.

Then there is the astonishing level of acrimony in so many published mainstream STS debates. Not that feminist always gets along - quite the contrary but, as Rose points, "feminists are committed to building alliances, not least with other feminists". Values subscribed to by many feminists - an ethic of care, respect for differences, the importance of community - are products of political efforts to build solidarity among women and to recognize and attend to feminists' own practices of exclusion, and they help to curb use of the kind of sarcasm and bullying that one sees within science studies. Respectful interaction doesn't solve the problem of difference, but it at least facilitates, rather than forecloses, productive debate.

But perhaps the most common feminist complaint is the lack of engagement of mainstream STSers with feminist work and issues of inequality. Donna Haraway has made this critique many times; her frustration is evident. They never ask how the practices of masculine supremacy, or many other systems of structured inequality, get built into and out of working machines. How and in what directions these transferences of 'competences' work should be a focus of rapt attention. Systems of exploitation might be crucial parts of the 'technical content' of science.

In her discussion of Harry Collins and Trevor Pinch, Rose adds that "For genuinely smart field workers, their inability to see such [structurally unequal] social relations at workis quite an achievement." Haraway relates this blind spot to mainstream STSers' attempts to counter assumptions that science simply 'reflects' social relations. But she argues that the issue is not simple reflection, but traffic between science and society; and she asserts that the "reified technical" is just as problematic as the "transcendental social" from which mainstream STSers seek to escape.

Gill and Grint note that ANT theorists are likely to argue that, if gender is relevant to the development of a scientific network, this will emerge as the network is analysed. But they point out that male ANT theorists may not be sensitive enough to issues of gender to see them, and that a lack of discussion about gender does not mean gender is not operating in the networks: "silence, like absence from networks, is itself gendered". The erasure of gender in mainstream STS accounts is clearly related to conceptualizations of politics in feminism and in mainstream STS.

Some mainstream STSers charge that politically-engaged perspectives which emphasize the stratifying effects of science take social concepts as unquestioned resource rather than empirical topic. For example, Latour attacks modern social movements for reifying the very categories they seek to oppose, thereby furthering modernity's artificial division of the natural and the social and unwittinglyly defending the natural sciences from thoroughgoing analysis. Proponents of the discursive turn in feminism have made similar points about the risks of reifying the inherited categories of women and gender upon which feminism depends.

But, while feminist postmodernists struggle to deal with the effects of 'gender' without reifying the category itself, mainstream STSers have tended to ignore the issues altogether by arguing that gender is a "'social' ghost that blocked real explanation of science in action". Haraway concludes that Latour "draw[s] a suspicious line around what gets to count as [scientific] practice".

Connected to debates about politics, symmetry and agnosticism are discussions regarding 'hard' and 'soft' science and the levels of difficulty associated with studying each. Consider Latour's analysis of Foucault:

> Yes, Foucault is asymmetrical. He is all for radical discontinuity and revolution, but all his work is in the social sciences. There is not a word on the natural sciences (except medicine, which is related to the natural sciences). Perhaps Foucault could have done the job if he had attended to the details of chemistry and physics but I think that by avoiding the hard sciences, he has shunned the hard cases, so we cannot really evaluate how useful he could be.

According to Latour, the 'hard' sciences are the hard cases because their connections to the social world are less immediately obvious. Certainly, feminists have tended to focus upon the 'soft' sciences precisely because they have more obvious political implications. But whether this makes the soft sciences easier to study is an open question: Eveleen Richards notes that it may be harder to remain politically agnostic when one studies 'soft' sciences (like medicine) which have clear effects on people's everyday lives.

The ethical and political dilemmas posed by the soft sciences may make analysing them more complex, not less so. Moreover, when studying the hard sciences, one may be able to stick to the inner circle of scientists; the involvement of various publics in debates about biological and medical science extends and complicates the field of analysis. In any case, by arguing that hard sciences are more difficult to analyse than soft ones, Latour extends the disciplinary hierarchy of the natural sciences to STS. Physics is the apex of the natural sciences; studies of physics represent the apex of STS.

Feminists who study the soft sciences are, by extension, relatively unskilled labourers doing inconsequential namby-pamby work. Here we have an extraordinary piece of boundary-work. Despite mainstream STS criticisms that feminism ascribes interests and identities a priori, Brian Wynne has argued that critiques of 'politics' in mainstream STS are themselves often simplistic, assuming monolithic 'sides' and pregiven identities and interests. Some mainstreamers have a tendency to reduce feminist scholarship in these ways and, in doing so, they erect a boundary between 'good' science studies and 'political' feminist work.

In the science wars, too, scientists have claimed that STS is politically motivated. This is a standard delegitimization tactic that depends, however implicitly, upon traditional ideals of 'good science.' But when mainstreamers use that tactic in regard to feminism, they contravene a first principle of contemporary STS: that the political and the scientific can't be neatly separated. Of course, there are some notable exceptions of mainstream STS scholars who do engage, to varying extents, with feminist work. Steven Shapin includes feminist work in a review of the sociology of scientific knowledge. But he argues that, because contemporary SSK is committed to avoiding grand narratives of any sort, it is incompatible with feminisms which view science as "'essentially masculinist'":

> To say that science, across a broad sweep of history and cultures, was "essentially" informed by gender preoccupations, or, with the "standpoint" theorists, that women-as-victims are "epistemologically privileged," represents much the same kind of sensibility as those that announced that science was "essentially" about class relations, or about the abstraction from common sense, or that a class of free-floating intellectuals existed and enjoyed epistemological privilege.

Shapin provides no examples of such works. The suggestion that essentialist readings of science are common in recent feminist work is unfair; as we have seen; contemporary feminist scholars practically have a phobia about essentialism. This would be like using the Edinburgh school of the 1970s as an example of contemporary STS. Shapin approves of "other versions of feminist science studies," and asserts that these "are perhaps best seen as tributaries of SSK and related streams". However, Shapin cautions the reader that such works have a "frankly political agenda", implying that mainstream SSK is not bound up with political agendas.

When Haraway's work is discussed in Andrew Pickering's book, *The Mangle of Practice,* she is described as a cultural studies theorist. Her feminism is mentioned in passing, when Pickering argues that Haraway's politics can be extricated from her analysis, of which he approves. But Haraway's feminism isn't just her politics; the work of other feminists is an integral part of her intellectual history and enables her theoretical insights, as she invariably and carefully acknowledges. Pickering is concerned to point out the complex interrelation of all the eclectic elements of scientific work.

Yet despite his talk of the 'mangle' of scientific practice, Pickering neatly separates out Haraway's feminism in an effort to show that we don't have to "hitch our analyses to particular political projects"-as if political projects aren't part of the mangle. A related point of contention has to do with 'interests' and readings of technology. Gill and Grint argue that feminists tend to see patriarchal interests as central to technological and scientific development, while mainstream constructivist STSers are more likely to argue that interests are products of scientific and technological practice.

Grint and Steve Woolgar, for example, criticize not only 'essentialist' feminist analyses of technology which argue that technology is intrinsically male, but also 'anti-essentialist' feminist analyses of technology which make the more modest claim that values and interests can become embedded in technologies. As an alternative, they propose that values and interests are only imputed to technologies by their users or audience, that there is no ghost in the machine.

Their approach is suggestive for feminism in that it, like many of the articles in a recent feminist collection, suggests that women can develop alternative readings and uses of technologies. But this has its limits. We cannot merely 'choose' to read the rack as, say, kitchen appliance rather than instrument of torture; and we (or at least I) don't want to suggest that women who read technologies as oppressive to them are just unimaginative readers or dupes of extant discourses. Some readings of technology are preferred and "we do not live in a semiotic democracy" where any reading is possible; readings that hold sway tend to be those whose advocates occupy particular positions.

Recently, Michel Callon and John Law have contested Langdon Winner's discussion of Robert Moses, a New York City planner who, in the interwar period, designed low bridges that could not admit buses so that blacks, most of whom did not own cars, could not go to Jones Beach. Callon and Law argue that "The new social group of blacks-who-cannot-go-to-the-Long-Island-beaches cannot be deduced ... from Moses' racism".

Their general point is that entities are what they are through heterogeneous networks of association; Pasteur-the-great-scientist or Andrew-the-businessman are the result not of the men-in-themselves but of the network of allies that support them - material objects, people, texts, organizations, and so on. Fair enough. But why can't racism be part of a heterogeneous network - especially when the racism of Moses was explicit and did not have to be read into his work by the analyst? Couldn't we imagine racism - or sexism or feminism - as elements of heterogeneous networks or n etworks in them, which support or undermine other networks?

A staunch refusal to consider that oppressive ideologies may be part of a network amounts to assuming the oppressive ideologies are not part of the network, a position which contradicts the principle of generalized agnosticism regarding interests and identities. In effect, mainstream STSers blackbox questions of social inequality when they refuse to open them to scrutiny.

Moreover, Andrew-the-businessman's secretary is part of the network; and in this piece by Callon and Law, at least, this is acknowledged. But as Star has pointed out, ANT has a tendency to focus on Great Men and Scientific Victors and to ignore support workers, those affected by science and technology, and especially those who refuse to be enrolled into scientists' networks. She argues that emphasizing the extension of networks and the blackboxing of scientific claims defines those who do not, cannot, or will not be standardized as deviant others whose existence is trivialized and whose suffering is ignored.

Networks create not merely insiders, but also outsiders and the partially enrolled. Attendance to practices of exclusion or avoidance and their effects are integral, not peripheral, to adequate descriptions of the process of network-building. The issue of outsiders and the partially enrolled relates to discussions of boundaries, prominent in both feminist and mainstream STS. In most feminist work, boundaries are described from the point of view of those who are outside or on the boundaries and the fractured identities that boundaries produce.

There is a tendency among feminists to celebrate marginalization, monsters, cyborgs, and the fragmented, decentred subject; the work of Donna Haraway is a good example. Haraway sometimes romanticizes marginalization, though the experience of marginalization is anything but romantic, and Emily Martin has suggested that marginalization and fragmentation are effects of the culture of late capitalism - something not to be celebrated, but critiqued. So the challenge is how to foreground marginalization and partial enrolment, taking advantage of the insights they can provide, while remaining critical of both the effects and causes of boundaries.

In mainstream STS, boundaries usually are described from the point of view of those who are inside - scientists - and how they bring some outsiders in and keep others out. Even most boundary-challengers described in mainstream STS are insiders of a sort - other scientists, government officials, or other types of experts, usually middle class pale males. Moreover, while the boundaries around feminism and practices of exclusion have been debated at length in feminist circles, those working in mainstream STS seem to discuss such issues in their own field rather less often.

The majority of explicit criticisms of feminism in the mainstream STS literature are epistemological. Steve Fuller's introduction to STS has little to say about feminist work, but he does question some feminists' assumption that subjectivist epistemology can lead to enlightened transformations of science. He notes that subjectivism, though associated with women, is not exclusive to women and in fact has been championed by several notable male philosophers.

He observes (correctly, I think) that it is the gendered division of labour that has attributed subjectivity to women and objectivity to men, such that subjectivist epistemology is just as much a symptom of oppressive social relations as is objectivist epistemology, and argues that substituting subjectivism for objectivism is "a bit like saying that the cure for sadism is masochism". He asks whether the project of feminists should rather be to develop a "dialectical synthesis" of objectivity and subjectivity, rather than a replacem ent of the former by the latter. Feminist epistemologists might reply that they have been working on this project for quite some time.

Other epistemological conflicts revolve around the realist-relativist problematic. Hilary Rose, for instance, criticizes mainstream STSers Harry Collins and Trevor Pinch for what she considers a contradictory position:

Thus while they show us the scientists actively socially constructing their "neat and tidy myths," we are invited to believe that C&P's own sociological accounts of science are real. They tell us their subjects construct science, while they offer one true sociological story which everyone should know. Arguably, C&P thus reproduce for sociology the authoritarian scientific voice they criticize.

Her critique applies more broadly. Pinch, among others, has pointed to a widespread relativist tendency in modern STS and has argued that "Few sociologists of scientific knowledge today would want to claim any special epistemic warrant for their own findings. Like all knowledge, that produced by the sociology of science can be understood as a social construct." Yet his own claim that contemporary sociology of science examines "the very content of scientific knowledge" employs a realist idiom. So do Pickering's description of the new STS as focussing upon "what scientists actually do" and Barry Barnes' assertion that new empirical studies of scientific work "tell it how it is".

In contrast, Rose notes, while Donna Haraway also constructs an account of science as story, "as a fully reflexive scholar she has the grace to acknowledge that her accounts are also stories." Reflexivity also is promoted by Grint and

Woolgar when they advocate a "post-essentialist" position that examines the discursive positioning of both the social and the technological and refuses to take either category as unquestioned resource. They advocate "new forms of writing and reflexivity, to invent new monsters and marginal beings which might displace standard units of analysis and transcend conventional categories and distinctions".

They cite Haraway's and Latour's work as examples. Ashmore, Myers and Potter likewise exhibit an appreciation for both feminist and mainstream STS works which use the "idea of competing discourses or registers or styles" and which celebrate multiple and fragmented identities in a reflexive fashion - and ask, "so why are [feminist and mainstream STS] so often separate?" Reflexive styles that trouble stable categories are a particular forte of feminist writing.

But Rosalind Gill notes that post-essentialism and anti-foundationalism leave untouched the adjudication of competing knowledge claims. She accepts that Grint and Woolgar want to demonstrate a political potential for post-essentialism and to counter critics who argue that epistemic relativism is equivalent to moral quietism. Yet, she argues, political commitments presuppose a realist perspective. In his ANT-inspired analysis of AIDS activism, Epstein makes the related point that health activist groups are committed to a realist vision of science for very good reasons:

> ...in the end, few activists, perhaps few people with AIDS or HIV infection, are fully sanguine about the prospect of" living with the reality of uncertainty." This is not surprising because activists, and people with AIDS and HIV, are confronted daily by a burning need to know whether given treatments "work" or not, and such need does not typically take comfort in relativism. The activist critique of the randomized clinical trial unseats that methodology from the pinnacle on which it is sometimes placed, but it also assumes a greater role for such trials than some STS analysts ... would recommend.

Sometimes we will want to be realists, such as when a scientific claim or a technological development helps to cure a fatal illness; sometimes, realism presents the moral dilemma of accepting the validity of science that causes suffering or oppression. On the other hand, adopting relativism can render us inconsistent (our own claims about science employ a realist idiom, while we relativize science s claims), unable to choose among competing accounts, or unable to make any firm claims. Even Grint and Woolgar, in presenting 'stories' about science, seem to suggest that their stories are the more accurate ones.

It may be better, then, to judge each scientific claim based upon its moral, political, and material implications and its fit with epistemological standards at the local level, and to recognize that these implications and standards may change, than to search for a consistent epistemo-political strategy (whether relativist or realist). The feminist empiricism of Lynn Hankinson Nelson suggests a way to do this: it recognizes that standards of evidence are negotiated locally within epistemological communities; that standards of evidence differ among epistemological communities; that, within a community, not all claims can be considered equivalent in merit; and that adjudications are based upon how well claims fit the evidence standards of the community. Nevertheless there is recognition that evidence - however much its definition may vary across communities - is required to support a claim.

In feminist communities, ethics and politics are core components of evidence standards: claims that are deemed h armful to women - however much scientific evidence or however many allies may be marshalled in their favour - simply will not be considered valid. I suspect that ethics and politics are relevant in other epistemological communities, too.

TOWARD A MORE PRODUCTIVE DIALOGUE

In this section, I discuss some recent attempts to combine feminist and mainstream STS (particularly ANT), some of which suggest ways in which the two bodies of literature can be combined to overcome the dilemmas in each. Susan Ormrod (1995) combines post-structuralism and ANT in an attempt to counter feminist 'blackboxing' of analytical categories such as gender, technology, patriarchy, identity, agency, and structure (though whether or not those issues have been blackboxed in feminism, rather than subjected to intense scrutiny, is debateable).

Ormrod argues that ANT can be used to demonstrate the ways in which gender relations and technological relations mutually enrol one another and consequently are renegotiated and transformed. She notes that there are a limited range of available gendered identities and that this limitation can help to account for the durability of networks: actors are constrained by their gendered subjectivity, so they often perform in predictable and relatively durable ways. She also shows, though, that sometimes actors can move between gendered identities to have varying effects on networks.

These are valuable insights that not only inject a concern with gender and subjectivity into ANT, but also help to explain change and continuity in networks over time. Unfortunately, her account appears to replace the agency/structure dualism with discursive determinism: discourse determines the available gendered positions of subjects, who appear to have no originary role in discourse. And in her appreciation of post-structuralism and her focus on actor-networks as systems of discursive association, she downplays ANT's emphasis on materiality - in my judgment, one of its greatest assets.

Vicky Singleton, too, has used ANT in her analysis of a cervical screening program (CSP). In one paper (1996), she attempts to answer a question posed to her at a conference: Should women participate in a CSP? She considers four answers to this question. She rejects a feminist empiricist answer because it would uncritically accept "the sexist foundations of ... science". She rejects a standpoint answer because it would falsely universalize women and occlude the perspectives of CSP opponents.

She argues that feminist postmodernists would reject faulty generalizations and would recognize their own partial, situated perspective (standpoint theorists would not?); but Singleton rejects feminist postmodernism because it is politically impotent and dodges the question of how women can engage with science. She formulates a modified ANT response, based upon her analysis of tactics used to redefine women's identities within the CSP and the degree to which women are enrolled into the network by taking on the se identities:

> In order to answer The Question in the terms in which it was put, I would need to speak for women and define their proper identity in the CSP: either they should or should not be participants. That is, I suggest that to engage in a 'should' discourse ('should women have the test?') is to engage in an oppressive and exclusionary discourse. Moreover, a definitive response to The Question conceals the negotiability and multiplicity of identity that characterizes the actors in the CSP, along with the complex and evolving ... relationship between those being defined and those doing the defining.

Her answer to the question, then, is "No women should have a cervical smear test but all women could". She acknowledges that women are unlikely to find this a helpful response; and it is curious that, while she rejects the feminist postmodernist response for its political impotence, she does not reject the political impotence of her own ANT-inspired response.

The point of the question, it seems to me, has little to do with excluding women who don't participate in CSPs or forcing women to participate in them. The question could quite as easily have been "Might women benefit from participating in the CSP?"; its point, I suspect, was to address the issue of evaluation. In worrying that their analyses might compel women to do anything, feminist academics both overestimate their impact on women's lives and underestimate women's ability to make their own judgments. I doubt that many women read feminist analyses as injunctions (that is, if they read them); they may view them as resou rces. Singleton's response to The Question provides no resources to women negotiating with science in their daily lives.

Certainly, ANT does not tell us how to make political and epistemological judgments. It is rather a methodological approach that might help us make them. "In order to make a diagnosis or a decision about the absurdity, the danger, the amorality or the unrealism of an innovation, one must first describe the network". Thus, it seems that ANT demands only a temporary agnosticism. Singleton stops at the ANT analysis rather than using it to make judgments about the truth, politics, and ethics of CSPs. A more politically-engaged adaptation of ANT would not shy away from making such judgments.

One such adaptation is suggested by David Hess. Drawing upon critical STS (including feminist work), he reworks four principles of mainstream STS - explanation, impartiality, symmetry, and reflexivity - to develop a more critically-engaged approach to science and technology studies based on power, culture, evaluation and intervention. First, STS should attend to the ways in which power relations help to constitute consensus and heterodoxies in the history of a field - which claims become part of the canon and which are systematically excluded, how, and why. Such analysis could attend to the marshalling of allies (ANT), the deployment of scientific capital, the effects of scientists' gender on their success, and the ways in which scientific orthodoxies might become so because they fit taken-for-granted assumptions about the social world (feminism).

Second, rather than providing a mechanical, reductive, instrumentalist analysis of interests and categories of difference, we should attend to the development of research cultures which make claims largely based on a system of "internal integrity" that is nevertheless connected to broader cultural and social trends. That is, rather than viewing scientists or technologists as 'Out to get women' (a rare view now anyway), we would acknowledge that scientists tend to conform to the ethical and political standards of their community; and we could examine the ways these standards reconfigure, but also (often unintentionally) are connected to, more widespread patterns of social interaction which, in turn, often are characterized by inequality.

Third, Hess argues, we should evaluate claims and the policies that derive from them based on the best available evidence, which is nevertheless open to cross-examination and interpretation. Hess's fourth principle, intervention, requires that we position ourselves as analysts to promote beneficial changes to research and institutional programs. Thus, we reco gnize our part in the controversy in a reflexive but politically engaged way: "I am better off positioning myself rather than letting someone else do it for me".

Hess's suggestions successfully combine some of the best elements of critical and mainstream STS, avoiding both the fixity of analytical categories, determinism, and instrumentalism found in some feminist work, and mainstream STS's blindness to issues of inequality, pretensions to political neutrality, and frequent lack of attention to network-building outside the confines of scientific communities. As Cynthia Cockburn has observed, in order for women's involvement in or exclusion from networks to become visible, the notion of network needs to be extended.

Susan Leigh Star (1991) combines the ANT notion of translation with feminist theories of marginality and split selves to develop a useful conception of resistance to practices of normalization. Donna Haraway has suggested that we move beyond mainstream STS conceptions of "interlocking agonistic fields, where practice is modeled as military combat, sexual domination, security maintenance, and market strategy".

She develops a metaphor of network-building as a game of cat's cradle, where shifting knots and patterns which can be passed from one actor to another yield new connections and reconfigure existing ones. Newly-created patterns become part of the game, can recur, and also pose interesting questions about how the patterns arose. Technoscience in this conception is an open-ended game which no on e 'wins'; it is "both local and global, distributed and knotted together". Like most of Haraway's work, her metaphor does not provide a clear program for science studies, but it might have some interesting applications.

Adele Clarke (1998) suggests another way to extend the notion of networks by combining ANT with feminism and symbolic interactionism. She particularly welcomes ANT's emphasis on the role of non-human actors in scientific practice.

But she points out some differences between ANT and her own social worlds analysis (SWA), which addresses some of the more common feminist critiques of ANT.

While ANT emphasizes the recruitment and enrolment of allies by scientists, SWA emphasizes the mutuality of negotiations and trade-offs between scientists and the entities they seek to enrol. Second, while ANT pays little attention to those affected by, silenced, or rendered invisible by science in action, SWA seeks to draw attention to them. Third, while ANT deemphasizes important differences among actors, SWA highlights these as crucial elements of the process of negotiation in scientific practice. Finally, while ANT employs an executive model, often suggesting (in spite of its claims to the contrary) that scientists are coord inating the action, SWA attends to the distribution of power and coordinating roles as an empirical topic.

Thus, Clarke argues, SWA bridges internal and external concerns, emphasizing not only scientific practice but the influence of social movements and social problems on the development of scientific claims and disciplines over time. The SWA approach addresses many feminist concerns about ANT: its focus on scientific victors; its marginalization of network outsiders, the partially enrolled, support workers, and those affected by scientific and technological developments; its 'take no prisoners' analysis of scientific network-building.

But Clarke also recognizes the utility of the ANT approach: its emphasis on the concrete practices that must be engaged in to extend scientific claims and have them regarded as true by diverse populations; its focus on materiality and the pivotal role assigned to machines and natural objects in network-building. ANT and related streams are particularly useful in explaining how particular scientific claims become successful - how scientists manage to convince people that their claims represent a view from nowhere.

They focus on strategies that scientists use: the rhetorical erasure of traces of authorship; the manipulation and strategic use of images to make a given interpretation appear to be a self-evident fact, rather than an argument; the accommodation and translation of interests and identities - in short, the drawing together of discursive and material elements to enrol a large and diverse group of allies essential to the acceptance of a claim. This basic model for analysis could be applied not only to science, but to other areas of social life in which one group gains preeminence over another, becoming empowered to speak and act authoritatively. ANT and related streams provide, it seems to me, crucial insights for feminist STS.

Granted, ANT analyses often are blind to the place of gender, race, class, and other axes of social difference in scientific work, and the insights of feminism and other critical STS perspectives can help to cure that blindness. Feminist work in STS has demonstrated the integral role of gender in the doing of science, and has provided crucial critiques of the scientific method and positivist epistemology's 'view from nowhere.' Feminist work also draws important attention to the effects of science and technology on non-scientists' lives, whereas most mainstream STS analysis stops at the point where a scientific claim has developed enough power to start affecting people's lives.

Extending the analysis further, as feminist work tends to do, would provide a more complete sociological analysis of science and its relation to the social. While ANT and related STS streams provide insights into the question of how, concretely, particular scientists make alliances and particular claims get extended, feminist work provi des insights into a still-unanswered question identified by Thomas Gieryn (1999): why science is granted such broad cultural legitimacy. Feminists draw our attention to the cultural and historical representing practices, especially dichotomizations that make scientists' strategies effective. For example, the erasure of traces of subjective authorship is only a successful strategy for scientists because objective distance has been identified so closely with reason and truth, in opposition to subjectivity, relatedness, and the emotional.

And Keller and Ludmilla Jordanova argue that these constructions appear to rely, in the final instance, upon the dichotomization of gender. In other words, cultural conceptions of gender ultimately may enable the cultural authority of science - which cannot be derived simply from particular episodes of scientific network-building. But, by the same token, the success of some scientific claims and the failure of others usually cannot be explained via reference to popular conceptions about science or gender. The insights of feminist and mainstream STS may be combined to attend to different dimensions of scientific credibility.

Combining feminist and mainstream STS insights may be particularly profitable for activists and the academics who support them. Drawing on feminist theory, social movement theory, ANT and other varieties of mainstream STS, Steven Epstein (1995) has shown that AIDS activists have been most successful in affecting the way scientific research is done not by pointing out that there is no such thing as a view from nowhere or by exposing the heterosexist assumptions of AIDS scientists (though these strategies have helped), but by using strategies that scientists themselves use.

These activists learned the language and culture of science, which compelled experts to engage in discussion. They established themselves as representatives of the entire HIV-positive population, thus making them obligatory passage points in scientists' efforts to recruit research participants for clinical trials and to develop research protocols with which the participants (according to their spokespeople) would comply. Activists tied their moral and political concerns to epistemological and methodological arguments, using accepted notions of good science to gain credibility and support from scientists and the general public. They took advantage of existing controversies about clinical trial methodologies to argue for a democratization of trial participation.

Recently, I conducted research on the maintenance and transgression of expert-lay boundaries by endometriosis patients and gynecologists. It is clear that gynecologists use and reify notions of the hysterical, subjective female to delegitimate endometriosis patients' claims about pain and to assert medical authority. But women with endometriosis are strategic claimsmakers too. Sometimes they appropriate standards of 'good science' and use certain medical claims to attack others which they find objectionable.

At other times, patients attack science as an insufficient basis for understanding endometriosis, and invoke their 'personal experience' with the disease to establish their cognitive authority (just as clinicians and gynecological researchers often cite their experience, and not just 'science,' to the same end). Through various patient networks, women with endometriosis have developed a set of core claims which they advance as constitutive of the collective experience of women with endometr iosis. Patients combine 'science' and 'experience' as the situation demands - drawing upon the epistemological resources of both medicine and women's health movements - to elevate the status of their own claims and to assert that most doctors don't know what they're talking about.

A patient organization called the Endometriosis Association (EA) has been extremely successful in enrolling eminent medical experts to assist in EA administered research and the advancement of EA claims. Medical experts are enrolled through offers of financial aid, access to research participants, and good publicity among endometriosis patients. The EA has formed alliances with other groups to direct attention to the effects of environmental pollutants on health. The Association uses cascades of inscriptions and standard social science research methods to represent the experiences of women with endometriosis.

These have proven useful in establishing the organization as the representative of women with endometriosis - which in turn has gained the EA access to expert decision-making processes about research and treatment protocols - seemingly because, through statistical representation, the social context and subjective nature of patients' experiential claims are erased. "A fact is nothing but a statement with no modality and no trace of authorship".

These kinds of analyses draw upon both feminist and mainstream STS to suggest concrete strategies that laypeople and activists can use to contest and reconfigure scientific practice and the development of scientific claims. As David Hess points out, "If science is politics by other means, then coalition politics can be actor-networks with other ends". In my estimation, Haraway is quite correct that the failure of feminist and mainstream STSers to engage with one another has not been symmetrical. However, the defenders of science in the 'science wars' also are correct that there are strong affinities among feminists and mainstream STS scholars.

Their linking of mainstream STS to feminism and 'left-wing politics' is clearly intended to portray STS as 'biased' and 'anti-science,' in contrast to the professed political neutrality of science. This, obviously, is apolitical strategy meant to delegitimate STS on traditional positivist terms. But mainstream STSers, in attempting to distance themselves from feminist and other overtly politically engaged forms of analysis, employ a not dissimilar strategy. By constructing feminist work as 'just politics' and science as 'politics by other means,' mainstream STSers seem to wind up suggesting that their own claims are less thoroughly political than either feminist claims or scientific practice - ironically, more in the tradition of transcendent, objective, value-free scientific rationality that they claim to contest. Thus mainstream STS is constructed as the obligatory passage point through which those seeking to understand science must work.

It seems that these constructions represent an attempt to gain for mainstream STS the cognitive authority that the natural sciences have so long enjoyed, and to forge alliances with scientists - a new attempt to hitch STS to the bandwagon of science a la Merton. In his analysis of the science wars, Thomas Gieryn has examined mainstream STSers' attempts to present themselves as the necessary allies of scientists who seek to repair their image in an era of public disillusionment with science. In his latest book, Latour protests scientists' construction of science studies as anti-science; emphasizes that mainstream STSers are scientists, too, and should be allowed into the club; and seeks to persuade scientists that he is friend, not foe - mainly by explicitly distancing himself from "sociologists," "militants," and "activists," the real enemies of science:

> I naively thought, if scientists have a faithful ally, it is we, the "science students" who have managed over the years to interest scores of literary folk in science and technology ... in this guerilla warfare being conducted in the no-man's-land between the "two cultures," we were the ones being attacked by militants, activists, sociologists, philosophers, and technophobes of all hues, precisely because of our interest in the inner workings of scientific facts. Who loves the sciences? I asked myself, more than this tiny scientific tribe that has learned to open up facts, machines, and theories with all their roots, blood vessels, networks, rhizomes, and tendrils? Who believes more in the objectivity of science than those who claim that it can be turned into an object of inquiry?

So talk of war has turned to talk of peace, and the politics of STS turns from critique to currying favour. A new Great Divide is suggested: scientists (including mainstream STSers) on one side, "humanists" and militants on the other. But those familiar with the history of social science will know that there is nothing very new about this. It strikes me as rather unlikely that mainstream STS will come to be seen as the obligatory passage point for scientists seeking to understand their own work. I suspect they feel they already understand what they are doing.

As Emily Martin (1996b) has pointed out, scientists have good reasons for rejecting science studies and embracing scientific rationality: not only is the latter the basis of their cultural authority, but it may be a necessary attitude in the performance of scientific work. Rather than attempting to enrol a huge, fairly epistemologically united, and infinitely more powerful and prestigious network of scientists, mainstream STSers might be better off concentrating upon ways to improve their understanding of the nature of scientific knowledge, culture, and practice. I have argued that the insights of feminist scholarship can help them do that, just as I believe that feminist scholarship is benefitting from its uptake of mainstream STS insights.

But feminists form a rather strong network themselves,

and need not be overly concerned if mainstream STSers disapprove of them. Feminist have long appropriated useful bits and pieces from mainstream authors, with or without approval. I very much doubt that, after reading my arguments, mainstream STSers who want nothing to do with feminists, 'humanists,' and 'activists' - or feminists who want no truck with mainstream STSers - will suddenly be converted.

Instead, my purposes here have been to counter representations to which I strenuously object; to help to flesh out, for those who are hostile to neither feminism nor mainstream STS, some fruitful ways in which the two may be combined; and to deconstruct some of the boundary-work that may lead us to think that cross-fertilization is impossible. The point is that there are no disinterested actors here. Just as there is no Great Divide between science and politics, there is no Great Divide between STS and political rhetoric, or between mainstream STS and feminism. Science studies, too, is politics by other means.

THORSTEIN VEBLEN'S NEGLECTED FEMINISM

Critics have rarely failed to remark that Thorstein Veblen was quite the gallant. The story goes, for example, that in 1905 the dean of the University of Chicago called Veblen into his office to inform the young professor that he was being dismissed for having dallied with the wives of various colleagues. The dean began by saying, "We have a problem with the faculty wives." "Oh yes, I know," Veblen allegedly rejoined, with a solemn shake of the head. "They're terrible. I've had them all." Veblen left the school at the end of that semester. Despite this presumably chastening experience, Veblen continued to philander. No sooner had he arrived at his new appointment at Stanford than he was forced to resign under circumstances similar to those at Chicago. The new episode led him to exclaim publicly, "What is one to do if the woman moves on you?" Following this incident, Stanford President David Starr Jordan wrote to University of Chicago President Harry Pratt Judson:

He seems unable to resist the "femme mecomprise." It is fair to say, that in my final talk with him, he... behaved in a manly fashion, with no attempt at denial or evasion. Veblen's reputation as a roue followed him everywhere. When in 1904 the notorious sexual liberationist Parker Sercombe proposed to begin publishing a new magazine named *Tomorrow*, his first invitation for the editorship went to Veblen. As much as his actual behaviour, it was Veblen's refusal to respect the canons of discretion that landed him in trouble and which, no doubt, accounts for his continued reputation as something of a campus Casanova. As C. Wright Mills remarked with envy, Veblen was never a "decent man".

It is striking how much of the biographical literature on Veblen has discussed this particular aspect of his private life. Unfortunately, many of those who have explicitly taken up the question of Veblen's womanizing have resorted to distasteful apologism. His biographer Joseph Dorfman, for example, attempts to pin the blame for Veblen's infidelities on the women:

Women were much attracted to Veblen, and he knew how to hold their interest. But in these friendships he seems to have been the pursued rather than the pursuer. His interest in women was usually only a passing desire for amusement and diversion, but their interest in him was often so tenacious that for him the affairs became baffling and in some cases even appalling. Veblen seems to have needed the maternal qualities in women....

On the other hand, Rick Tilman offers a different exculpation by suggesting that Veblen's wives may themselves have been responsible for his infidelity. He writes, "Much has been made of Veblen's 'womanizing,' but insufficient attention has been paid to the mental state of his wives as a plausible explanation of this." As evidence, Tilman cites the testimony of Veblen's brother Andrew as to the theosophical tendencies of Veblen's first wife, as if this were somehow proof of her psychological instability. Even if Veblen's wives suffered from greater mental infirmity than Tilman demonstrates, this would in no way prove that these instabilities caused or justified

Veblen's womanizing. It might be just as well to assume that the causal process was precisely the reverse.

Though we might dismiss such attention as so much prurient curiosity, the notoriety of Veblen's habits helps to explain why some commentators have ignored the centrality of gender in Veblen's theories and the egalitarian vision of gender relations that grounds his ethology. This critical lacuna seems even odder when we consider that Veblen's contemporaries championed (or scorned) him as a feminist. In the eyes of his critics, his erotic activities may have undermined the legitimacy of his feminist stance. Paradoxical as it may seem, however, I would suggest that Veblen's rakish qualities may have been intimately connected to his feminist theories. Veblen's best-known critics, however, have not drawn out these connections.

For example, Dorfman's failure to relate Veblen's erotic behaviour to his theories led him to conclude that "Veblen seemed to feel that women were intended either to serve men's pleasure or to look after their comfort", a conclusion that this chapter will demonstrate is patently false. In calling Veblen a feminist, I should define what I mean by this much-contested word.

To begin, as Nancy Cott's recent work has noted, the term "feminism" only came into common usage in the United States around 1913, and thus to call Veblen a feminist is a bit anachronistic. However, using a less historical and more theoretical definition of feminism, I believe that labeling Veblen a feminist remains justified. It seems to me that the minimum definition of a feminist would be, first, a belief in the equality of men and women; second, a belief that the differences in men's and women's social status are socially constructed; and third, that imposing an inferior social position on women is morally wrong.

All of these ideas were fundamental to Veblen's thought. Moreover, what set twentieth-century feminism apart from the women's movement of the late nineteenth century was the rejection of Christianity and conventional respectability, and in this sense, Veblen was very much of the twentieth century and not of the nineteenth. Indeed, in his shameless practice of erotic freedom, and more crucially, his foregrounding of female sexual assertiveness (the bete noire of anti-feminists), Veblen adumbrated one of the great issues that feminists would elaborate in the years preceding World War I. In 1905, Veblen's comment, "What is one to do if the woman moves on you?" had radical implications.

At this juncture, I should emphasize that this chapter concerns the centrality of gender in Veblen's thought and is not an argument about late nineteenth-century American feminism. To my knowledge, Veblen never pronounced himself on the question of contemporary feminism, and my argument in this chapter rests on a close reading of Veblen's concepts, rather than on an account of his life as a political activist. My point is not that Veblen was a campaigner for women's emancipation in the mold of a Frank Lester Ward, but rather that Veblen's intellectual agenda cannot be understood apart from his attack on socially constructed gender inequality, which provided a conceptual cornerstone for his intellectual edifice.

Though clearly a shameless Lothario, Veblen was also one of the first and shrewdest critics of women's subordination in a commodified culture. Despite his carnal proclivities and whatever prejudices we might bring to bear on such behaviour, Veblen certainly realized that women were more than mere objects. Veblen's attitudes toward women were no doubt informed by having grown up in a family of emancipated women.

His mother, according to Max Lerner, "was a talented woman who often served as an amateur doctor for the frontier community," and his father distinguished himself from his neighbors by sending not only all of his sons to college, but also all of his daughters. Not surprisingly, criticism of contemporary gender relations and the historical genesis of these relations occupied a major place in his writings. In this chapter, I will set out the place of gender in Veblen's thought, beginning with his most celebrated work, The Theory of the Leisure Class.

In Theory of the Leisure Class, Veblen first delineated his famous (and by now rather hackneyed) idea of "conspicuous consumption," and it is this analytical concept that remains the point of departure for much of the continued interest in his work. What did Veblen mean by this term? In the first instance, consumption is merely part of normal human sustenance, including such basic activities as eating, drinking, and the provision of shelter.

These activities can be attended to with a greater or lesser degree of pleasure, but they are necessary activities and can be satisfied in purely functional ways. Veblen's criticism of consumption focused not on the basic human need for consumption, but rather on the unnecessary consumption intended primarily as a form of social display. Examining the world of his day, Veblen charged that the majority of consumption did not aim at the fulfillment of human needs, but rather took place as a form of symbolic exchange, in particular, as a way of demonstrating social superiority over those unable to consume in the same manner. It was this form of consumption that Veblen labeled "conspicuous."

Conspicuous consumption focuses primarily on "luxury" goods - commodities that serve no useful purpose in sustaining life, but instead show the superior wealth of the consumer and his or her concomitant ability to engage in wasteful, i.e., nonuseful, consumption. "The means of showing pecuniary strength, and so of gaining or retaining a good name," Veblen explained, "are leisure and a conspicuous consumption of goods". Because of the generally competitive and opulent nature of contemporary society, no one, not even the most abject, escapes the process of inherently wasteful conspicuous consumption; no one is so poor that they cannot engage in the essentially upper-class game of consumption for display.

What sets people apart socially, therefore, is the quantity and quality of conspicuous consumption they engage in: the more waste, the more honor. So, for example, serving caviar rather than salt cod at a dinner has as its primary aim not nutritional enhancement, but rather the demonstration of wealth and social superiority. These habits of social display through commodities are so ingrained that "we instinctively insist upon at least some measure of wasteful expenditure in all our consumption, even in the case of goods which are consumed in strict privacy and without the slightest thought of display". Veblen described as "barbarian" communities that organized their consumption around such "invidious" forms of social display, thereby implying that they were the opposite of progressive and enlightened.

This view of consumerism took sharp aim at contemporary economic wisdom. To understand the view of consumerism against which Veblen was reacting, consider the work of economist Simon Patten. In his 1889 essay, "The Consumption of Wealth," Patten started from the classic utilitarian assumption that human beings were essentially motivated by pleasure-seeking, but he observed everywhere the corrupting effect of this pleasure-seeking. For him, the chief problem with contemporary consumerism lay in its debased taste.

The masses seemed to prefer "cheap amusements" like sports, drinking, and smoking. In Patten's view, this tendency to choose the meretricious over the sophisticated did not occur because of lack of education or an inability to "play the game" of conspicuous consumption, but simply because the more refined pleasures were priced out of reach. In other words, Patten believed that the class-based differentiation of commodities was merely a side effect of the price system. The solution to this class differentiation, therefore, was to tax these cheap pleasures to the point where the more sophisticated pleasures would become preferable. Patten saw culture as the solution to the problem of economic distinctions and class conflict.

Veblen, however, rejected this view of contemporary consumerist practices. Positing an instinct for emulation, rather than for utilitarian need, as the driving force behind contemporary consumerism, Veblen concluded that the rich used price distinctions to set themselves apart from their social inferiors. The different cultural choices made by the various classes were the result of deliberate distinction-making. What made high culture "high" was not anything intrinsic in that culture, but rather the simple fact of its being exclusive. Thus, to Veblen, proposals such as Patten's to elevate the morals of the masses by raising the price of low cultural activities failed to comprehend the true purpose of the price system.

In contrast to Patten, Veblen believed that the fundamental point of the price system was to create invidious social distinction. Commodities could never bridge the cultural or social gap between the upper and lower classes. On the contrary, the former Minnesota farm boy realized, commodities were differentiated with the express intent of providing a means to rearticulate economic distinctions on a cultural level.

The Theory of the Leisure Class not only traced the rise of conspicuous consumption out of the desire for social differentiation, but also described the contemporary manifestations of it, and it was this aspect of his book that received the most attention. One of the most striking aspects of Veblen's characterization of contemporary consumer practices was his awareness of women's central role in the new consumer civilization. Veblen pointed out the paradox that, although women earned less than men, women did a disproportionate amount of the conspicuous consuming.

Despite patriarchal values that deemed that woman "should consume only what is necessary to her sustenance," women were the primary conspicuous consumers. Veblen explained that women's consumption actually did serve male wage-earners' needs in that women, in their consumption, served as vehicles for the exhibition of male wealth. With the decline of large servant staffs with which men could furnish evidence of their economic power, the role of display had been assigned to women. In other words, a woman's large engagement ring, while ostensibly evincing her taste and privilege, functioned socially as a marker of her husband's pecuniary prowess.

Rather than conclude, as did many of his contemporaries (such as Balzac or Dreiser, for example), that women were "naturally" more inclined than men to ostentation, Veblen showed that women's consumption worked to glorify the men who provided them with the means to consume. Even though women often performed the act of consumption, in a patriarchal society where women "belonged" to men, every act of consumption by a woman served to increase the prestige of her possessing male.

Consumerism did not liberate women, but rather reinscribed within the sphere of consumption their dependence on male benefactors. In the gendered division of labour, men adopted the role of producer, while women "consume[d] vicariously for the head of the household". This latter role was particularly important for women of the middle class, whose less prosperous husbands could afford to have only one conspicuous consumer attached to him; his wife therefore became increasingly important as a tool for display of not only consumption, but leisure: "As we descend the social scale, the point is presently reached where the duties of vicarious leisure and consumption devolve upon the wife alone. In the communities of the Western culture, this point is at present found among the lower middle class".

In that portion of the middle class where having the wife work outside of the home would have been most useful, women found their activities most restricted. Thus, according to Veblen, the subjugation of women reached its nadir in the lower-middle class. It should be noted, however, that Veblen did not dismiss all of women's work about the house as being merely about the display of conspicuous waste. He was well aware of the utility of much household work: "So far as these services conduce to the physical efficiency or comfort of the master or the rest of the household, they are to be accounted productive work. Only the residue of employment left after deduction of this effective work is to be classed as a performance of leisure".

Veblen's criticism of women's position in consumer society was more than just a component of his general theory; the entire theory emerged directly out of a critique of women's subjugation. In one of his earliest substantive essays, dating from 1894, Veblen explored the development of that most basic aspect of consumerism - fashion. In "The Economic Theory of Women's Dress," Veblen began by positing an essential difference between "dress" and "clothing."

Whereas clothing had the functional role of protecting a person from the elements, dress stemmed from "the principle of adornment." Although adornment "in the naive aesthetic sense" was of little economic importance, it soon "emerged from the primitive efforts of the savage to beautify himself with gaudy additions to his person," to become "an economic factor of some importance" in "its function as an index of the wealth of its wearer - or, to be more precise, of its owner, for the wearer and the owner are not necessarily the same person".

Because the ultimate purpose of dress was to demonstrate the capacity for expenditure, it soon became customary to change fashions on a regular basis. By not only making clothes expensive, but also requiring that these expensive items be changed regularly, the divisions between those who could afford this waste and those who could not were etched clearly into any social structure. Here was the embryonic idea that Veblen would develop into a general social theory in The Theory of the Leisure Class.

"Under the patriarchal organization of society," Veblen explained, "the dress of women was an exponent of the wealth of the man whose chattels they were," and the same situation persisted to Veblen's day. With the accumulation of possessions (what Marx called "primitive accumulation"), social consideration derived from the display of pecuniary strength, which was best demonstrated by needless consumption. As soon as this social habit emerged, a differentiation of gender roles ensued, whereby "it became the function of the woman, in a peculiar degree, to exhibit the pecuniary strength of her social unit by means of unproductive consumption of valuable goods".

This exhibition of non-productivity condensed in the physical nature of women's clothes, which according to Veblen were designed specifically to betoken that a woman had no productive function. It soon became customary not only "among the wives of the magnates of the African interior," but also in "the best, most advanced, most highly developed societies of our time," to require that women adorn themselves with all manner of ridiculous accouterments and appurtenances that served to hobble her gait, to inhibit her breath, and most crucially to render her non-productiveness apparent to all. As evidence, Veblen pointed to the particularly incommodious persistence of the skirt "and of all the cumbrous and otherwise meaningless drapery which the skirt typifies."

While social waste was the primary object of Veblen's scorn, he was also clear about its victims:

> That women must appear to be idle in order to be respectable, is an unfortunate circumstance for women who are compelled to live by their own livelihood. They have to supply the means of living, but also the means of advertising the fiction that they live without any gainful occupation.

In other words, fashion victimized working-class women most severely. Thus, we can see that Veblen's idea of conspicuous consumption emerged out of a dual critique of women's social and economic positions in contemporary society. Having established that, far from serving as a sign of aesthetic sophistication or as a diversion for rich wives, women's fashion instead functioned as a form of patriarchal male display, Veblen next turned his attention to the social origins of patriarchy.

He did this in two key essays, "The Beginnings of Ownership" and "The Barbarian Status of Women," which appeared just months before the publication of The Theory of the Leisure Class and which should be read as prolegomena to the Theory. Although he had published book reviews, as well as some articles on wheat production, these were the first works of the mature Veblen who would become famous after the publication of the Theory. Moreover, these essays confirm that Veblen's social theory stemmed from a critique of the place of women in modern society.

"The Beginnings of Ownership" commenced with a critique of the Lockean view that ownership derives from the productive labour of the owner. In his "Second Treatise on Civil Government," Locke explained and justified the origins of private property by claiming that an individual established ownership over an undifferentiated piece of nature by improving the land through his labour.

According to Locke, value derived from the labour inherent to a commodity. Veblen began his critique of this classic account of ownership and value with an explicitly gendered example: "Even very recently - culturally speaking - there was no suspicion that a woman's work, in the patriarchal household, should entitle her to the products of her work." In contrast to the labour theory of ownership, Veblen proposed that the possession of land began with a collective, communal act of seizure and was maintained by "a tenure of prowess." For Veblen, this original act of seizure constituted the protean moment in property relations. But this communal act of seizure did not yet constitute individual ownership.

Individual ownership emerged through the exclusive, institutionalized consumption of specific goods by the barbarian warrior, whose prowess gained him first rights to disposal of the seized property. Although some goods were consumed collectively, other articles (those pertaining "organically to the person of the user") came to belong exclusively to the person who originally seized them. The most typical object of the latter sort, according to Veblen, was the captive, who could not be communally used by the group. Moreover, Veblen remarked, "the captives taken under rude conditions are chiefly women." In other words, ownership, which was nothing but the institutionalization of the right to exclusive consumption, arose directly out of the capture of women in warfare.

The subjugation of women was thus the foundational act, one might say, of a consumer society. That Veblen turned to gender at this point in his argument reveals a great deal about the theoretical underpinnings of his work. Veblen did adduce "good reasons for this," for example, that women were "more easily controlled," that their labour was worth more, and that they therefore served better than men as trophies. But these arguments seem rather odd. Why is men's labour worth less? Why not the totem of one would's opposing tribe serve as a wonderful trophy? Is a male slave really any harder to control than a female one?

What is most noticeable, from our viewpoint, is that in explaining why women were preferred as captives, Veblen left out the issue of sex, except obliquely, at the end of his essay, by turning to the issue of marriage. In the essay he published in the subsequent issue of The American Journal of Sociology, he went on to explain at length this question of "The Barbarian Status of Women" and particularly how the institution of marriage figured into that status. Before turning to the issue of marriage among the barbarians, however, it behooves us to review Veblen's definition of barbarism. For Veblen, the institution of ownership emerged with the shift from peaceful primitivism to bellicose barbarism:

Defined as the transition from a peaceable to a predatory habit of life. Throughout barbarian culture, where this tenure of prowess prevails, the population falls into two economic classes: those engaged in industrial activities, and those engaged in such non-industrial pursuits as war, government, sports, and religious observances.

The domination of exploit, coercion, and seizure distinguished barbarian societies from their primitive predecessors. Like his spiritual forebear Rousseau, Veblen assumed that the state of nature was one of peace and harmony. In contrast to this "naive primitivism" that came before, barbarism celebrated exploit, wastefulness, and warfare. Honor, rather than industry, was its chief value. Like Rousseau, Veblen's assumption that there existed a peaceful state of nature led directly to a misanthropic view of modern man.

Under the antecedent primitive conditions, there was no hierarchy of economic classes; everyone engaged in productive labour in order to survive. Under the spur of technological innovation promoted by a combination of workmanlike effort and idle curiosity, however, barbarism emerged through the habit of the hunt, which Veblen conflated with warfare.

Defined as "the habit of coercion and seizure reduced to system and consistency", ownership of property was what distinguished barbarian from savage cultures. It was under barbaric conditions that the division of labour first arose. By distinguishing those employed in useful work from those engaged in such leisurely activities as warfare and worship, the division of labour turned on "a profound disparity between man's and woman's work". Whereas men's work was predatory in nature, women's work continued in the old vein of workmanlike drudgery. Men's hunting and warfare came to be extolled, while "women's assiduous and uneventful shaping of materials" began to be seen as a second-class activity.

According to Veblen, the members of the leisure class were nothing more than sophisticated barbarians. Since, under barbaric conditions, leisure functioned as a sign of high status, this leisure class on the one hand engaged in conspicuous consumption and on the other hand partook of activities that served as a symbolic extension of warfare. The ruder elements of barbaric violence having been purged from society, the neo-barbarians of the leisure class still partook of the spirit of barbarism, namely honor, but without engaging in the Ur-barbaric act of killing.

All that had changed, according to Veblen, was that the "aristocratic virtues" celebrated by barbarian cultures were now disguised by a certain kind of fraud. Despite the claims of ideologists like Patten, "cultured" traits, such as athleticism, intimidation, posturing, and administrative ability, remained rooted in the predatory impulse. In contrast to creative production, all of these activities shared as their primary motivation the desire for display. According to Veblen, the institution of display remained most imbedded in contemporary society through the unreconstructed role of women as typified by that most barbaric of institutions, marriage.

Marriage, according to Veblen, constituted little more than the ownership and barter of women, and as the most fundamental form of ownership, patriarchy was the model for all further forms of private property. For Veblen, patriarchy and private property were inseparable social phenomena. The true origins of the marriage relations thus lay in the capture of women in barbarian raids:

All the women in the barbarian group will share in the

class of repression and depreciation that belongs to them as women, but the status of women taken from hostile groups has an additional feature. Such a woman not only belongs to a subservient and low class, but she also stands in a special relation to her captor. She is a trophy of a raid, and therefore the evidence of his exploit.

In order for the woman to retain her value as a living sign of his exploit, her captor guarded her jealously. Over time, the barbarian habit of capture and exclusive ownership over women solidified into the institution of marriage. Eventually, as even women came to accept marriage, it became the only permissible form of relation between men and women, so that coercion became the legitimate attitude of men toward women. "None but the brave," quotes Veblen, with venomous irony, "deserve the fair."

For final proof that capture was at the bottom of all late barbarian (i.e., bourgeois) marriage, Veblen described the way in which the modern marriage ritual practiced "a mock-seizure or mock-capture" by demanding the formal profession of fealty and submission on the part of the woman....This form of household is almost always associated with some survival or reminiscence of wife-capture. In all such cases, marriage is, by derivation, a ritual of initiation into servitude. In the words of the formula, even after it has been appreciably softened under the latter-day decay of the sense of status, it is the woman's place to love, honors, and obey.

Veblen supposed that the maternal household of "unattached women" probably antedated the development of the predatory male household. Though matriarchal households sometimes persisted in the contemporary world, he noted that these households were habitually accorded a lower status than patriarchal ones. "The purpose of the argument," he concludes, "is to point out that there is a close connection, particularly in point of psychological derivation, between individual ownership, the system of status, and the paternal household".

It is worth pausing at this point in our discussion of

Veblen's works to point out the strong autobiographical motive discernible behind this account of marriage as atavism. Whether he intended it or not remains an open question, but no doubt his attack on the institution of marriage provided moral sanction for his libertine lifestyle and unfaithfulness to his wives, permitting him certain self-righteousness as he "poached" his colleagues' beds, perhaps allowing him to believe that he was liberating his colleagues' wives.

However, Veblen must have also been aware that, although society restricted "official" capture of women to one (at a time), many patriarchal circles readily granted prestige to those who possessed, however temporarily, many women; thus, one might interpret his own behaviour as a form of status-seeking. Despite castigating the patriarchal prestige associated with woman-capture, he must have known how his own womanizing would win him prestige among his fellow patriarchs.

As we have seen, Veblen considered patriarchy (as sanctified by marriage) to be the most basic institutional aspect of what he called barbarism. Lerner has described Veblen's theory of institutions as covering "habits and customs, ways of doing things and ways of thinking about things, both of them sanctioned by long practice and by the community's approval." Insofar as they helped to establish a horizon for understanding social activities, Veblen's "institutions" functioned in the same way as Emile Durkheim's "cosmologies" or Pierre Bourdieu's "habitus."

Each of these categories functions conservatively in that, as social practices, they serve to slow social change. This conservative dimension made Durkheim take a positive view of cosmologies and Bourdieu take a neutral view of habitus. But for Veblen, institutional conservatism was the most basic of social ills. If technological transformation was a positive good, the tenacious persistence of old ways of doing things always retarded the full flowering of new technological potentials. Society and culture, in other words, served as a brake on the full development of human life through technology.

Like his recent predecessor in theories of social evolution,

E. B. Tylor, Veblen regarded his work as guided by an ethical imperative. Both hoped their social theories would provide a blueprint for social change. But whereas Tylor was a Victorian meliorist, Veblen maintained the more ironic, typically modernist belief that persistent institutional backwardness would inevitably dog technological change. Useless personal habits would remain because they helped service the vested interest of institutions.

Veblen took four basic ideas from Tylor: a reliance on the comparative method; a philosophy of history in which all societies moved through the same series of linear and rankable stages from primitivism through barbarism and up to civilization; an attention to the way certain cultural traits "survived" their point of origins; and a conviction that all religious beliefs stemmed from animism. The first two, of course, were general principles common to nineteenth-century North Atlantic thought and had ideological roots in Aristotle.

Although many contemporary historians would today reject Veblen's philosophy of history, the notion of cultural lag is one of Veblen's enduring legacies. It was at this point in particular that he superseded Tylor, who believed that cultural survivals could be effectively overcome. Veblen gave his most detailed account of historical lag in his Imperial Germany and the Industrial Revolution.

Veblen had visited Germany several times around the turn of the century and, like most foreign visitors to the country, could not help puzzling over the curious sight of little boys in lederhosen playing next to high-tech chemical factories, or, in other words, the combination of social and political backwardness with immense industrial productivity. In large part, the book consisted of a comparison of industrialization and the cultural impact thereof in England and Germany.

Veblen began his argument with the premise that technologies necessarily developed within a given set of institutions, i.e., within a given cultural matrix of habits and ways of doing things. The difficulty was that "these standing conventions out of the past unavoidably act to retard, deflect, or defeat adaptation to new exigencies that arise in the further course" of development. However, when transferred to another nation, these technologies were brought over only in their physical aspect, while the cultural baggage inhibiting their optimal implementation could be left behind: "It is, in other words, taken over in a measure without the defects of its qualities". Thus, the new technologies could be imported without the productive inefficiencies associated with their cultural context in the country of origin.

Veblen illustrated his case with his usual assortment of provocative examples, of which the following is particularly striking in the context of this chapter:

> Certain facts of no questionable taste may be brought in to point a comparison between British and continental customs bearing on the industrial efficiency of the community at large. It has, e.g., become improper, not to say immoral, for English women to do fieldwork; whereas in Continental countries, and perhaps especially in German countries, women work in the field without moral restraint. Various arguments are advanced for the "exemption" of women from outdoor work. So far as these arguments are fit to survive scrutiny they turn out to be considerations of conventional propriety. They appear to be of the nature of an impulsive imitation of that exemption of well-to-do women from all useful work, that constitutes one the chef infirmities of the English social code and one of its chief exemplifications of the principle of conspicuous waste.

Again, denying women the right to labour stood as a chef example of social inefficiency. For Veblen to call something inefficient represented more than simply an analytical fact; it represented a moral condemnation. Inefficiency was the result, according to Veblen, of a perversion of moral instincts, or rather, the result of the predominance of the "bad" instincts over the "good" ones.

Veblen asserted that mankind was imbued with a number of characteristically human instincts. Instinct was distinguished from mere mechanistic functioning - what Veblen called "tropism," following the usage of his biologist friend Jacques

Loeb - in that it was the conscious pursuit of an objective end, in other words, in that it was teleological in intention (though not necessarily in effect). In other words, a bird hunting a worm was instinctive, while a fertilized egg splitting was not.

Unlike most social theorists of the instinctual life, Veblen took a strongly non-determinist view of instinctual functioning. Veblen realized that any instinct could have a variety of contrasting and even contradictory manifestations, both between cultures and within a given culture. Instincts could be classified normatively into two categories: on the one hand the "good" instincts, including the instinct of workmanship and the parental bent, on the other hand the "bad" instincts of predation and emulation. While instincts established the desired ends, institutions established the standard means within any given culture for attaining those ends.

These institutions for governing the instincts evolved out of specific historical contexts, but as we have seen, under the conditions of rapid economic development, institutional delimitations of socially acceptable instinctual expression could easily become anachronistic. Veblen claimed that ownership was the institutional manifestation of the dominant instinct in barbarian civilization, namely, predation and its subcategory, pugnacity.

Defined by the desire to accumulate either money or goods, the "pecuniary impulse" was the modern institutional form of the predatory instinct. The typical form of the pecuniary impulse was ownership, which in turn was "of a personal, invidious, differential, emulative nature". In essence, the instinct of emulation functioned as a desire for recognition similar to that enunciated by Hegel in the Phenomenology of Spirit. In other words, property in its emulative aspect functioned chiefly as a way to garner social recognition, which was why even poor people felt compelled to follow fashion.

According to Veblen, under savage conditions the emulative instinct had served as the basis for the animistic religious impulse, but under contemporary circumstances, it impelled men toward the consumerist and female-subjecting habits that would provide evidence of their pecuniary prowess. Thus, in modern life, predation and emulation combined to encourage conspicuous consumption. In addition to the negative instincts of predation and emulation, Veblen claimed that mankind was also endowed with more positive instinctual traits: "Chief among those instinctive dispositions which conduce directly to the material well-being of the race, and therefore to its biological success, is perhaps the instinct of workmanship.

The only other instinctive factor which could with any likelihood dispute this primacy would be the parental bent." The instinct for workmanship had deep roots in the long history of human savagery, when consistent work toward a given end was a human necessity:

Through long ages of work and play men (perhaps primarily women) learned the difficult and delicate crafts of husbandry and carried their mastery of these pursuits to such a degree of proficiency...that...virtually all the species of domesticable animals in three continents had been brought in and bred into improved races.

The instinct of workmanship was therefore not the same thing as the instinct for work. Striving for excellence, not mere banausic labour, defined human beings. The hope for humanity, the redemptive quality of the instinct of workmanship, resided in the desire for qualitative improvement, not merely accumulation. Because Veblen valued this qualitative dimension of work, he supported the arts and crafts movement around the turn of the century; its valorization of skilled labour and its demand that work be enjoyable resonated with his own sensibilities about workmanship.

Moreover, the exclusion of women from the workplace, which prevented the instinct of workmanship from flourishing, outraged Veblen. In this, he was at one with the majority of the women's movement of his day. As one historian has noted, "the right to labour became in the late 1880s a cardinal principle of women's advancement". As we saw with the example of the English women, Veblen's intellectual stance on the importance of work for full human development paralleled this dimension of the women's movement.

The parental bent, so closely related to the instinct of workmanship that it would be "a matter of extreme difficulty to draw a line between them", was more than anything a communal instinct - a desire to further the life-ends of the group, which in practice congealed in the desire of group elders to ensure the success of their young. Given that Veblen devalued both marriage and monogamy, it is unsurprising that he believed the parental bent signified a communal, rather than familial, impulse.

Nonetheless, Veblen could affirm nurturing without limiting women to the role of mothering. Even this most tough-minded of critics was capable of a tenderhearted moment when he observed that women's "wordless communion with their own young is perhaps the most notable and engaging trait of their own motherhood". Note that Veblen, unlike the vast majority of his contemporaries, did not claim that women manifested the parental bent more strongly than men; the child's nursing was the most engaging trait of motherhood, not of womanhood.

While the parental bent - hose great end was to maintain the group's life - was shared equally by both sexes, the instinct of workmanship was historically the peculiar domain of women. Though Veblen did not reduce women to their fecundity, he did argue that women bore an organic relationship to agriculture in the minds of savages. In his hands, however, rather than being a denigration, this characterization became a compliment. During the peaceful, pre-barbaric phase, which Veblen believed characterized early human society before the emergence of barbaric predatory habits, women occupied "the chief place in the technological scheme...[and had] come to take the leading role in the industrial community of the early time, and the community's material interests [had] come to centre about them and their relation to the natural products of the fields . . ."

As evidence for this "magical" connection between women and fecundity, Veblen noted the prevalence of fertility cults among primitive peoples. This brings us to the heart of Veblen's thought. Veblen was a vitalist, a member of that turn-of-the-century movement that claimed that ethical and social standards should be judged for their life-enhancing or life-detracting qualities.

He celebrated increase and hated wastefulness. More than anything else, Veblen hated modern barbarism for the wastefulness typified, for example, by the maintenance of large servant staffs that had no purpose other than to demonstrate a chief's ability "to sustain large pecuniary damage without impairing his superior opulence". Veblen realized that the idea of "waste" was entirely normative and yet insisted on its utility as a device for analyzing societies. Wastefulness, according to Veblen, was "an illegitimate expenditure of human product or human life...This expenditure is here called waste because it does not serve life or human well-being on the whole, not because it is waste or misdirection of effort or expenditure as viewed from the standpoint of the individual consumer".

This basic vitalist impulse pulsated at the core of all of Veblen's work. What distinguished Veblen from most other vitalists, however, was his emphasis on collectivist notions of life. Veblen insisted that vitality be judged on the basis of group, rather than individual, well-being. Veblen rejected "the wholly illegitimate teleological" reading of Darwin that claimed "that the expression 'survival of the fittest'" meant the "survival of socially desirable individuals." Veblen derived his own "collectivist" notion of Darwinism from the work of Enrico Ferri, who by interpreting "fittest" in group terms used Darwinism to justify socialism.

By adding this collectivist reading of Darwin to the typical lebensphilosophische ideas, Veblen transcended the somewhat stale (and often misogynist) vitalism of his day. In this regard, it is instructive to compare Veblen with another famous vitalist, Friedrich Nietzsche. Nietzsche's vitalism, of course, was highly individualistic, perhaps as individualistic as any vitalism could be, and the resulting differences between his ideas and Veblen's are highly instructive.

For where Nietzsche celebrated barbarism, Veblen scorned it; while Nietzsche was deeply suspicious of the collectivist possibilities dormant within Darwin's theories, Veblen embraced this then-unfashionable reading of Darwin; when Nietzsche emphasized will, Veblen emphasized reason. Given all this, it is not surprising that Nietzsche was the most notorious of misogynists, whereas Veblen was a feminist. In short, a collectivist vitalism tends to accord women an equal place with men while an individualistic vitalism denigrates them.

The most basic instinct of all was the instinctive drive of all social groups to sustain and reproduce themselves. In a way, Veblen was advocating a kind of fertility cult of his own, but a fertility cult embedded in a society without distinctions between men and women. According to Veblen, modern barbaric conditions had misdirected the life-enhancing instincts of mankind by perverting both the parental bent and the instinct of workmanship. Rather than labour productively, the modern barbarian preferred the idleness made possible by technological advance.

With leisure as the barbarian ideal, industriousness had become dishonorable and productive labour therefore irksome. Reversing the usual causal analysis, Veblen argued that labour, rather than being intrinsically tedious, only became considered so as a result of the institutionalization of the leisure class. At the same time, labour, in its socially constructed irksomeness, became associated with femininity. Eventually, the ultimate sign of pecuniary prowess became the ability to waste a woman's working potential by using her merely as a display object.

The instinct of workmanship was also the locus of agency in Veblen's writings. Although Veblen acknowledged that instincts could manifest themselves in a variety of institutional forms, he remained a determinist in regard to individual functioning. Pinned between instincts and institutions, individual members of society were not accorded much agency in Veblen's theory. Insofar as he gave any credence to the idea of individual agency, however, Veblen located that freedom in the free development of the instinct of workmanship, since it was from this instinct that humans gained their proclivity for "creative work and technological mastery of facts".

In the primitive era (the period of human history that Veblen revered most), the instinct of workmanship and the parental bent had brought "women into the chief place in the technological scheme'", and it was women who had probably generated the technologies of the agricultural revolution. Even though Veblen's writings on dress and the leisure class might have seemed to reduce women to mere pawns in men's games, his analysis had shown that men were just as will-less as women in a commodified world, skewered by their desire for invidious distinction to the same degree as women were manipulated by men. Insofar as Veblen ascribed agency to any social actors, he did so to the women of an earlier period.

Veblen loathed the position of women in the leisure class because of what I would call his productivist ideology, by which I mean his tendency to value production over consumption or distribution, which in turn involved a nascent critique of domesticity. Veblen's caustic criticism of the spatio-economic reordering that accompanied modern consumer civilization encompassed a critique of contemporary gender relations. This reordering involved removing production from the home mostly to ease employers' efforts to enforce stricter work discipline with a concomitant restriction on women's activity. The home was redefined as a place of family and privacy, in contrast to the strictly economic role of such spaces as offices or factories.

In part to compensate for the intensified work schedules made possible by factories and offices, the home was glorified as a kind of sanctum. According to this ideology of domesticity, the home became a sacred site, free from the quotidian realities of economics. Veblen, however, would have none of this. For Veblen, domesticity was not the contrary of economy, but rather involved the redefinition of the home's economic significance from a unified site of production and consumption to one devoted exclusively to consumption.

In this respect, Veblen's criticism of the role of women in contemporary society resonated with Charlotte Perkins Gilman's Women and Economics, published in 1898, just a year before The Theory of the Leisure Class. The parallels between Gilman and Veblen have not gone unnoticed. One historian of the women's movement called Gilman the "Veblen of the movement" not only for her style, but for her method. Both Veblen and Gilman relied on contemporary anthropological theories to help justify their work and both characterized the present social position of women as the result of a fall from some archaic state of prelapsarian community, and both tended to dismiss the relevance of individual human agency in historical affairs.

Furthermore, Gilman saw in Veblen a kindred spirit, claiming that his work was "illuminated by the most brilliant penetrating satire I ever saw". Rosalind Rosenberg observed that Gilman agreed with Veblen "that women's subordinate status in modern society illustrated not the rational, coherent heterogeneity of Spencer's system but the irrational, and ultimately destructive, byproduct of men's baser instincts". Modern women, for Gilman as for Veblen, remained dependent on men.

Gilman attacked contemporary society for limiting women's role to a passive source of erotic pleasure for men. Little more than sex objects at home, women found that their gender was invariably the most important part of their social identity. Gilman laid particular stress on how the normative model of womanhood literally constricted the physical mobility of women. The ideal of the "absolutely stationary female," Gilman wrote, directly reduced women's perceptual and intellectual range.

A woman's "restricted impression, her confinement to the four walls of her home, have done great execution, of course, in limiting her ideas, her information, her thought-processes, and power of judgment....But this is innocent in action compared with her restricted expression, the denial of the freedom to act". Likewise, Veblen criticized female passivity via the conceptual category of the "instinct of workmanship." based on a twin rejection of the normative model of utilitarian man and the passive psychology that went with it, the instinct of workmanship represented an assault on the psychological foundations of neoclassical economics.

In its place, Veblen proposed an activist psychology derived from the ideas of Charles Peirce, with whom he had studied at Yale. This activist psychology grounded his radical reversal of the passive, consumerist assumptions subtending utilitarianism. Where the utilitarian claimed that man's ceaseless efforts to maximize his pleasures and minimize his pains led him inevitably to consume as much as possible while moving as little as possible, Veblen instead proposed that man was driven instinctively to produce.

That contemporary civilization made women the vehicles of consumerism meant that women were necessarily being forced into the passive economic and psychological role that both Veblen and Gilman abhorred. But where Gilman limited her sociology to an attack on the place of women in contemporary American society, Veblen located his criticism of women's enforced passivity in a more general assault on the epistemological foundations of contemporary economic theories justifying the relegation of women to such positions.

Although Veblen's criticism of women's position in modern society took place at a more philosophically profound level than Gilman's, Gilman did exceed Veblen in one crucial way. Gilman's attention to the sexual component of women's subjection revealed an important hole in Veblen's conceptualization of women's subordination. Indeed, throughout his writings and allusions to the status of women in our barbarian society, there is an almost studied silence about the role of sexuality in general and sexual slavery in particular.

The critical absence of any discussion of erotic sexuality in Veblen's thought is all the more surprising now that we have seen how crucial gender was in the formulation of the categories and dynamics of his thought. Such an omission, I propose, must be autobiographically significant for a man of Veblen's sexual notoriety. I will finish this chapter with some frank speculations as to the possible significance of this theoretical gap.

In his personal life, Veblen seemed to favour what the Saint-Simonians years before had called the "intimate affections," those moments of erotic and emotional bliss that were equally profound whether of long or brief duration. Indeed, one is struck by the degree to which Veblen's thought mirrored the Saint-Simonians'. Like them, his main hero was the engineer in whose hands both they and he trusted the future of social organization. Like them, his condemnation of contemporary social arrangements focused on the subjugation of women. Even his analytical categories paralleled theirs.

What Veblen called "predation" echoed the Saint-Simonian term "antagonism." Likewise, where the Saint-Simonians celebrated "association," Veblen exalted "the parental bent," an essentially communal vision of sociability. However, in other significant ways, Veblen differed from the Saint-Simonians. First, he saw institutions as the primary source of social dysfunction, whereas they believed that existing institutions (other than the state, for which they had little use) could be progressive forces when given over to the right leaders. Second, and more pertinently to our discussion, the Saint-Simonians saw the primary oppression of women as sexual rather than social.

As we have seen, Veblen ignored the issue of sexuality, but by focusing on other areas of repression, he also avoided the fatuous error of believing that women's oppression consisted only in sexual oppression, as the Saint-Simonians often seemed to believe. Some commentators have examined Veblen's generally hostile attitude toward consumer culture and concluded that Veblen was something of a killjoy, a man who failed to appreciate the true pleasures of consumption or, alternatively, condemned pleasure of all kinds. To T. J. Jackson Lears, for example, Veblen was a "utilitarian moralist, impervious to the psychological and religious attractions of 'barbaric' art and ritual."

As we have seen, however, Veblen was in no way a utilitarian and spent much of his career attacking the basic utilitarian precepts that governed (and continue to govern) mainstream economic thought. To agree with Lears that

Veblen was against the sybaritic excesses of his age misrepresents the essential thrust of Veblen's argument. Veblen acknowledged that "the desire for comfort and security" was a motive in every stage of social evolution and he took no issue with this desire. Veblen had no problem with those "articles of...consumption [in which] the motive principle...is personal comfort or well-being".

Only when the "habit of pecuniary emulation" polluted this pleasure-seeking did Veblen take up arms. In other words, it was not pleasure-seeking per se that bothered Veblen, but rather the invidious motives that grounded many of the social practices associated with sybaritism. Wastefulness to impress others, not enjoyment in it, was Veblen's villain. Thus, while he might criticize the "manly" drinking contests of a college fraternity, he did not in any way criticize the material phenomenon of drinking itself. Veblen understood and tacitly affirmed the bodily pleasures and, in his practice, most especially applauded the pleasures of feminine company.

For Veblen, there were essentially two sorts of pleasures, which were radically distinct from one another. The first could be described as social pleasure. Grounded in the parental bent and the instinct of workmanship, social pleasures included such things as attention to family, the desire to produce for the community, and, I would argue, sexual union. What unified all of these pleasures was that they were essentially productive rather than destructive; they did not involve the use and exhaustion of limited goods, but rather were conducive of increase in themselves. Such was the pleasure in watching the babe nurse at the mother's breast.

This was what Marx would have called the realm of unalienated human activity, an authentic sociability entirely at odds with the asocial sociability of commodities. In contrast to the emulative pleasures of consumerism, erotic pleasure in theory is without limit; indulgence of this pleasure does not require the destruction of scarce resources that could be put to a more life-enhancing use. To dismiss Veblen as an ascetic thus misses the radical sexual-liberationist implications embedded in his work. In this respect, Veblen's personal life represented an active and shameless affirmation of anti-consumerist sources of pleasure.

I will call Veblen's second form of pleasure "consumptive pleasure." These pleasures, in Veblen's opinion, were grounded in the "negative" instincts of emulation and predation. A typical example of this sort of pleasure would be the ostentatious public display of women, for this pleasure was based on useless social norms, rather than biological necessity. Veblen never denied the "peculiar" (read: erotic) pleasures of the barbarian regarding his female captive, but insofar as the barbarian's pleasure in his woman restricted her social activity and ability to contribute to the life of the group, this barbaric pleasure involved decrease and death.

Although Veblen rejected this form of pleasure-seeking as socially unhealthy, it would be a mistake to see his rejection of consumerism as a rejection of pleasure altogether, as Theodor Adorno [1981] came close to claiming. Contrary to Adorno's criticism, Veblen was not simply partaking of a Lutheran asceticism in his rejection of consumerism. He never rejected pleasure altogether or denied the pleasure of female company in particular.

Although Adorno may have been a bit flip in citing Veblen's religious background as an explanation for his position on consumerism, he was at least one of the few early commentators on Veblen who recognized him "as a late apologist of the feminist movement," and he intuited that what Veblen hoped for was "a state in which all that survives the disgrace of the difference between the sexes is the happiness that difference makes possible". Nonetheless, Adorno took issue with Veblen's practical attitude that erotic pleasure was the private business of consenting adults.

For Adorno, social mediation was an inevitable aspect of all pleasure since all desire was socially constituted. No truly private happiness could exist for Adorno (even for the pre-Auschwitz Adorno of this chapter); hence Veblen's reduction of marriage to its display value and his implicit celebration of more diversified and private sexual relations denied the fact that all erotic encounters must be reflected through a social prism. To describe marriage as an example of invidious display was only to denigrate mankind as a whole. Again like Rousseau, Veblen's unwillingness to countenance the necessity of mediation in all social relations led him to a deeply misanthropic worldview.

Adorno also highlighted Veblen's fundamental suspicion of aesthetics that accompanied his hostility to display. According to Adorno, "Culture...was never anything for Veblen but advertising, a display of power, loot and profit." Adorno quite rightly pointed out that Veblen failed to acknowledge that cultural phenomena could go beyond their "display function." Veblen's extreme embrace of a hermeneutic of suspicion resulted in a denigration of the autonomy of the aesthetic. By vaunting technology as the source of all positive change, Veblen failed to appreciate the redemptive qualities inherent in certain aesthetic practices.

As Veblen's life and theory testify, he was no killjoy; he demonstrated that it is possible to enjoy sexual congress without having "sole ownership" over the woman in question. Nonetheless, by limiting his appreciation of social relations to the functional aspect of the interactions, Veblen seems to have missed a crucial component of the human experience, namely, beauty. However, I would propose that perhaps the feminist in Veblen understood something profound when he rejected the aesthetic. Justification of the subordination of women on aesthetic grounds is, after all, one of the oldest traditions in Western thought.

Like his contemporary Henry Adams, Veblen may well have intuited that what set femininity off from masculinity was precisely its aesthetic dimension. Veblen may have believed that to unfetter women, aesthetics might have to be sacrificed. Veblen reacted with hostility only to the idea of women as objects of social display, as part of his general subordination of form to function. If we may judge the subversiveness of ideas by the degree to which they lead others to interfere in the thinker's life, then clearly Veblen's criticism of domesticity was the most radical aspect of his thought. Unlike many intellectuals, Veblen practiced his ideas: he led a hard-working, decommodified life whose primary pleasures were social, rather than material.

Although his shabby clothes perhaps led to hallway snickers, it was his practice of his ideas about gender that led to his dismissal from one university after another. Veblen's ideas were deeply intertwined with his womanizing habits. If he was dangerous, it was because he attacked both in theory and in practice the bastion of all conservatism - the patriarchal family. As Lerner commented, "The Philistines knew that he was a giant among them, but he was the wrong kind of giant, whose strength they feared, and they were glad to see him go packing before he pulled the temple down around their heads." While his theories gave his conservative colleagues grounds to distrust him, his practice gave them the excuse to dismiss him. Fundamentally, however, they were of a piece.

Bibliography

Anker, R. and C. Hein, 'Why Third World Urban Employers Usually Prefer Men', *International Labour Review*, Vol. 124, No. I, Geneva, 1985.

Beech, C., *Women and Women into Information Technology*, a report by the British Computer Society, 1990.

Byrne, E., *Women in Science and Technology: The Institutional Ecology Approach*, Interim Research Report, Department of Education, University of Queensland, 1988.

Chew. S.B. and R. Chew, 'Information Technology as a Strategy Human Resource Development', in E.C.Y. Kuo, C.M. Loh and K.S. Raman, *Information Technology in Singapore Society: Trends, Policies and Applications*, Singapore University Press, 1990.

Davidson, M.J. and C.L. Cooper (eds), *Women and Information Technology*, Psychology and Productivity at Work Series, London, John Wiley and Sons, 1987.

Deakin, R., *Women and Computing: The Golden Opportunity*, London, Macmillan Press, 1984.

Eriksson, I.V., B.A. Kitchenham and K.G. Tijdens (eds), *Women, Work and Computerization: Understanding and Overcoming Bias in Work and Education*, Amsterdam, North Holland, 1991.

Faruqui, A.M., M.H.A. Hassan and G. Sandri (eds), *The Role of Women in the Development of Science and Technology in the Third World*, proceedings of the conference organized by CIDA and the Third World Academy of Sciences, Trieste, Italy, October, 1988.

Harrison, P. (1983), *The Third World Tomorrow*, NY, Pilgrim Press and Harmondsworth, Penguin

Irvine, J., 'Women into Information Technology', *Information Technology and Public Policy*, Vol. 8, No. 3, Summer, 1990.

Kluzer, S., *Computer Diffusion in Black Africa: A Preliminary Assessment*, unpublished paper, SPRU, University of Sussex, Brighton, UK, 1988.

Lim, G.K., 'Women's Participation in the Computer Industry in Singapore', in Ken Tijdens *et al.* (eds), *Women, Work and Computing: Forming New Alliances*, Amsterdam, North Holland, 1989.

Lovegrove, G. and B. Segal (eds), *Women into Computing: Selected Papers*, 1988-1990, London, Springer, 1991.

Mitter, S., 'Computer Aided Manufacturing and Women's Employment: a Global Critique of Post Fordism', in I.V. Eriksson, B.A. Kitchenham and K.G. Tijdens (eds). *Women, Work and Computerisation: Understanding and Overcoming Bias in Work and Education*, Amsterdam, North Holland, 1991.

Mumford, E., *Where are Tomorrow's Top Women Executives* ?, Manchester Business School Review, Vol. 4, No. 3, 1980.

Ng, C. (ed.), *Technology and Gender: Women's Work in Asia*, Women's Studies Unit, UPM and Malaysian Social Science Association, 1987.

Ng, C. and J. Othman, 'Information Technology, Gender and Employment in Malaysia', in S.C. Bhatnagar and M. Odedra (eds) *Social Implications of Computers in Developing Countries*, New Delhi, Tata-McGraw Hill, 1992.

Odedra, M., *Information Technology Transfer to Developing Countries: Case Studies from Kenya, Zambia and Zimbabwe*, unpublished Ph.D. thesis, London School of Economics, 1990a.

Odedra, M., 'Poor Management leads to Gross Under-utilization', *Computer in Africa*, Vol. 4, No. 5, July, 1990b.

Parikh, I., *Women in Management: an Annotated Bibliography with Emphasis on Commonwealth Sources*, London, Commonwealth Secretariat, 1987.

Stamp, P., *Technology, Gender and Power in Africa*, Ottawa, international Development Research Centre, 1989.

Subramaniam, P.R., *The Future for Women in Information Technology*, M. Sc. dissertation, London School of Economics, 1991.

Tijdens, K., M. Jennings, I. Wagner and M. Weggelaar (eds), *Women Work and Computing: Forming New Alliances*, Amsterdam, North Holland, 1989.

Virgo, P., 'The Case for Women into Information Technology Campaign', *Information Technology and Public Policy*, Vol. 6, No. 3, Summer, 1988.

World Bank, *Sub-Saharan Africa: From Crisis to Sustainable Growth*, Washington DC, World Bank, 1989.

Wright, B.D. (ed.), *Women, Work and Technology: Transformations*, Chicago, University of Michigan Press, 1987.

Index